THE OFFICIAL

2006
BLACKBOOK
PRICE GUIDE TO
UNITED STATES
PAPER
MONEY

THIRTY-EIGHTH EDITION

BY MARC HUDGEONS, N.L.G.
& TOM HUDGEONS, Jr.
& TOM HUDGEONS, Sr.

HOUSE OF COLLECTIBLES

Random House Reference • New York

This book is available for special discounts for bulk purchases for sales promotions or premiums. Special editions, including personalized covers, excerpts of existing books, and corporate imprints, can be created in large quantities for special needs. For more information, write to Special Markets/Premium Sales, 1745 Broadway, MD 6–2, New York, NY, 10019 or e-mail specialmarkets@random house.com.

 House of Collectibles and colophon are trademarks of Random House, Inc.

Published by: House of Collectibles
               Random House Reference
               New York, New York

Distributed by Random House Reference, a division of Random House, Inc., New York, and simultaneously in Canada by Random House of Canada Limited, Toronto.

www.HouseofCollectibles.com

Printed in the United States of America

Buy It • Use It • Become an Expert is a trademark of Random House, Inc.

ISSN: 0195-3540

ISBN: 1-4000-4845-1

Thirty-eighth Edition: June 2005

10 9 8 7 6 5 4 3 2 1

CONTENTS

iv / CONTENTS

OFFICIAL BOARD OF CONTRIBUTORS

The authors would like to express a special thank you to:

W. R. "Bill" Rindoné, Bank Notes North West, PO Box 790, Aurora, OR 97002, for his collaboration and Market Review,

and **Regina Banks and Larry Felix at the Department of the Treasury,** Bureau of Engraving and Printing, Washington, D.C., for the articles on the BEP, and David Koble of Mid-American Currency.

PUBLISHER'S NOTE

The Official® Blackbook Price Guide to United States Paper Money is designed as a reference aid for collectors, dealers, and the general public. Its purpose is to provide historical and collecting data, as well as current values. Prices are as accurate as possible at the time of going to press, but no guarantee is made. We are not dealers; persons wishing to buy or sell paper money, or have it appraised, are advised to consult collector magazines or the telephone directory for addresses of dealers. We are not responsible for typographical errors.

NOTE TO READERS

All advertisements appearing in this book have been accepted in good faith, but the publisher assumes no responsibility in any transactions that occur between readers and advertisers.

Market Review

Collector interest continues at an all time high! Couple this with the upside value performance of currency and you have a formula for continuing increased interest in this fascinating field of collectibles.

Continued rising prices have tempted the owners of several major collections to dispose of their holdings. Several outstanding offerings have recently surfaced at auction and been rapidly absorbed by an appreciative collecting fraternity. Although the collections have been extensive, seveal knowledgeable collectors have been disappointed when they were unable to obtain a particular desired item. Rare notes which may not reappear for several years create fierce bidding wars and often exceed the catalog estimates. A high percentage of collectors appear determined to acquire the material they seek and this has continued to drive the market in an upward price spiral.

Among the most noteworthy collections to appear were the Krause Collection of Scrip, (fifty years in the making) and the Schingoethe holding of Scrip/Obsoletes which represented decades of accumulating. The FUN Show auction contained a depth of rare Fractionals greater than any offering since the Friedberg collection came to market. Several collections of rare Nationals also came to the market along with the Malcolm Trask Collection of Large Size Type. Most of the notes in the Trask collection had not been seen in several decades and were basically unknown to the fraternity. This tremendous volume of rarities merely whetted the appetite of both collectors and investors. Rumors of a monumentally extensive Fractional collection and a "one of everything" Large Size Type Note collection abound and both will probably appear at auction this year as "new" material finds it's way into the market place.

Dealer inventories are generally very low and most activity is centered around auctions. In 2001 most dealers dramatically reduced their inventory in anticipation of a stock market fiasco. What they failed to realise was that the fall of the stock market did very little harm to the currency field and aside from a small hiccup at the time of 9/11, the upward spiral of interest and value continued unabated. This left a lot of dealers unable to replace inventory.

The auction houses of Lyn Knight, R.M. Smythe and Heritage's CAA took up the slack and today they field the brunt of material reaching the marketplace.

One of the most exciting areas of increased interest is in the field of Western Scrip Notes. Always a rarity, they have now come into their own as a highly collectible field which has emerged over the past five years. During the Krause Collection sale most lots were hammered at well above their estimates. Depression Scrip notes broke the $1000 barrier for the first time and bidding was heated for most items. The scrip field can be particularly rewarding as there are still a lot of unknown notes yet to be discovered. It is also an area where Territorial Notes can still be found at reasonable prices and where rare notes can be found at bargain prices in dealer stock.

One additional comment on Western Scrip: Grading is NOT an important factor with these notes as their very existence is the major concern. That they exist is sufficient for most collectors and it is certainly not a field for anyone seeking only pristine condition notes! "One two known" notes are much more prevalent then in other fields.

Over the past seven years we've seen a tremendous influx of new collectors who've become interested in currency. Some are investors who realize the potential for growth in our hobby, but most are dyed-in-the-wool collectors who appreciate the history associated with these notes and the sheer beauty of the engraver's art. Others are attracted by the rarity or by the concept of researching unusual financial items. What ever your interest the basic underlying concern is to enjoy what you're doing!

A word on grading; Grading is a highly subjective field and certainly not a science. One man's VF is another's XF. If grading is a concern to you, then there is no substitute for experience. Spend time looking at the various definitions and take currency out of your wallet and grade it! There has been a great deal written about what constitutes any single grade. Find one that you agree with. The only real grade is one of dollars and cents. That is the bottom line! I can show you three different notes of the same exact series that all grade a strict Extremely Fine and none of them will be the same value. Beauty is always in the eye of the beholder and each person will view the notes as differently as witnesses to a traffic accident would. Another thing to remember, grading services will also vary in their assessments. This can occur for the reasons already outlined or for a variety of other concerns. Most of the services are owned and operated by currency dealers and their personal interests can get involved. Unlike the securities industry, there is no governing watch dog on these grading services. They can grade their own purchases and sell them to the public accordingly. Complaints are routinely heard that notes submitted fell far short of the expected grade while seemingly nicer then others graded by the same service. From time to time we see notes graded by these services that fall far short of reality. "Buyer beware" is still the best approach. The happiest collecors are those who are knowledgeable and seek out notes that they personally like. In the end, the chances are that a pretty note is much more desirable that a technically graded note of the same caliber. Grade alone should not be the only factor in a sale or purchase.

Large Size Notes (1861–1923 Series). This sector of collecting has long been the most popular area and it continues as such. Prices continue to rise and nice material gets scarcer each year. Dealer stocks are very low, especially in the nicer grades and all notes regardless of grade are collectable. Only long standing dealers still have a wide selection and most "new" material comes out at auction.

Federal Reserve Notes were overlooked in past decades and in previous issues we identified them as "sleepers". This is no longer true and rarer combinations of FRN district/signature now bring substantial premiums. Today, the best areas for bargains will be found in Gold Certificates and in the Legal Tenders of 1874–1880 where it is still possible to find rare notes at prices inconsistent with their rarity. Several excessive rare notes came out in 2005, including one of only two $500 1880 Legal Tenders known to be in public hands.

Small Size Notes (1928–Present). All areas of small size currency are strong with a single exception. Small Size Federal Reserve notes from the period of 1934 to present are showing weakness. Uncirculated Federal Notes from the 1950's are available at slightly over face and seem to be readily available. More recent issues are also suffering from lack of interest while Federal notes of 1928 series are still highly sought after and often difficult to obtain. Collections due to appear later in the year will undoubtedly prove to be a barometer of future expectations. At this point in time, it's still early to discern what's going to happen to the current prices.

The focus of Small Size collectors is generally on strong type material such as R & S Experimentals, early Red Seals and Hawaii/North Africans. The more specialized collector is avidly seeking rare blocks, plates and star notes plus low or unusual serial numbers.

National Bank Notes: (1865–1929). Interest in this area along with prices has risen sharply. The Horwedel Sale of California

Nationals pushed the envelope to still higher and countless record sales have occurred during the past year. Current prices are at multiple of just five years ago. There are, however, a few states where the number of available rare notes exceeds the number of serious collectors. In such states a few new collectors could radically change the value on R4–R6 (1–12 known) notes. Look for a continued high interest level in this area.

Fractionals: (1862–1876). Prices continue to move up on better notes. More common notes such as the Fifth Series are stable and show little change. As in the Large and Small Size Type, rarity and condition are the prime factors. There are a high number of collectors who are obsessed with perfect centering and absolutely pristine condition. This is somehwat feasible due to the high number of notes that are extant. Various sources quote the outstanding in the range of $220,000.00.

Specimen and Proof Fractional Notes command excellent prices in the market place. Most specimen notes have been removed from Fractional Shields that were distributed as anticounterfeiting aids to banks. As such these notes have extremely narrow margins. Proofs can be easily recognized as they are usually wide margined and both types are printed on only a single side. Proofs command substantially higher prices and are much rarer than the narrow margin specimens. Both are in heavy demand and highly sought after. Fractional Shields still appear at auction and the value is primarily dependent on their condition. Remember this if you decide to acquire one.

Western Scrip Notes: (1840–1939) A great deal of interest has been focused on this area over the last few of years and auction records show a sharp increase in both price and demand. In the past, availability of issues has been virtually unknown except to a few collectors and then only in their personal area of expertise. With the advent of internet sales it has finally become possible to track these otherwise scarce notes. The probability of a large number of hitherto unknown notes surfacing is definitely strong and in the last year we've seen a goodly number of these come into the market place. In all but the most common issues, condition plays a very small part in value. The collectors basic concern is in just obtaining a representative note. Most realize that a high grade example may not even exist. If you're interested in a field where great discoveries are still possible and bargains abound, Western Scrip should be a definite consideration.

Error Notes: (1862–present). Prices remain stable. The overwhelming majority of errors found come from the Small Size series of 1928 to date and a great variety of unusual notes is available. Due to low quality control a great profusion of error notes escape the Bureau of Engraving each year. Since some errors are "manfactured" after they leave the BIP. we strongly recommend studying the process of how notes are printed BEFORE purchasing any Errors. Armed with knowledge, you will develop a sense of rarity for notes which cross your path. The primary basis for value is rarity and their visual impact.

Obsolete Notes: (1800–1877). Often referred to as "Broken Bank" have had solid gains across the entire spectrum! These are extremely colorful examples of a byegone banking era when banks and businesses issued their own currency. The range from wildcat banking venturs to state issued notes and are usually collected on a geographical basis. A denomination collection is also a consideration as notes were issued in a plethora of values such as $1.75, $6, $300, etc. One gentlemen we know collects "First, Last and Only" issues, that's the first type issued by a given bank, the last known and anything "unique". Whatever your interest, this is a popular area of our fraternity and sure to have "something for everyone". Prices are generally affordable.

Depression Notes (1933). Popularity for these issues has climbed substantially over the past years as they reach a "collectable age". These notes were issued to supplant Federal currency at a time when the banks were closed national. Without these notes commerce would have ground to a halt and the depression would have been even more severe. The were issued by civic groups, cities, counties and even states and usually were based on monies previously deposited and then frozen in the nations banks. The amount of issue usually represented 40-50% of the deposit assets and most issues were directly tied to banks.

Colonial Notes: (1690–1799). In the 38 years I've watched this market it has remained stable and without any up's and downs. Most collectors in this field due so based on historical significance. Well known colonial gentlemen often signed the notes and it's possible to find the signatures of Governor's, famous men and signers of the Declaration of Independence. You can also obtain notes printed by Benj. Franklin and Paul Revere. Most of the notes are readily available as their value, while in circulation, was constantly going down. For many years the term "Not worth a colonial" was used to denote worthless items.

Military Payment Certificates: (1947–1973). MPC's are popular and quite colorful. They were issued for the use of U.S. military personnel in foreign countries. The market for this material is conditional on grade and highly collected in Uncirculated grade. Replacement notes are also sought after by specialists in this field. Sales of single notes in excess of $1000 now occur with regularity.

Related Areas: Early Checks (1800–1899) are quite popular and highly collecteable. Recently, we've seen rarer checks go to auction for $150–$200. That figure would have been impossible two or three years ago.

Encased Postage is one of the more elusive fields of interest. They were issued during the American Civil War to offset the general lack of coinage created by the committment of valuable metals to the war effort. Close to forty different issues exist and most consist of a round silver plated case containing a U.S. Postal Stamp covered by a thin sheet of clear mica which allowed the stamp to be visible. Condition, denomination and issuer are the prime value factors. They were all isued by private merchants and bear their names on the case. The more common pieces such as "Ayer's Pills" range in the $200 to $250 range while rare issues command substantially more.

CONCLUSION; We close this year's Market Review with the same accurate statement as in the past: "Although interest is at an all time high, the collectible currency field should continue to expand for many years. The entire spectrum of currency-related materials is extremely healthy. Will it stay that way? Past history says it will, and what better way to be involved in the history of a nation than with its money"

PUBLICATIONS

Get a global perspective on paper money collecting from *The Bank Note Reporter*. This monthly tabloid is devoted entirely to U.S. and world paper money, notes, checks, and all related fiscal paper. Find current prices for national and international bank notes, plus an active buy/sell marketplace. *12 monthly issues are $32.00.*

The *Numismatic News* delivers weekly news and information on coin and paper money collecting with exclusive reports from the hobby's only full-time Washington Bureau. Accurate retail/wholesale value guide, current events, and up-to-date calendar make this the most comprehensive numismatic forum available. *52 weekly issues are $32.00.*

For more information, please contact:

Krause Publications
700 East State Street
Iola, WI 54990
Phone 715-445-2214, Subscription Services 1-800-258-0929

USING COMPUTERS TO ENHANCE COIN AND PAPER MONEY COLLECTING

by Tom Bilotta,
Carlisle Development Corporation

Computers are now in widespread use by coin and paper money collectors. Properly exploited, they offer the collector many ways in which to enhance the enjoyment of collecting. They also provide the opportunity for enhanced buying and selling.

In order to take advantage of what computer can do for the collector, it is important to have some basic understanding of what capabilities a computer can bring to collecting. Many collectors first use of a computer consists of a connection to the Internet through one of the service providers such as America Online. This opens up a gateway to the world of collecting, but often leaves collectors at a loss as to where to start. The Internet provides access to much useful information, but it is often surrounded by misinformation.

A second common use of computers among collectors is organizing an inventory of their coins and paper money collection. In addition to helping you to catalog your collection, software can aide you in identifying collection objectives that are aligned with your interests and financial resources. In addition to inventory software, there are a number of educational software products available to assist in specialized aspects of collection such as coin grading and identification of varieties.

In this article, we will examine each of the two uses in more detail, hoping to provide some guidance in the most effective ways to approach these applications.

USING THE INTERNET

Access to the Internet opens up a world of opportunity to the collector of coins and paper money. Probably the three major areas of use are access to information, communication with other collectors, and buying and selling venues.

COMMUNICATION WITH OTHER COLLECTORS

Prior to the existence of the Internet, communications with other collectors was quite limited. Attendance at major coin and paper money shows and participation in local coin clubs presented some opportunity to meet and exchange ideas with other collectors. The Internet, however, has changed the ground rules for communication. Using this obiquitous communications channel, it is possible to converse with other collectors all over the world, unaffected by geographic differences and time zones. There are three basic approaches to such communication.

E-mail provides a vehicle for effective communication across time zones where detailed communications, accompanied by attached pictures and documents, may be carried out with a modest time delay. This is an appropriate medium for detailed communications with other collectors, experts, and dealers.

Instant messaging provides for real-time communication with others. Since it is real time, the issue of time zone differences remains, but in most instances the communication is free, as compared to long distance telephone charges. It does requires some basic typing ability and this often limits the depth of discussion that can be had on this medium.

Online bulletin boards and forums provide a third means of communication. Though it is often difficult to ask a question and get a quick answer, browsing of prior discussion topics can often be very informative and also help to identify others with whom you might wish to communicate directly.

INFORMATION ACCESS

Over the past several years, usage of the Internet has continued to grow. The number of coin and currency sites has grown exponentially. Web sites covering almost any imaginable specialty of coin or currency collecting may be found. These sites are often maintained by very knowledgeable sources. The American Numismatic Association (ANA) maintains a major website dedicated to coin and currency collecting (www.money.org). This site offers a variety of useful information, and links to many other coin and currency related websites. Most major mints have a strong web presence. The United States Mint, for example, has a highly successful website (www.usmint.gov) which has become the preferred way for its customers to purchase coin offerings.

A key aspect of information access is learning to use search engines effectively. This implies both an understanding of how to formulate a search and alos how to interpret the results. A detailed discussion of this topic is beyond the scope of this article, but here are a few basic tips:

- Start with a broad query and add more words to narrow it down until the sites found appear well targeted.
- Don't limit yourself to Google, which is the most-used search engine. Often other specialized search engines will return additional sites or filter more accurately.
- When looking at a results list, quickly scan the first few entries to make sure your search is on target. For example, if you type the word "coin" you might see results for companies that make coin counting machines, when you are looking for coin collecting related sites. Even "Coin collecting" might return results so broad that you need at least one additional word such as "Canadian coin collecting" or "ancient coin collecting"
- Use phrases, such as "coin collecting," rather than the separate words "coin" and "collecting". This will only return responses which contain the two words "coin collecting" together, rather than sites which happen to have the two words separated and with meanings unrelated to coin collecting.

BUYING AND SELLING COINS ON THE INTERNET

Online access provides the collector with the opportunity to buy, sell, and trade coins with many other parties using several different methods. Whereas before the Internet, a collector was limited to a few local coin shops and mail order firms, it is now possible to establish relationships with dealers and collectors all over the world, using the Internet to transmit the detailed information needed to consummate a transaction and establish good working relationships.

This increased access to the marketplace allows the buyer/seller to better understand the marketplace for collectibles activity and should result in more effective transactions. Additionally, online auctions provide an opportunity for both buyers and sellers to participate in a real-time auction not limited by their ability to travel.

The impact of computer technology on coin and paper money collecting on your access to the collecting community is only limited by your imagination.

COIN AND PAPER MONEY INVENTORY SOFTWARE

When collectors think of using computer software to assist their collecting, they first think of an inventory program. Their goal is to catalog their collection and then use this information to generate a variety of printed reports. These reports include a wide variety of sorted and filtered listings to assist in managing a collection, want lists which identify items one is seeking, sales lists of items to be sold or traded, detailed inventories for insurance purposes, and many other purposes.

ORGANIZING YOUR COLLECTION WITH COIN AND PAPER MONEY INVENTORY SOFTWARE

Collectors of coins and currency fall into several categories. There is the serious coin collector, who enjoys the hobby and pursues personally defined collecting objectives. Accumulators retain many of the coins that they receive in normal commerce and build up large quantities of unsorted coins. Investors use coin collecting to build portfolios intended to produce profits. Inheritors receive a coin collection or accumulation from their families and must decide how they will handle a potentially valuable asset.

All of these collectors have a common need to catalog their items and understand their value. Most collectors also have accumulated many items with a very wide range of values.

A modern inventory program can adapt to meet the needs of all types of users, from novice collectors to experienced experts. It will incorporate a comprehensive database of coins and/or paper money to assist the user in identifying and defining their collections as well as a flexible set of functions to enable them to organize their collection in a manner consistent with their collection methodology.

Most collectors will want to organize their collections into several groupings that mirror their physical collections. For example, someone with coin albums of common series such as Mercury dimes, statehood quarters, or Buffalo nickels will want to have software albums organized in a similar fashion. Other coins might be grouped into coins for sale, duplicates, partial collections for other family members, or any other categorization which suits the collector.

USING YOUR TIME WISELY

When using computer software to catalog a coin or paper money collection, it is important to use it in a manner consistent with your purposes and which will enhance your enjoyment. You should spend your time, therefore, working with the portions of your collection in which you have the most interest or where the primary financial value exists.

For example, if you are collecting a complete set of Mercury dimes, you may wish to scan an image of each individual piece so that you can print picture catalogs of your collection. For these coins, you might choose to enter complete information including purchase price, source, certification information, origin, etc. For this type of grouping you will also likely want to include coins that you don't have that are required to complete your collection, enabling you to generate want lists. This will also assist you in identifying the cost to complete your collection and planning your approach.

For large quantities of relatively inexpensive items or coins worth only bullion content, and where you have no particular collecting interest, you might choose to only enter a single line item and not bother to take the time to list each coin individually. For example, if you have several hundred silver Washington quarters in circulated condition from the 1950s and 1960s you might enter the single line item "225 Washington Quarters" with a date range and average value. In this way, large accumulations can be tracked with minimum effort and your attention can be focused on your real collecting interests. Your coin inventory program should adapt to all of these possible approaches to organizing your collection.

EVALUATING COIN AND PAPER MONEY INVENTORY SOFTWARE

The quality of the software that you purchase will greatly impact the success of your efforts.

One of the most important parts of a coin inventory program is the database. The database contains standard information about coins and paper money and saves the user from having to type this information manually. The greater the amount of information in the standard database, the easier the task of data entry. A modern coin collecting program, should at a minimum include coin type, date, mint mark, denomination, and variety. Comprehensive programs, such as those made by Carlisle Development Corporation also include such information as designer/engraver, coinage metal, size, weight, edge, and mintage. The organization of the database should reflect commonly used groupings and thereby provide user with guidance in organizing their collection.

Some inventory programs include current market values. It is important that these are updated frequently and produced by reliable sources. Coin values should evolve to include areas of high market interest. For example, over the past year, the market interest in high grade recent coin issues has become very high. It is also important to allow the user the ability to extend the database to include items that are not listed. These may be specialized varieties, private mint products, or other coin-related collectibles.

Ability to share data with other programs and people is also very important. Most computerized collectors are connected to the

Internet and will want to share some information with other collectors and dealers. The ability to export listings in common text readable formats for transmission over the Internet or for input into a word processor or spreadsheet is of great value in buying and selling coins and paper money.

Carlisle Development's inventory software *Collector's Assistant* provides a comprehensive database of all coins ever minted by the United States Mint. This includes all type coins by date and mint mark, bullion coins, sets, old, and new commemoratives. Recent additions to the database are the 50 states circulating quarters and the new Sacagawea dollar. Coin values are licensed from Coin World, Inc., an industry leader in providing coin valuations. Quarterly updates are available by subscription allowing collectors to maintain trends of their values. Carlisle Development's *Currency Collector's Assistant* has a complete database based on *Friedberg's Paper Money of the United States, 16ᵗʰ Edition*. This database includes all U.S. Paper Money, including Confederate notes, and Encased postage stamps. A relationship with CDN, publisher of the *Greensheet,* makes value information available to the paper money collector in electronic format.

For collectors of ancient coins, Carlisle offers an add-on database containing color images of several hundred ancient coins and a specialized interface containing data entry fields appropriate for ancient coins. For example, the date field can handle and sort mixed AD/BC dates and has long fields for obverse and reverse inscriptions. The most recent additions to Carlisle Development's databases include the Euro Coin Database and World Currency Database.

REPORT GENERATION

Once you have entered your coin collection into an inventory program, the most important function will become its ability to generate a wide array of reports and/or exports for informational purposes.

You will probably want to have a detailed listing, identifying items, their value, and where they are stored for insurance purposes. You will want to generate partial lists of your collections for sales and trading. You may want to generate labels to aide in identifying your coins. You may want to look at your collection in many different ways, such as sorted by value, metal content, or collection completeness.

One common need of coin collectors is the printing of inserts for 2" flips. Once catalogued, computer software can allow you to produce customized flip inserts in a standard format of your own design.

Report generation is the subset of an inventory program which produces the listings that you view on the screen, print on paper, or export to other computer applications. Its flexibility will greatly impact its utility. For example, you may want to generate two listings of coins that you have for sale, one which includes your cost and target price (your copy), and one which does not include this information for general distribution to prospective buyers.

At various times, you will probably want to be able to list any subset of the information fields, filter based on a wide array of parameters and sort using different criteria.

OTHER FUNCTIONALITY YOU SHOULD EXPECT FROM YOUR INVENTORY SOFTWARE

Inventory software should be able to store all of the information in which a collector is interested. Specific fields will vary based on collector interest and purpose. Some will require detailed certification and descriptive information, others comprehensive purchase and sales history. Some collectors will want to have comprehensive recording of storage location and insurance information. Modern programs provide sufficient information fields to meet all of these needs.

Backup and restore functionality should allow the user to easily protect the data they have meticulously entered. History charting enables the user to track the changes of value of a part of their collection over time.

Good software must be easy to use and supported by context sensitive help which provides the user with detailed instructions in a "how-to" format on all of the basic functions that they will wish to perform.

AVAILABILITY OF TIMELY UPDATES

Once you have taken the time to catalog your collection in a computer program, you will want to preserve your investment by having access to database updates incorporating information on new coin releases as well as changes in value. Your supplier of inventory software should have a timely program for availability of annual database and value updates.

EDUCATIONAL SOFTWARE FOR COLLECTORS

Adding significantly to your enjoyment of collections are electronic information sources that exploit the power of the computer to present you with high quality information in an easily accessible format. These programs can provide comprehensive knowledge of all aspects of coin collecting, detailed information on grading coins, and specialized information such as collecting coin varieties.

COIN GRADING

Most coin collectors will want to be able to grade their coins, at least to an approximate grade. This enables them to have an understanding of value as well as identify coins that might be appropriate for certification. Coin grading skill is built up through time and experience.

The Grading Assistant, offered by Carlisle Development is based on the official grading guide of the American Numismatic Association. It enables the user to view side-by-side images of their own coins along with various grades from the ANA grading set. These images are supported by detailed descriptions of the wear points for each grade. Using software such as the *Grading Assistant*, a user can develop their skill in grading coins and establish approximate grades for their collection.

VARIETY COLLECTING

The collecting of coin varieties is an exciting area of the hobby currently experiencing some growth. Varieties are the result of differences in the minting process or dies which produce design differences and/or errors. These include such effects as doubling of some features or letters, extra pieces of metal on the coin surface and die breaks. Variety collecting requires the collector to identify subtle differences in coin designs.

The Morgan dollar series is one of the most commonly collected and is categorized by many varieties. Carlisle Development offers a *Top 100 Morgan Dollar* CD, based on the book written by Michael Fey and Jeff Oxman. This work provides pictures, identification information, and values for the most sought after and valuable Morgan dollar varieties. It provides a spectacular set of high quality pictures to assist you in identifying these coins and also the full text and information provided in this work.

GENERAL EDUCATIONAL WORKS ON COLLECTING

There is much to learn about coin collecting, whether it is technical knowledge such as grading and authentication or practical knowledge such as buying and selling coins, attending trade shows, or participating in auctions. Educational computer software offers advantages over printed works in that the contents may be searched and indexed allowing the user to rapidly retrieve valuable information.

Carlisle Development offers the *Coin Collector's Survival Manual,* an interactive edition of the work by Scott Travers. This work provides a set of information that every collector of coins should have. The entire contents of this book are provided in a searchable, interactive format. This allows the user to easily locate information based on word searching, topics, illustrations, bookmarks, a table of contents, or index. In addition to the contents of the book, a set of high quality NGC PhotoProof images have been included for such topics as identifying MS-63, MS-65, and MS-67 coins and toning. An interactive grading calculator brings to life the grading methods described in the book.

WELL-DESIGNED COMPUTER SOFTWARE WILL ADD TO YOUR ENJOYMENT OF COLLECTING

Carlisle Development Corporation publishes the most comprehensive line of collector software available, especially regarding coins and paper money.

Central to Carlisle's product line is the *Collector's Assistant,* the most advanced and comprehensive collection software available. It is sold in a variety of configurations to serve collectors of over thirty collectible types from autographs to toys. Most extensive is support for coins and paper money. The Collector's Assistant family includes:

- **United States Coin Database**—complete listings of all U.S. coinage from 1793 to the present. 50 State quarter program and Sacagawea dollar are recent additions. This also includes Colonial and Hawaiian coinage.
- **World Coin Database**—A listing of over 5000 coin types from over forty-five countries, which may be extended by the user.
- **Ancient Coin Database**—includes several thousand listings of Byzantine, Judaic, Roman, and Greek coinage along with several hundred images. Data entry screens are optimized for ancient coin collectors including long fields for inscriptions and preloaded choice lists of rulers, ancient denominations, towns, mints and others.
- **United States Currency Database**—A complete listing of all United States currency based on Friedberg's 16th Edition, *Paper Money of the United States.* This also includes 120 high quality color images of early US currency.

To learn more about Carlisle Development's product line, visit our website at www.carlisledevelopment.com. You will find current product information and may also place orders. You can reach us by e-mail at support@carlisledevelopment.com or by phone at 800-219-0257.

COLLECTING ORGANIZATIONS

PROFESSIONAL CURRENCY DEALERS ASSOCIATION (PCDA)

Looking for a reliable paper money dealer? . . . Collecting rare paper money can be an enjoyable hobby. Imagine being able to own an example of fractional currency printed during the Civil War era, or a National Bank Note issued by a financial institution in your own state.

Whatever your collecting interests, the members of the Professional Currency Dealers Association (PCDA) will be pleased to assist and guide you. The members of this prestigious trade association specialize in virtually all the areas of paper money collecting.

Once you've started to collect, it can sometimes be a challenge to locate a dealer with a significant inventory. Members of the PCDA are the market makers for currency collectors. Whatever your interest, a PCDA member is certain to be able to supply you. Whether you are a beginner on a limited budget or an advanced collector of many years' experience, you can be certain that you'll find fair, courteous, and reliable treatment with a member of the Professional Currency Dealers Association.

CONTACT INFORMATION

General Information and Correspondence

James A. Simek
PCDA Secretary
P.O. Box 7157
Westchester, IL 60154
(630) 889-8207
E-mail: nge3@attbi.com

PCDA Publication

Ron Horstman
PCDA
P.O. Box 2999
Leslie, MO 63056

THE SOCIETY OF PAPER MONEY COLLECTORS (SPMC)

The Society of Paper Money Collectors (SPMC) invites you to become a member of our organization. SPMC was founded in 1961 with the following objectives: (1) Encourage the collecting and study of all paper money and financial documents; (2) Provide collectors the opportunity to meet and enjoy fraternal relations with their fellow collectors; (3) Furnish information and knowledge about paper money; (4) Encourage research about paper money and financial documents and publish the resulting information; (5) Promote legislation favorable to collectors; (6) Advance the prestige of the hobby of numismatics; (7) Promote rational and consistent classification of exhibits, and ENCOURAGE participation by our members; (8) Encourage realistic and consistent market valuations.

Paper Money, SPMC's bimonthly journal now in its 36th year, has repeatedly been selected by the ANA as the Best Specialty Publication in numismatics; the Numismatic Literary Guild has also selected *Paper Money* for first-place recognition. Virtually every article in every issue is written by an SPMC member, who receives no monetary compensation. SPMC coordinates and judges the exhibits at the largest all-paper show every year. SPMC co-sponsors many large all-paper shows held in the U.S. each year.

Information about membership may be obtained by writing to:

Frank Clark
P.O. Box 117060
Carrollton, TX 75011

PCDA MEMBERSHIP DIRECTORY

Rick Allard
Cashmans Currency
3453 Green Pine Place
Simi Valley, CA 93065
(805) 579-0339
Cellular: (805) 279-1641
FAX: (805) 579-0339
Web Site: www.cashmanscurrency.
com
E-Mail: cashmanscurrency@aol.com

United States Large Size Type Notes
United States Small Size Type Notes
Fancy and Low Serial Numbers
Notes
Error Notes

Robert Azpiazu
First City Currency & Collectibles,
Inc.
P.O. Drawer 1629
St. Augustine, FL 32085
(904) 794-0784
Fax: (904) 824-1018
Web Site: www.fstctycurr.com
E-mail: fstctycurr@aug.com

United States Small Size Type Notes
Star Notes
Error Notes
Fancy and Low Serial Number Notes
FRN Blocks
Auction Representation
Estate Appraisals

Pat Barnes
Pat Barnes Paper Money
P.O. Box 25114
Lansing, MI 48909

(517) 333-9980
Fax: (517) 333-9980
E-mail: patbarnes@voyager.net

United States Large Size Type Notes
United States National Bank Notes
United States Small Size Notes - By
Type and Variety

Doris Bart
Bart, Inc.
P.O. Box 2
Roseville, MI 48066
(586) 979-3400
Fax: (586) 979-7976
Web Site: www.ErrorNotes.com
E-mail: bartinccor@aol.com

Auction Representation
Rare United States Small Size
Notes
United States Large Size Type Notes
Error Notes
Autographed Notes

Frederick J. Bart
Bart, Inc.
P.O. Box 2
Roseville, MI 48066
(586) 979-3400
Fax: (586) 979-7976
Web Site: www.ErrorNotes.com
E-mail: bartinccor@aol.com

Error Notes
Serial #1 National Bank Notes
Uncut Sheets
Rare Small Size Notes
Large Size Type Notes

Keith S. Bauman
TNA Associates
P.O. Box 250027
Franklin, MI 48025-0027
(248) 647-8938
E-mail: TNAksbauman@earthlink.net

*United States Large Size Type
Notes
United States Small Size Type
Notes
United States Fractional Currency
United States Military Payment
Certificates
Confederate
World Paper Money
Numismatic Related Art Work*

David A. Berg
Dave Berg, Ltd.
P.O. Box 348
Portersville, PA 16051
(724) 452-4586
Fax: (724) 452-0276
E-mail: davbergltd@aol.com

*Error Notes
Mail Order Price Lists
United States Fractional Currency
United States Large Size Type Notes
United States National Bank Notes
United States Small Size Type Notes*

Carl Bombara
P.O. Box 524
New York, NY 10116
(212) 989-9108
(888) 449-9268
Fax: (212) 989-9108
E-mail: CBcurrency@aol.com

*United States Large Size Type Notes
United States Small Size Type Notes
United States National Bank Notes
Error Notes
Mail Order Sales
Auction Representation
Want Lists Serviced*

Q. David Bowers
American Numismatic Rarities
P.O. Box 1804
Wolfeboro, NH 03894
Toll Free: (866) 811-1804
Fax: (603) 569-3875
Web Site: www.anrcoins.com
E-mail: qdavid@anrcoins.com

*Auction Services for American
Colonial, Obsolete, Confederate,
Federal Related Paper Money of all
Eras
Celebrating 50 years in professional
numismatics 1953-2003
Past president Professional
Numismatists Guild (1977-1979)
Past president American Numismatic
Association (1983-1995)*

Jason W. Bradford
**Heritage / Currency Auctions of
America**
3500 Maple Avenue, 17th Floor
Dallas, TX 75219-3938
Toll Free: (800) 872-6467, Ext. 280
Fax: (214) 443-8425

Jennifer Cangeme
Denly's of Boston
P.O. Box 51010
Boston, MA 02205
(617) 482-8477
(800) HI DENLY (Orders Only)
Fax: (617) 357-8163
Web Site: www.denlys.com
E-mail: jen@denlys.com

*Colonial and Continental
United States Fractional Currency
United States Large Size Type Notes
United States Small Size Type Notes
Confederate
Obsolete Notes
United States National Bank Notes
Error Notes
Books and Supplies
Military Payment Certificates
World Paper Money
Auction Sales - Bidder Representative
Mail Order Price Lists
Encased Postage
Mylar D† Currency Holders
United States & Foreign Coins*

I. Nelson Clark
I. Nelson Clark Banknotes
P.O. Box 883
Los Alamitos, CA 90720
(714) 761-3683
Cell: (714) 809-5120
Fax: (714) 761-3683
E-mail: inellclark@attbi.com

*United States Currency
United States National Bank Notes*

Arthur D. Cohen
Penfield Note Exchange
P.O. Box 311
Penfield, NY 14526-0311
(585) 377-4677
Fax: (585) 377-4677
E-mail: adcohen@frontiernet.net

World Paper Money
Mail Order Price Lists
Custom Labels For Currency
Holders,
Flips and Slabs

Terry Coyle
Alex Perakis Coins & Currency
P.O. Box 246
Lima, PA 19037
(610) 627-1212
Fax: (610) 891-1466

United States National Bank Notes
United States Large Size Type Notes
United States Small Size Type Notes

Paul Cuccia
C $ H Coins & Collectibles, Inc.
P.O. Box 326
Belvidere, NJ 07823
(908) 475-1026

United States Large Size Type Notes
United States Small Size Type Notes
Obsolete Notes
United States National Bank Notes
Error Notes
Small Size Stars

Pat Cyrgalis
A.P. Cyrgalis Currency
P.O. Box 141235
Staten Island, NY 10314-0008
(718) 448-7615
Fax: (718) 448-7615
E-mail: apcyrgalis@att.net

United States Large Size Type Notes
United States Small Size Type Notes
United States National Bank Notes

John DeMaris
P.O. Box 72
Boys Town, NE 68010
(402) 334-2756
E-mail: siramed@aol.com
Colonial and Continental
United States Fractional Currency

United States Large Size Type Notes
United States Small Size Type Notes
Confederate
Obsolete Notes
United States National Bank Notes

Thomas M. Denly
Denly's of Boston
P.O. Box 51010
Boston, MA 02205
(617) 482-8477
(800) HI DENLY (Orders Only)
Fax: (617) 357-8163
Web Site: www.denlys.com
E-mail: denlys@aol.com

Colonial and Continental
United States Fractional Currency
United States Large Size Type Notes
United States Small Size Type Notes
Confederate
Obsolete Notes
United States National Bank Notes
Error Notes
Books and Supplies
Military Payment Certificates
World Paper Money
Auction Sales - Bidder
Representative
Mail Order Price Lists
Encased Postage
Mylar D† Currency Holders
United States & Foreign Coins

Tom Durkin
P.O. Box 328
Walland, TN 37886
(865) 448-3290
E-mail: tdurkin@bellsouth.net

United States Large Size Type Notes
United States Small Size Type Notes
Confederate
Obsolete Notes
United States National Bank Notes

Lawrence Falater
P.O. Box 81
Allen, MI 49227
(517) 437-8977
(888) FALTER (Toll Free)
Fax: (517) 437-8978

Stock and Bonds
Obsolete Notes
United States National Bank Notes
United States Currency - All Kinds
Including Errors

Confederate
Colonial and Continental
World Paper Money
Specialized Price Lists
Books on Paper Money and Stocks
Specialist: Michigan Paper; Stocks;
Automobile,
Aviation, Banking, and Beverages

Don Fisher
Currency Unlimited
P.O. Box 481
Decatur, IL 62525
(217) 692-2825
Fax: (217) 692-2825

Obsolete Notes
United States National Bank Notes
World Paper Money

Tom Flynn
801 Kerper Court
Dubuque, IA 52001
(563) 583-6494
Fax: (563) 583-7453
E-mail: flynngroup@aol.com

United States Small Size Type Notes
Federal Reserve Notes
Auction Representation

Kevin Foley
Currency Auctions of America. Inc.
P.O. Box 370650
Milwaukee, WI 53237
(414) 421-3498
(800) USCOINS, ext. 256
Fax: (414) 423-0343

Auction Sales
Auction Representation
Internet Sales
Colonial and Continental Notes
Confederate Notes
Error Notes
Low and Fancy Serial Numbers
Obsolete Notes
Serial #1 Notes
United States Fractional Currency
United States Large Size Type Notes
United States National Bank Notes
United States Small Size Type Notes
Numismatic Conventions and Show
Management

Dennis Forgue
Harlan J. Berk, Ltd.
31 North Clark Street
Chicago, IL 60602
(312) 609-0016

Fax: (312) 609-1305
Web Site: www.harlanjberk.com
United States Large Size Type Notes
United States Small Size Type Notes
Confederate
Obsolete Notes
United States National Bank Notes
Error Notes
Autographs

Stephen Goldsmith
R.M. Smythe & Co., Inc.
2 Rector Street, 12th Floor
New York, NY 10006-1844
(212) 943-1880 or (212) 312-6304
Toll Free: (800) 622-1880
Fax: (212) 908-4670
E-mail: sgoldsmith@smytheonline.com

Auction Sales
Autographs
Colonial and Continental
Confederate
Financial Documents
Mail Order Sales
Mail Order Price Lists
Obsolete Notes
Stocks, Bonds and Fiscal Documents
United States Fractional Currency
United States Large Size Type Notes
United States Small Size Type Notes
United States National Bank Notes
World Paper Money

Bruce R. Hagen
P.O. Box 836
Bowling Green Station
New York, NY 10274-0836
(212) 721-2028

Appraisals
Auction Representation
Colonial and Continental
Consulting Services
Financial Documents
Obsolete Notes and Proofs
United States Federal Proofs, Essays
& Vignettes
Stocks, Bonds and Fiscal Documents
Security Printing Archives, Histories
& Artifacts
United States National Bank Notes
World Paper Money

Larry Hanks
Hanks & Associates
415 North Mesa
El Paso, TX 79901
(915) 544-8188

Fax: (915) 544-8194
United States Large Size Type Notes
United States Small Size Type Notes
United States National Bank Notes

Quintin H. Hartt
Red River Rarities
P.O. Box 12444
Alexandria, LA 71315
(318) 443-4405
(800) 314-4405
Fax: (318) 484-3939

United States Large Size Type Notes
United States Small Size Type Notes
World Paper Money

James R. Hatch
P.O. Box 978
Londonderry, NH 03053-0978
(603) 434-3635
Web Site: www.frn-ones.com
E-mail:jim61@frn-ones.com

Specializing in High Grade $1 FRN's

Joe L. Hensley
Char's Paper
P.O. Box 234
Madison, IN 47250
(812) 273-1683

United States Large Size Type Notes
United States National Bank Notes

Roland Hill
Rare Choice Currency
P.O. Box 6426
Fort Myers, FL 33911
(239) 549-7267
E-mail: Hillco@aaacoll.com

United States Large Size Type Notes
United States Small Size Type Notes
United States National Bank Notes
United States Fractional Currency
Obsolete Notes
Colonial and Continental
Confederate
Civil War Photos
Rare Autographs
Canadian
Western Americana
Early Railroad
Star Notes
F.R.N. Red Seals

Gregg Hoffman
Premier Precious Metals Coins &
Currency

P.O. Box 28100
Santa Fe, NM 87592-8100
(505) 989-7680
(800) 557-9958
Fax: (505) 989-7685
Web Site: www.premierprecious
metals.com
E-mail: cindy@premierprecious
metals.com

United States Large Size Type Notes
United States Small Size Type Notes
Silver Dollars
Bust Type Silver Dollars
Older Type Coin

Honorary Life Member
Ronald Horstman
P.O. Box 2999
Leslie, MO 63056
(573) 764-4139

St. Louis National Bank Notes
St. Louis Obsolete Notes
St. Louis Checks
St. Louis Merchants and Bank
Tokens

Lowell C. Horwedel
P.O. Box 2395
West Lafayette, IN 47996
(765) 583-2748
Fax: (765 583-4584
Web Site: www.horwedelscurrency.
com
E-mail: lhorwedel@insightbb.com

United States National Bank Notes
Colonial and Continental
United States Large Size Type Notes
United States Small Size Type Notes
Confederate
Obsolete Notes
Error Notes
Checks
Books and Supplies
World Paper Money
Mail Order Price Lists

Steve Ivy
Heritage / Currency Auctions of
America
3500 Maple Avenue, 17th Floor
Dallas, TX 75219-3938
(214) 528-3500
(800) 872-6467
Fax: (214) 448-8409
Web Site: www.heritagecoin.com
E-mail: steve@heritagecoin.com

Auction Sales of:
United States Large Size Type Notes
United States Small Size Type Notes
United States National Bank Notes
United States Fractional Currency
Error Notes
Colonial and Continental
Confederate
Obsolete Notes

Peter Johnson
Staples Numismatics, Inc.
P.O. Box 541255
Lake Worth, FL 33454-1255
(561) 383-6631
Fax: (561) 383-6621
E-mail: staplescoin@earthlink.net

World Paper money
United States Large Size Type Notes
United States Small Size Type Notes

Harry E. Jones
Harry E. Jones Rare Currency
7379 Pearl Road
Cleveland, OH 44130
(440) 234-3330
Fax: (440) 234-3332
E-mail: hjones6671@aol.com

Error Notes
United States Large Size Type Notes
United States Small Size Type Notes
United States National Bank Notes
Obsolete Notes
Serial #1 Notes
Uncut Sheets

Jeffrey S. Jones
The Small Size Shop
P.O. Box 2007
Westerville, OH 43086
(614) 899-1803
Fax: (614) 899-1557
E-mail: jeff.jones@gnorth.com

United States Small Size Type Notes
Especially High Grade and Rare
Ohio National Bank Notes
Ohio Obsolete Notes

Glen I. Jorde
**Lake Region Coin & Currency
Exchange**
323 Fourth Street
P.O. Box 48
Devils Lake, ND 58301
(701) 662-5770

(800) 803-2322
Fax: (701) 662-5775
E-mail: lrcc@stellarnet.com

United States Large Size Type Notes
United States Small Size Type Notes
United States National Bank Notes
Confederate
Obsolete Notes
Checks
Mail Order Price Lists

A.M. "Art" Kagin
A.M. Kagin, NEWCO, Inc.
505 Fifth Avenue, Suite 1001
Des Moines, IA 50309
(515) 243-7363
Fax: (515) 288-8681

United States National Bank Notes
United States Large Size Type Notes
and Varieties
Handled over 95% of U.S. Notes in
Friedberg
United States Small Size Type Notes
and Varieties
Error Notes
Rarities - Gem to VF
Star Notes - Large and Small
Uncut Sheets - Large and Small
Encased Postage
Odd and Unusual Serial Number
Notes

Donald H. Kagin
Kagin's
98 Main Street, Suite 201
Tiburon, CA 94920
(415) 435-1627
(888) 8KAGINS
Fax: (415) 435-1627
E-mail: kagins@earthlink.net

Gem United States Type Notes
United States Fractional Currency

Judith Kagin
Kagin's
98 Main Street, Suite 201
Tiburon, CA 94920
(415) 435-1627
(888) 8KAGINS
Fax: (415) 435-1627
E-mail: kagins@earthlink.net

High Quality and Rare United States
Paper Money
Mail Order Sales

Allen Karn
Allen's Coin Shop
399 South State Street
Westerville, OH 43081
(614) 882-3937
(800) 848-3966
Fax: (614) 882-0662
Web Site: www.allensinc.com/coins

Colonial and Continental
United States Large Size Type Notes
United States Small Size Type Notes
Confederate
Obsolete Notes
United States National Bank Notes
Books and Supplies
Military Payment Certificates
World Paper Money
United States Fractional Currency
Mail Order Price Lists

Don C. Kelly
Paper Money Institute
P.O. Box 85
Oxford, OH 45056
(513) 312-4760
Web Site: www.donckelly.com
E-mail: don@donckelly.com

United States Paper Money
Colonial and Continental
Obsolete Notes
United States National Bank Notes

Lyn F. Knight
Lyn Knight Currency Auctions
P.O. Box 7364
Overland Park, KS 66207-0364
(913) 338-3779
(800) 243-5211
Fax: (913) 338-4754
Web Site: www.collectors.com/
lynknight/
E-mail: lynfknight@aol.com

Auction Sales for National
Conventions
United States Large Size Type Notes
United States National Bank Notes
United States Small Size Type Notes
United States Fractional Currency
Mail Bid Sales

David R. Koble
Mid America Currency
P.O. Box 1282
Bartlesville, OK 74005
(918) 335-0847

Cellular: (918) 914-1496
Fax: (918) 335-3110
E-mail: dkoble@cableone.net

United States Large Size Type Notes
United States Small Size Type Notes
United States National Bank Notes
United States Fractional Currency
Error Notes
Auction Representation

Paul L. Koppenhaver
Thalpa, Inc. / The Coin Haven
P.O. Box 34056
Granada Hills, CA 91394
(818) 832-8068
Fax: (818) 832-8987
E-mail: plkopp@as.net

United States Large Size Type Notes
United States Small Size Type Notes
United States National Currency
Sutler Scrip
Western Americana
Autographs
Exonumia

Robert J. Kravitz
Rob's Coins & Currency
P.O. Box 303
Wilton, CA 95693
(916) 687-7219
E-mail: robsfractional@aol.com

Specialist: United States Fractional
Currency
All United States Currency
United States Large and Small Size
Gold Certificates
Error Notes
Colonial and Continental Currency

Tim Kyzivat
P.O. Box 451
Western Springs, IL 60558
(708) 784-0974
Web Site: www.kyzivatcurrency.com
E-mail: tkyzivat@kyzivatcurrency.
com

Chicago Area National Bank Notes
Illinois National Bank Notes
United States Large Size Type Notes
United States National Bank Notes
United States Small Size Type Notes
Confederate Currency
Obsolete Notes
Error Notes

Jay Laws
Scotsman Coins
11262 Olive Blvd.
St. Louis, MO 63141
(314) 692-2646
(800) 642-4305
Fax: (314) 692-0410

United States National Bank Notes
United States Large Size Type Notes
United States Small Size Type Notes
Confederate Currency
Military Payment Certificates

Stuart Levine
P.O. Box 217
Sudbury, MA
(978) 443-9070
E-Mail: smlevine@ix.netcom.com

Colonial and Continental Currency

Scott Lindquist
R.M. Smythe & Co., Inc.
26 Broadway, Suite 973
New York, NY 10004-1703
(212) 943-1880, ext. 4677
(800) 622-1880
Cellular: (602) 741-3385
Fax: (212) 908-4670
E-mail: slindquist@smytheonline.com

United States and Canadian
Currency - Large and Small
Canadian Charter Bank Notes
World Paper Money
Colonial and Continental
United States Fractional Currency
Confederate
Obsolete Notes
United States National Bank Notes
Error Notes
Books and Supplies
Military Payment Certificates
Auction Sales - Bidder
Representative

Dana Linett
Early American Numismatics
P.O. Box 675390
Rancho Santa Fe, CA 92067
Early American History Auctions, Inc.
P.O. Box 3507
Rancho Santa Fe, CA 92067
(858) 759-3290
Fax: (619) 374-7280
Web Site: www.earlyamerican.com
E-mail: dana@earlyamerican.com

Colonial and Continental
United States Fractional Currency
United States Large Size Type Notes
United States Small Size Type Notes
Confederate
Stocks, Bonds and fiscal Documents
Checks
Books and Supplies
Auction Sales
Mail Order Price Lists
Mail Bid Sales
Encased Postage Stamps
Historic Maps
Rare Autographs

Jess Lipka
Numismania
P.O. Box 847
Flemington, NJ 08822
(908) 782-1635
Cellular: (908) 500-1885
Fax: (908) 782-6235

United States National Bank Notes
United States Large Size Type Notes
United States Small Size Type Notes
Rare Coins

William Litt
William Litt Rare Coins & Currency
P.O. Box 6778
San Mateo, CA 94403
(650) 458-8842
Fax: (650) 458-8843
E-mail: billlitt@aol.com

United States National Bank Notes
United States Large Size Type Notes
National Bank Memorabilia

Claire Lobel
Coincraft
44 & 45 Great Russell Street
London WC1B 3LU
ENGLAND
(44) 20 7636 1188
Fax: (44) 20 7323 2860
E-mail: clairlob@aol.com

England, Scotland, Ireland, Channel
Islands, Isle of Man
General World

Ray Marrello
Antique Currency LLC
P.O. Box 807
Mundelein, IL 60060
(847) 566-2620

Fax: (847) 566-2620
Web Site: www.rmcurrency.com
E-mail: rmcurrency@aol.com

United States Large Size Type Notes
United States Small Size Type Notes
United States National Bank Notes

David V. Messner
Constellation Numismatics
P.O. Box 209
Akron, OH 17501-0209
(717) 721-9504

Error Notes
Colonial and Continental
United States Error and Die Variety
Coins

James W. Miller
Deuceman Currency.com
P.O. Box 2452
Statesboro, GA 30458
(912) 284-1586
Cellular: (912) 614-4980
Web Site: www.deucemancurrency.
com
E-mail: jwmiller11@aol.com

Obsolete Notes
Confederate
Colonial and Continental
United States National Currency
United States Large Size Type Notes
United States Small Size Type Notes
Internet Auction Sales
Auction Bidder Representation

Thomas J. Modzelesky, Jr.
Gemini Coin
P.O. Box 344
Suffield, CT 06078
(860) 668-2838
Fax: (860) 668-2838
E-mail: Geminicoin@aol.com

United States National Currency
United States Large Size Type Notes
United States Small Size Type Notes

Charles D. Moore
Charles D. Moore, Inc.
P.O. Box 5233
Walnut Creek, CA 94596
(925) 946-0150
Fax: (925) 930-7710

Auction Sales
Mail Bid Sales

Canadian and Related Paper Money
Canadian Cheques
Canadian Fiscal Documents

Stanley Morycz
P.O. Box 355
Englewood, OH 45322
(937) 898-0114

United States Large Size Type Notes

V.H."Ossie" Oswald, Sr.
Ossie's Coin Shop
June to December
P.O. Box 304
Emmaus, PA 18049
(610) 965-9485
(610) 433-4474
Fax: (610) 967-5852
January to June
P.O. Box 810423
Boca Raton, FL 33498
(561) 483-9626
Fax: (561) 483-8390

United States Large Size Type Notes
United States Small Size Type Notes
United States National Bank Notes
Error Notes
Confederate
Better Broken Bank Notes
Mail Order Price Lists
Please Send Want Lists

Thomas N. Panichella
Stack's
123 West 57th Street
New York, NY 10019
(212) 582-2580
Fax: (212) 245-5018

Auction Sales
Appraisals
United States Currency of All Types
United States Coins of All Type
World Coins and Paper Money

Charles C. Parrish
P.O. Box 481
Rosemount. MN 55068
(651) 423-1039

United States Large Size Type Notes
United States Small Size Type Notes
United States National Bank Notes
Obsolete Notes
All Minnesota Nationals

Huston Pearson, Jr.
P.O. Box 13559
Arlington, TX 76094-3559
(817) 274-5971

United States Large Size Type Notes
United States Small Size Type Notes
Republic of Texas Notes
Texas National Bank Notes
United States Fractional Currency
Colonial and Continental Currency
Confederate
Military Payment Certificates
Obsolete Notes
Books and Supplies

Alex G. Perakis
Alex Perakis Coins & Currency
P.O. Box 246
Lima, PA 19037
(610) 627-1212
(610) 565-1110
Fax: (610) 891-1466
and
12941 North Pioneer Way
Tucson, AZ 85737
(520) 544-7778
Fax: (520) 544-7779
E-mail: alperakis@aol.com

United States Fractional Currency
United States Large Size Type Notes
United States Small Size Type Notes
United States National Bank Notes
United States Obsolete Notes

Stephen Perakis
Alex Perakis Coins & Currency
P.O. Box 246
Lima, PA 19037
(610) 627-1212
(610) 565-1110
Fax: (610) 891-1466

United States Fractional Currency
United States Large Size Type Notes
United States Small Size Type Notes
United States National Bank Notes

Earl N. Petersen
USA Coins
419 Nebraska Street
Sioux City, IA 51101
(712) 252-9876
(800) 872-2660
Fax: (712) 252-6130
E-mail: usaco@pionet.net

Iowa and Nebraska National Bank Notes
All Midwest National Bank Notes

James Polis
4501 Connecticut Avenue, N.W.
Suite 306
Washington, DC 20008
(202) 363-6650
Fax: (202) 363-4712
E-mail: jpolis7935@aol.com

Colonial and Continental
United States Fractional Currency
United States Large Size Type Notes
United States Small Size Type Notes
Confederate and Southern States
Currency
Confederate Bonds
Mail Order Price List

Richard H. Ponterio
Ponterio & Associates, Inc.
1818 Robinson Avenue
San Diego, CA 92103
(619) 299-0400
(800) 854-2888
Fax: (619) 299-6952

World Paper Money
Mexican Paper Money
Auction Sales
Mail Bid Sales

Vern Potter
Vern Potter Rare Fiscal Documents
P.O. Box 10040
Torrance, CA 90505-0740
(310) 326-0406
Fax: (310) 326-0406
E-mail: VernPotter@aol.com

United States Large Size Type Notes
Obsoletes Notes
Confederate Currency
Gold Rush and Civil War Documents
Historic Maps
Western Americana and Paper
Ephemera
Stocks, Bonds, Checks and Fiscal
Documents
Western Express and Postal History
Mining and Railroad Certificates and
Documents

Lou Rasera
Southland Coins & Currency
P.O. Box 403

Woodland Hills, CA 91365
(818) 348-5275
Fax: (818) 348-5275
E-mail: ljrasera@aol.com

United States Large Size Type Notes
United States Small Size Type Notes
United States National Bank Notes
Confederate
Error Notes
Professional Auction Representation

Kent Robertson
U.S. Currency
P.O. Box 631250
Irving, TX 75063
(404) 229-7184

United States Large Size Type Notes
United States Small Size Type Notes
Obsolete Notes
Confederate Notes
Confederate Bonds
Political Memorabilia
Auction Representation

Edward M. Rothberg
Emporium Coin & Currency
P.O. Box 606
Moorhead, MN 56560
(800) 248-9751

United States National Bank Notes
United States Fractional Currency
Colonial and Continental
Errors
Obsoletes Notes
Canadian Currency
United States Coins

John N. Rowe III
Southwest Numismatic Corp.
6301 Gaston Avenue, Suite 650
Dallas, TX 75214
(214) 826-3036
Fax: (214) 823-1923

United States Large Size Type Notes
United States Small Size Type Notes
Confederate
Obsolete Notes
United States National Bank Notes
Republic of Texas

O. E. "Dusty" Royer
Notes of Note
34 Lake Charles
St. Peters, MO 63376
(636) 441-0481

Web Site: www.geocities.com/dusty
royer
E-Mail: dustylB@netscape.net

World Currency
German Notgeld
Military Items

Bob Rozycki
Sycamore Coin Gallery
320 West State Street
Sycamore, IL 60178
(815) 895-6669
E-mail: sycamorecoin@tbcnet.com

United States Large Size Type Notes
United States Small Size Type Notes
United States National Bank Notes

Gaylen Rust
Rust Rare Coin Co.
252 East 300 South
Salt Lake City, UT 84111
(801) 363-4014
(800) 343-7878
Fax: (801) 364-0929
Web Site: www.rustcoin.com
E-mail: grust@rustcoin.com

Mormon and Related Items
Utah and Intermountain Area Notes

Sergio Sanchez, Jr.
Sergio Sanchez, Jr. Currency
P.O. Box 44-1490
Miami, FL 33144-1490
(305) 567-1515

United States Large Size Type Notes
United States Small Size Type Notes

Joe Sande
Joe Sande - Professional
Numismatist
P.O. Box 211
Nichols, FL 33863-0211
(863) 607-6337
Fax: (863) 607-6337

United States Large Size Type Notes
United States Small Size Type Notes
United States National Bank Notes
United States Fractional Currency
Mail Bid Sales

Jim Sazama
Jim Sazama, Inc.
P.O. Box 1235
Southern Pines, NC 28388

(910) 692-9357
Fax: (910) 692-9357
Web Site: www.jimsazama.com
E-mail: jimsazamainc@pinhurst.net

United States Large Size Type Notes
United States Small Size Type Notes
United States National Bank Notes
Obsolete Notes
Confederate

George Schweighofer
Currency Quest
P.O. Box 384
Reynoldsberg, OH 43068
(614) 864-8875
E-mail: currencyquest@aol.com

All United States Currency

Joel Shafer
P.O. Box 170985
Milwaukee, WI 53217
(414) 228-7351
E-mail: grbaypa@aol.com

World Paper Money

Amanda Sheheen
A & O Auctions
P.O. Box 1711
Camdan, SC 29020
(803) 432-2435
Fax: (803) 713-9048
Web Site: www.AOAuctions.com

Confederate Notes
Obsolete Notes and Scrip
South Carolina National Bank Notes
Colonial and Continentals Notes
United States Fractional Currency
Military Payment Certificates
Books and Supplies
Auction Representative

Austin M. Sheheen, Jr.
P.O. Box 428
Camden, SC 29020
(803) 432-1424
Fax: (803) 432-1831

South Carolina Colonial Notes
South Carolina Obsolete Notes
South Carolina National Bank Notes
Eastman College Scrip

Micky Shipley
Lake Region Coin & Currency Exchange
P.O. Box 48

Devils Lake, ND 58301
(701) 662-5770
(800) 803-2322
Fax: (701) 662-5775
E-mail: lrcc@stellarnet.com

United States National Bank Notes
United States Large Size Type Notes
United States Small Size Type Notes

Hugh Shull
P.O. Box 761
Camden, SC 29020
(803) 432-8500
Fax: (803) 432-9958

Confederate Notes
Obsolete Notes and Scrip
South Carolina National Bank Notes
Colonial and Continentals Notes
United States Fractional Currency
Stocks, Bonds and Fiscal Documents
Mail Order Catalogs
Books and Supplies
Auction Sales - Bidder Representative

James A. Simek
Numisgraphic Enterprises
P.O. Box 7157
Westchester, IL 60154
(630) 889-8207
Fax: (630) 889-1130
E-mail: nge3@attbi.com

United States Large Size Type Notes
United States Small Size Type Notes
United States National Bank Notes
Error Notes
Hawaiian Related Material
Autographs and Documents
Numismatic Photography

James Sorn
Family Coins, Ltd.
12232 South Harlem Avenue
Palos Heights, IL 60463
(708) 923-0100
Fax: (708) 923-0151

United States Large Size Type Notes
United States Small Size Type Notes
United States National Bank Notes
Colonial and Continental
Confederate
Obsolete Notes

David Steckling
Gold-N-Silver Rarities
1615 Division Street

St. Cloud, MN 56301
(302) 259-0233

Minnesota National Bank Notes
Minnesota Obsolete Notes
Obsolete Notes
United States Large Size Type Notes
United States Small Size Type Notes

Mike Storeim
Numismatic Professionals, LLC
2922 Evergrenn Parkway, Suite 203
Evergreen, CO 80439
(303) 670-3212
Cellular: (303) 903-9932
Fax: (303) 670-3216
E-mail: mike@numispro.com

United States Large Size Type Notes
United States Small Size Type Notes
United States National Bank Notes

David M. Sundman
Litttleton Coin Company
1309 Mt. Eustis Road
Littleton, NH 03561-3735
(603) 444-3524
Fax: (603) 444-3512
Web Site: www.littletoncoin.com

United States Large Size Type Notes
United States Small Size Type Notes
United States National Bank Notes
United States Fractional Currency
United States Coins
Fixed Price Lists and Catalogs

Allan L. Teal
P.O. Box 429
Chester Heights, PA 19017
(610) 459-5265
Fax: (610) 459-8821
Sunday at Store 7:30 AM - 4 PM
Renninger's Antique Market
Adamstown, PA
(717) 336-6622

Pennsylvania National Bank Notes
Delaware National Bank Notes
Confederate
Obsolete Notes
United States Large Size Type Notes
United States National Bank Notes

Leon Thornton
P.O. Box 726
Eminence, MO 65466
(573) 226-5536

United States Large Size Type Notes
United States Small Size Type Notes
United States National Bank Notes
Obsolete Notes
Confederate
World Paper Money
Foreign Exchange

Robert L. Vandevender II
American Paper Connection, Inc.
P.O. Box 2816
Joliet, IL 60424-2816
(815) 886-9451
E-mail: rvpaperman@aol.com

United States Large Size Type Notes
United States Small Size Type Notes
United States Fractional Currency
United States National Bank Notes

Frank Viskup
Frank Viskup Collectables
P.O. Box 90122
Dayton, OH 45490
(937) 440-8888
E-mail: fviskup@hotmail.com

United States Large Size Type Notes
United States Small Size Type Notes
Mail Order Price List

George K. Warner
P.O. Box 842
Sheridan, WY 82801
(307) 751-3230

United States Small Size Type Notes
Military Payment Certificates
United States Fractional Currency

Harry Warren
Mid-South Coin Co., Inc.
3894 Park Avenue
Memphis, TN 38111
(901) 324-2244
Fax: (901) 324-2249

United States Large Size Type Notes
United States National Bank Notes

Barry Wexler
Numisvalu
P.O. Box 185
Jamison, NY 18929
(215) 444-0550
Fax: (215) 444-0550
E-mail: nimisvalu@bestweb.net

United States Large Size Type Notes
United States Small Size Type Notes

United States National Bank Notes
Colonial
Confederate
Obsolete Notes
Stocks, Bonds and fiscal Documents
Checks

Louis Whitaker
River Hollow Coins
925 South Mason Road #327
Katy, TX 77450
(281) 829-5097
E-mail: Riverholl@pdq.net

All United States Notes

Harlan White
2425 El Cajon Blvd.
San Diego, CA 92104
(619) 298-0137
Fax: (619) 298-7966

United States High Denomination Notes
United States Paper Money

Gary Whitelock
Whitelock Rare Currency
P.O. Box 6263
Lakewood, CA 90714
(562) 731-0562
Cellular: (562) 673-0794
E-mail: whiteloc@ktb.net

All United States Notes

William Crutchfield Williams II
Crutchfield's Currency
P.O. Box 521
Kemah, TX 77565
(281) 334-3297
Fax: (281) 334-3297
Cellular: (281) 455-2511
Web Site: www.crutchwilliams.com
E-mail: crutchfieldwilliams-csa@
worldnet.att.net

Republic of Texas
Confederate States of America

Southern States Currency
Mexican Bancos & Revolutionary
Paper Money

Scott Winslow
P.O. Box 10240
Bedford, NH 03110
(603) 641-8292
(800) 225-6233
Fax: (603) 641-5583
Web Site: www.scottwinslow.com

Autographs
Stock, Bonds and Fiscal Documents

John Yasuk
Caribbean Sun Gold
P.O. Box 924533
Princeton, FL 33092-4533
(305) 256-7201

Florida Obsolete Currency
United States Large Size Type Notes
United States Small Size Type Notes

William Youngerman
William Youngerman, Inc.
95 South Federal Highway, Suite
203
Boca Raton, FL 33432
(561) 368- 7707
(800) 327-5010 (Outside Florida)
(800) 826-9713 (Within Florida)
Fax: (561) 394-6084
Web Site: www.williamyoungerman.
com
E-mail: wymoney@aol.com

Specialist: United States National
Bank Notes
Florida National Bank Notes
Florida Obsolete Notes
United States Large Size Type Notes
United States Small Size Type Notes
United States Fractional Currency
Confederate
Mail Order Price Lists

BUYING PAPER MONEY

Browsing in coin shops is the usual way in which beginners start buying paper money. Just about every coin dealer—and many stamp dealers—stock paper money to one degree or another, from a single display album with elementary material to vaults filled with literally millions of dollars worth of specimens. Be observant of condition when shopping from dealers' stocks. Get to know the dealer and become familiar with his grading practices. Some dealers will grade a specimen higher than another dealer, but this may be offset by the fact that they charge a lower price.

Bargains. Is it possible to get bargains in buying paper money? To the extent that prices vary somewhat from dealer to dealer, yes. But if you're talking about finding a note worth $100 selling at $50, this is unlikely to happen. The dealers are well aware of market values, and the slight price differences that do occur are merely the result of some dealers being overstocked on certain notes or, possibly, having made a very good "buy" from the public. What may appear to be a bargain will generally prove, on closer examination, to be a specimen in undesirable condition, such as a washed bill on which the color has faded.

Auction sales. Many coin auctions feature selections of paper money, and there are occasional sales (mostly of the postal-bid variety) devoted exclusively to it. There is much to be said for auction buying if you have some experience and know how to read an auction catalog.

Shows and conventions. Paper money is offered for sale at every coin show and exposition. These present excellent opportunities to buy, as the dealers exhibiting at such shows are generally out-of-towners whose stock you would not otherwise have a chance to examine. As many sellers are likely to be offering the same type of material, you have the opportunity to make price and condition comparisons before buying.

COLLECTING DO'S
AND DON'TS

Paper money is not at all difficult to care for, store, and display attractively.

There is not much question that albums are the favorite storage method of nearly all paper money enthusiasts. Many ills to which paper money falls prey result from not being housed in a suitable album, or any album at all. Framing and mounting present some risk, as the item may then be exposed to long periods of direct sunlight, almost sure to cause fading or "bleaching" of its color.

Faded color. There is no known restorative for faded color.

Holes. It is suggested that no effort be undertaken to repair holes, as this will almost certainly result in a further reduction in value.

Missing corners. Missing corners can seldom be restored in a manner that is totally satisfactory. The best that can be done is to secure some paper of approximately the same color and texture, trim a small piece to the proper size, and glue it in place as described below. If a portion of printed matter is missing, this can be hand-drawn, in ink, after restoration. Obviously, this kind of repair is not carried out to "fool" anybody, but simply to give a damaged specimen a less objectionable appearance.

Repairs to paper money. Repair work on damaged or defaced paper money is carried out strictly for cosmetic purposes; to improve its physical appearance. Repairs, even if skillfully executed, will not enhance the value of a specimen, as it will still be classified as defective. Amateurish repair efforts can very possibly make matters worse.

Tears. Tears can be closed by brushing a very small quantity of clear-drying glue to both sides of the tear, placing the note between sheets of waxed kitchen paper, and setting it under a weight to dry. A dictionary of moderate size serves this function well. Allow plenty of drying time and handle gently thereafter.

Wrinkles. Wrinkles, creases, and the like can sometimes be improved by wetting the note (in plain water) and drying it between sheets of waxed paper beneath a reasonably heavy weight—five pounds or more. This should not be done with a modern or recent specimen if there is danger of losing crispness.

SELLING YOUR COLLECTION

Selling to a dealer. All dealers in paper money buy from the public, but not all buy every collection offered to them. Some are specialists and are interested only in collections within their fields of specialization. Some will not purchase (or even examine) collections worth under $100, or $500, or whatever their line of demarcation happens to be. Obviously, a valuable collection containing many hard-to-get notes in VF or UNC condition is easier to interest a dealer in than a beginner-type collection. If a dealer is interested enough to make an offer, this is no guarantee that another dealer would not offer more. In the case of a collection worth $50,000, offers from several dealers might vary by as much as $5,000. This is not an indication that the dealer making the lowest offer is unscrupulous. Dealers will pay as much as the material is worth to them, and one dealer may be overstocked on items that another badly needs. Or one dealer may have customers for certain material that another doesn't. For this reason it makes good sense, if you choose to sell to a dealer, to obtain several offers before accepting any. But should you sell to a dealer at all? The chief advantage is quick payment and reduced risk. The price may not be as high as would be obtained at auction, however, depending on the property's nature and pure luck.

Selling by auction. Auction selling presents uncertainties but at the same time offers the possibility of gaining a much better return than could be had by selling to a dealer. It is no easy matter deciding which route to follow. If your collection is better than average, you may be better advised to sell by auction. This will involve a waiting period of, generally, four to six months between consigning the collection and receiving settlement; over the summer months it may be longer. However, some auctioneers will give a cash advance, usually about 25 percent of the sum they believe the material is worth. In special circumstances a larger advance may be made, or the usual terms and conditions altered. One auctioneer paid $100,000 under a special contract, stipulating that the money was not to be returned regardless of the sale's outcome or even if no sale took place. But this was on a million-dollar collection. Auctioneers' commissions vary. The normal is 20 percent, but some houses take 10 percent from the buyer and 10 percent from the seller. This would appear to work to the seller's advantage, but such a practice may discourage bidding and result in lower sales prices.

Selling to other collectors. Unless the owner is personally acquainted with a large circle of collectors, this will likely involve running ads in periodicals and "playing dealer," which runs into some expense. Unless you offer material at very favorable prices, you are not apt to be as successful with your ads as are the established dealers, who have a reputation and an established clientele.

GLOSSARY

BROKEN BANK NOTE (a.k.a. obsolete note)

Literally, a Broken Bank Note is a note issued by a "broken" bank—a bank that failed and whose obligations could therefore not be redeemed. It may be presumed, by those who recall passing of legislation establishing the Federal Deposit Insurance Corporation, that banks failed only in the financial panic of 1929. During the 19th century, bank failures were common, especially in western and southwestern states. These were generally small organizations set up in frontier towns which suffered either from mismanagement or a sudden decline in the town's fortunes. Some collectors make a specialty of Broken Bank Notes.

DEMAND NOTES

Demand Notes have the distinction of being the first official circulating paper currency of this country, issued in 1861. There are three denominations: $5, $10, and $20, each bearing its own design on front and back. Demand Notes arose out of the coinage shortage brought about by the Civil War. A total of $60,000,000 in Demand Notes was authorized to be printed, amounting to several million individual specimens. Though this was an extraordinary number for the time, it was small compared to modern output, and only a fraction of the total survived. These notes were signed not by any specially designated Treasury Department officers, but a battery of employees, each of whom was given authority to sign and affix his name by hand in a slow assembly-line process, two signatures to each note. Originally the spaces left blank for signatures were marked "Register of the Treasury" and "Treasurer of the United States." As the persons actually signing occupied neither of these offices, they were obliged to perpetually add "for the . . ." to their signatures. In an effort to relieve their tedium, fresh plates were prepared reading "For the Register of the Treasury" and "For the Treasurer of the United States," which required nothing but a signature. This created a rarity status for the earlier specimens, which are now very desirable collectors' items.

ENGRAVING

Engraving is the process by which designs are printed on U.S. paper money. Bank note engraving involves the use of a metal plate, traditionally steel, into which the design is cut with sharp instruments called "burins" or "gravers." Ink is smeared over the surface and allowed to work into the grooves or lines comprising the design. The ink is then cleaned away from raised portions (intended to show blank in the printing). The engraving is pressed against a sheet of moistened paper, and the ink left in these grooves transfers to the paper, resulting in a printed image. When done by modern rotary press, it's a fast-moving process.

FEDERAL RESERVE BANK NOTES

Federal Reserve Bank Notes were issued briefly in 1915 and 1918. Like National Bank Notes they were secured by bonds or securities placed on deposit by each Federal Reserve Bank with the U.S. government. While issued and redeemable by the member banks of the Federal Reserve system, these notes are secured by—and are obligations of—the government.

FEDERAL RESERVE NOTES

Federal Reserve Notes, the notes in current circulation, were authorized by the Federal Reserve Act of December 23, 1913. Issued under control of the Federal Reserve Board, these notes are released through twelve Federal Reserve Banks in various parts of the country. Originally they were redeemable in gold at the U.S. Treasury or "lawful money" (coins) at a Federal Reserve Bank. In 1934 the option of redemption for gold was removed.

FREAK AND ERROR NOTES

These are bills which, by virtue of error or accident, are in some respect different from normal specimens. See the chapter on Error or Freak Notes.

GOLD CERTIFICATES

When gold coinage became a significant medium of exchange, the government decided to hold aside quantities of it and issue paper notes redeemable by the Treasury Department. The first Gold Certificates for public circulation were released in 1882. The series lasted until the era of small-size currency, ending in 1928. In 1933 all were ordered returned to the Treasury Department for redemption, including those in possession of collectors. A new law in 1964 permitted their ownership by collectors, though they can no longer be redeemed for gold.

LARGE SIZE CURRENCY

Large Size currency is the term generally used to refer to U.S. notes issued up to 1929, which were somewhat larger in size than those printed subsequently. The increased size permitted more elaborate design, which seldom fails to endear Large Size currency to beginners. Some of the earlier examples (especially of the 1870s, 1880s, and 1890s) are works of art. Though economic considerations were mainly responsible for the switch to a reduced size, there is no doubt that today's notes are far more convenient to handle and carry. Large Size notes are sometimes referred to as "bedsheet notes."

NATIONAL BANK NOTES

This is the largest group of notes available to the collector. They were issued from 1863 to 1929 and present collecting potential that can only be termed vast. More than 14,000 banks issued notes, in all parts of the country. While the approach to collecting them is usually regional, sets and series can also be built up, virtually without end. The National Banking Act was instituted in 1863, during the Civil War, to permit chartered banks to issue and circulate their own currency. Printing was done at the U.S. Government Printing Office and the designs were all alike, differing only in names of the banks, state seals, bank signatures, and the bank's charter number. Each charter bank was limited to issuing currency up to 90 percent of the value of bonds that it kept on deposit with the government. Charters remained in force for twenty years and could be renewed for an additional twenty years. National Bank Notes circulated in the same fashion as conventional currency and, thanks to the bond-deposit system, gained public confidence. The financial panic of 1929, which brought ruin or near-ruin to many banks, put an end to National Bank Notes.

NATIONAL GOLD BANK NOTES

These notes were issued exclusively by California banks during the 1870s under the same terms as ordinary National Bank Notes, their values backed by bonds deposited with the government. Events surrounding their origins form a unique chapter in the history of American economy. Following the discoveries of substantial quantities of gold in California in the late 1840s, that metal soon became the chief medium of local exchange, largely because it was more readily available in that remote region than coinage. Later, when gold coins and tokens began to circulate heavily in California, banks became so swamped with them that they petitioned Washington for authority to issue Gold Notes that could be substituted for the actual coinage. On July 12, 1870, Congress voted favorably on this measure, giving the right to issue such notes to nine banks in California and one in Boston. The Boston bank, Kidder National Gold Bank, appears not to have exercised its right, as no Gold Notes of this institution have been recorded.

The California banks wasted no time in exercising their authority, the result being a series of notes ranging from $5–$500. All were printed on yellow-toned paper so as to be instantly identifiable. The banks issuing these notes were permitted to redeem them in gold coins.

REFUNDING CERTIFICATES

Refunding Certificates, a sort of hybrid between currency and bonds or securities, were issued under a Congressional Act of February 26, 1879. These were notes with a $10 face value which could be spent and exchanged in the fashion of ordinary money but drew interest at the rate of 4 percent per year. The purposes behind Refunding Certificates were several. They were chiefly designed to encourage saving and thereby curb inflation, which even at that time was becoming a problem. Also, they provided a safe means of saving for persons who distrusted banks (safe so long as the certificates were not lost or stolen), and, probably more important, were readily obtainable in areas of the country not well served by banks. In 1907 the interest was halted. Their redemption value today, with interest, is $21.30.

SERIAL NUMBER

The serial number is the control number placed on all U.S. paper bills, appearing below left-center and above right-center. No two bills in the same series bear repetitive serial numbers. The use of serial numbers is not only an aid in counting and sorting bills as printed, but a deterrent to counterfeiting.

SIGNATURES

The inclusion of signatures of Treasury Department officials on our paper bills, a practice as old as our currency (1861), began as a mark of authorization and as a foil to counterfeiters. The belief was that the handwriting would be more difficult to copy than an engraved design. Persons whose signatures appear on notes did not always occupy the same office. From 1862 to 1923, the two signers were the Treasurer and the Register (or Régistrar as it appears in old writings) of the Treasury. Subsequently, the Treasurer and the Secretary of the Treasury were represented. These signatures are of great importance to collectors, as some notes are relatively common with certain combinations of signa-tures and others are rare. A "series" collection is not considered complete until one obtains every existingcombination, even though the specimens may be in other respects identical.

SILVER CERTIFICATES

Silver Certificates were authorized in 1878. America's economy was booming at that time, and the demand for silver coinage in day-to-day business transactions outdistanced the supply. Silver Certificates were not intended to replace coinage but to create a convenient medium of exchange, whereby the government held specific quantities of Silver Dollars (later bullion) and agreed to redeem the notes or certificates against them. In 1934 the Treasury Department ceased redemption of these notes in Silver Dollars, and on June 24, 1968, redemption in all forms was ended. The notes are still, however, legal tender at their face value. When printing of Silver Certificates was discontinued, a flurry of speculation arose and many persons began hoarding them. This was done not only in hope of eventual redemption for bullion but in the belief that such notes would become valuable to collectors. Though Silver Certificates are popular with hobbyists, they have not increased sufficiently in price to yield speculators any great profits—especially since many collectors saved specimens in circulated condition.

STAR NOTES

United States Notes, Silver Certificates, and Gold Certificates sometimes have a star or asterisk in place of the letter in front of the serial number. Federal Reserve Notes and Federal Reserve Bank Notes have it at the end of the serial number. These notes are known as "Star Notes."

When a note is mutilated or otherwise unfit for issue, it must be replaced. To replace it with a note of the same serial numbers would be impractical, and Star Notes are therefore substituted. Other than having their own special serial number and a star, these notes are the same as the others. On United States Notes and Silver Certificates, the star is substituted for the prefix letter; on Federal Reserve Notes, for the suffix letter. All defective notes are accounted for and destroyed by burning them in an incinerator.

Large stars after the serial number on the 1869 Series of United States Notes, and 1890 and 1891 Treasury Notes, do not signify replacement notes as are known in later and present-day Star Notes.

Serial numbers on early Large Size Notes were preceded by a letter and were ended by various odd characters or symbols. These characters are not known to have any significance, except to show that the number was terminated, and prevented any elimination or addition of digits. The suffix characters were replaced by alphabet letters on later issues of notes.

TREASURY OR COIN NOTES

Treasury Notes were authorized by Congress in 1890. Their official title was Coin Notes, as they could be redeemed for silver or gold coins. The series did not prove popular and was discontinued after the issue of 1891.

TREASURY SEAL

The Treasury Seal is the official emblem of the U.S. Treasury Department, which has appeared on all our currency since 1862. It is missing only from the early Demand Notes, issued in 1861, and some Fractional Currency. Two versions have been employed, distinguished readily by the fact that one (the original) bears a Latin inscription, while the current Treasury Seal is in English. The basic motif is the same, a badge displaying scales and a key. The original Seal, somewhat more decorative, was in use until 1968.

UNITED STATES NOTES

Also known as Legal Tender Notes, this substantial and ambitious series followed Demand Notes and constitutes the second earliest variety of U.S. paper currency. There are five distinct issues, running from 1862 to 1923. Though United States Notes are all "Large Size" and their designs not very similar to those in present use, they show in their successive stages the evolutionary advance from this nation's first efforts at paper money to its currency of today. The first issue is dated March 10, 1862. Denominations are $1, $2, $5, $10, $20, $50, $100, $500, $1,000, $5,000, and $10,000. Individuals portrayed included not only presidents but other government officials: Salmon P. Chase (Lincoln's Secretary of the Treasury), Daniel Webster, and Lewis and Clark. Some of the reverse designs are masterpieces of geometrical linework. A number of rarities are to be found among Legal Tender Notes, but in general the lower denominations can be collected without great expense.

WILDCAT NOTES

Wildcat Notes are the notes that were issued by so-called "wildcat banks" in the era of State Bank Notes before the Civil War. Numerous banks sprang up around the middle part of the 19th century, mostly in the west and southwest, operated by persons of questionable integrity. Some never had capital backing and were instituted purely as a front for confidence swindles. After issuing notes, the bank shut down, its directors disappeared, and owners of the notes were left with worthless paper. As news traveled slowly in those days, the same persons could move from town to town and work the scheme repeatedly. Notes issued by these banks, or any banks that became insolvent, are also called Broken Bank Notes. Apparently the origin of the term "wildcat" derives from public sentiment of the time, which held that owners of such banks had no greater trustworthiness than a wild animal. "Wildcat" may also refer to the rapid movement of swindling bank officials from one locality to another.

DEPARTMENT OF THE TREASURY, BUREAU OF ENGRAVING AND PRINTING

Reprinted with permission of the Department of the Treasury, Bureau of Printing and Engraving, Washington, D.C.

BUREAU FACTS

- Since October 1, 1877, all U.S. paper currency has been printed by the Bureau of Engraving and Printing, which began as a six-person operation using steam-powered presses in the Department of the Treasury's basement.
- Now 1,900 Bureau employees occupy 25 acres of floor space in two Washington, D.C. buildings flanking 14th Street. Currency and stamps are designed, engraved, and printed 24 hours a day, 5 days a week on 23 high-speed presses. An additional 600 Bureau employees are at the Western Currency Facility in Fort Worth, Texas, where currency is printed 24 hours a day, 5 days a week on 12 high-speed presses.
- In Fiscal Year 1999, at a cost of 4.5 cents each, the Bureau of Engraving and Printing produced for the Federal Reserve System a record 11.3 billion notes worth approximately $142 billion. Ninety-five percent will replace unfit notes, and five percent will support economic growth. At any one time, $200 million in notes may be in production.
- Of total production, notes currently produced are the $1 (48% of production time), $2 (1%), $5 (9%), $10 (11%), $20 (19%), $50 (5%), and $100 (7%).
- The Bureau also prints White House invitations and some 500 engraved items, such as visa counterfoils, naturalization documents, commissions, and certificates for almost 75 federal departments and agencies.

TOURS

BEP Public Tour Contact Information
Bureau of Engraving and Printing
14th and C Streets, S.W.
Washington, DC 20228
Telephone: 1.866.874.2330 (toll-free), 202.874.2330 (local)
School Group Tours Fax: 202.874.6331
Congressional Tours Fax: 202.874.0968

VISITORS' CENTER

- At the Visitors' Center, history, production, and counterfeit exhibits showcase interesting information about U.S. currency.
- Many unique items can be purchased at the sales counter. Items include uncut currency sheets of 32, 16, 8, or 4 $1, $2, and $5 notes; a premium portfolio containing a new series 1996 $20 note with a low serial number and one of the last previous series $20 notes; a deluxe single note in the series 1996 with a low serial number; $150 worth of shredded currency in plastic bags that are sold for $1.50; engraved collectors' prints; souvenir cards; and Department of the Interior Duck Stamps.
- If you are planning a trip to Washington, please call our information number at 1.866.874.2330 (toll-free) for updated information or program changes.

MAIL ORDER SALES

The Bureau of Engraving and Printing (BEP) is experiencing extended delays in the delivery of incoming mail. At this moment, it is unknown when timely mail deliveries will resume. In order to get timely delivery of numismatic products, it is recommended that customers order by telephone, fax, or Internet.

- For telephone orders, call toll free at 1-800-456-3408.
- For fax orders, call toll free at 1-888-891-7585.
- For Internet orders, the BEP web site is

INTERNET

The Bureau's **Internet address** is *www.bep.treas.gov/*. We also offer an **interactive website** at www.moneyfactory.com/.

THE FEDERAL RESERVE BANKS

Reprinted with permission of the Department of the Treasury, Bureau of Printing and Engraving, Washington, D.C.

The Federal Reserve System is divided into twelve Federal Reserve districts, in each of which is a Federal Reserve Bank. There are also twenty-four branches. Each district is designated by a number and the corresponding letter of the alphabet. The district numbers, the cities in which the twelve banks are located, and the letter symbols are:

1-A—Boston	5-E—Richmond	9-I—Minneapolis
2-B—New York	6-F—Atlanta	10-J—Kansas City
3-C—Philadelphia	7-G—Chicago	11-K—Dallas
4-D—Cleveland	8-H—St. Louis	12-L—San Francisco

○ Reserve Bank Cities
• Branch Bank Cities
— District Boundaries
— Branch Territory Boundaries
★ Board of Governors of the Federal Reserve System

FEDERAL RESERVE SYSTEM

The Federal Reserve System was created by the Federal Reserve Act, which was passed by Congress in 1913, in order to provide a safer and more flexible banking and monetary system. For approximately 100 years before the creation of the Federal Reserve, periodic financial panics had led to failures of a large number of banks, with associated business bankruptcies and general economic contractions. Following the studies of the National Monetary Commission, established by Congress a year after the particularly severe panic of 1907, several proposals were put forward for the creation of an institution designed to counter such financial disruptions. Following considerable debate, the Federal Reserve System was established. Its original purposes were to give the country an elastic currency, provide facilities for discounting commercial credits, and improve the supervision of the banking system.

ECONOMIC STABILITY AND GROWTH

From the inception of the Federal Reserve System, it was clear that these original purposes were aspects of broader national economic and financial objectives. Over the years, stability and growth of the economy, a high level of employment, stability in the purchasing power of the dollar, and a reasonable balance in transactions with foreign countries have come to be recognized as primary objectives of governmental economic policy.

CURRENCY CIRCULATION

An important function of the Federal Reserve System is to ensure that the economy has enough currency and coin to meet the public's demand. Currency and coin are put into or retired from circulation by the Federal Reserve Banks, which use depository institutions as the channel of distribution. When banks and other depository institutions need to replenish their supply of currency and coin—for example, when the public's need for cash increases around holiday shopping periods—depository institutions order the cash from the Federal Reserve Bank or Branch in their area, and the face value of that cash is charged to their accounts at the Federal Reserve. When the public's need for currency and coin declines, depository institutions return excess cash to the Federal Reserve Bank, which in turn credits their accounts.

UNFIT AND COUNTERFEIT NOTES

The Federal Reserve Banks and the U.S. Department of the Treasury share responsibility for maintaining the physical quality of U.S. paper currency in circulation. Each day, millions of dollars of deposits to Reserve Banks by depository institutions are carefully scrutinized. The Reserve Banks are responsible for receiving, verifying, authenticating, and storing currency and shipping it as needed. Currency in good condition is stored for later distribution. Worn or mutilated notes are removed from circulation and destroyed. Counterfeit notes are forwarded to the U.S. Secret Service, an agency of the Treasury Department.

FEDERAL RESERVE NOTES

Virtually all currency in circulation is in the form of Federal Reserve Notes, which are printed by the Bureau of Engraving and Printing of the U.S. Treasury. The Reserve Banks are currently authorized to issue notes in denominations of $1, $2, $5, $10, $20, $50, and $100. Coins are produced by the Treasury's U.S. Mint.

CASH TRANSFERS

Currency and coin are used primarily for small transactions. In the aggregate, such transactions probably account for only a small proportion of the value of all transfers of funds.

32-SUBJECT SHEET LAYOUT

All U.S. currency is now printed with 32 subjects (notes) to a large sheet. The first printing is the greenback. The second printing is the face of the note, in black. This includes the portrait and border, the series year, the check letter and quadrant number, two signatures, and the face plate number. The sheet is then cut in half vertically for the third printing. This includes the black Federal Reserve seal, the four Federal Reserve district numbers, the green Treasury seal, and two green serial numbers.

The 32-subject sheet is divided into four quarters called quadrants for numbering and other controls. Each quadrant has its own numbering sequence for the eight notes, with serial numbers advancing by 20,000 to the next note. The quadrant number and check letter in the upper left section indicate the first, second, third, or fourth quadrant and the position of the note in the quadrant. In the lower right corner the position letter is shown again with a plate number. On the back of the note the same small number in the lower right is the back plate number.

	FIRST QUADRANT						THIRD QUADRANT				
A1			E1			A3			E3		
A00000001A	A100		A00080001A	E100		A00320001A	A100		A00400001A	E100	
B1			F1			B3			F3		
A00020001A	B100		A00100001A	F100		A00340001A	B100		A00420001A	F100	
C1			G1			C3			G3		
A00040001A	C100		A00120001A	G100		A00360001A	C100		A00440001A	G100	
D1			H1			D3			H3		
A00060001A	D100		A00140001A	H100		A00380001A	D100		A004600001A	H100	
A2			E2			A4			E4		
A00160001A	A100		A00240001A	E100		A00480001A	A100		A005600001A	E100	
B2			F2			B4			F4		
A00180001A	B100		A00260001A	F100		A00500001A	B100		A00580001A	F100	
C2			G2			C4			G4		
A00200001A	C100		A00280001A	G100		A0050001A	C100		A00600001A	G100	
D2			H2			D4			H4		
A00220001A	D100		A00300001A	H100		A00540001A	D100		A00620001A	H100	
	SECOND QUADRANT						FOURTH QUADRANT				

NUMBERING SYSTEM

The system of numbering paper money must be adequate to accommodate a large volume of notes. For security and accountability purposes, no two notes of any one class, denomination, and series may have the same serial number. The two serial numbers on each note have a full complement of eight digits and an alphabetical prefix and suffix letter. When necessary, ciphers are used at the left of the number to make a total of eight digits.

Whenever a numbering sequence is initiated for United States Notes or Silver Certificates, the first note is numbered A 00 000 001 A; the second A 00 000 002 A; the hundredth A 00 000 100 A; the thousandth A 00 001 000 A; and so on through A 99 999 999 A. The suffix letter A will remain the same until a total of twenty-five groups, or "blocks," of 99 999 999 notes are numbered, each group having a different prefix letter of the alphabet from A to Z. The letter "O" is omitted, either as a prefix or as a suffix, because of its similarity to zero. The 100 000 000th note in each group will be a Star Note, since eight digits are the maximum in the mechanical operation of numbering machines.

At this point, the suffix letter changes to B for the next twenty-five groups of 99 999 999 notes, and proceeds in the same manner as the suffix letter A. A total of 62,500,000,000 notes could be numbered before a duplication of serial numbers would occur. However, it has never been required to number that many notes of any one class, denomination, and series.

The Federal Reserve Notes printed for the twelve districts are numbered in the same progression as United States Notes and Silver Certificates, except that a specific alphabetical letter identifies a specific Federal Reserve district. The letter identifying each district is used as a prefix letter at the beginning of the serial numbers on all Federal Reserve Notes and does not change. Only the suffix letter changes in the serial numbers on Federal Reserve currency.

PORTRAITS AND BACK DESIGN ON SMALL SIZE NOTES

DENOMINATION	PORTRAIT	BACK DESIGN
$1	Washington	Great Seal of the United States
$2	Jefferson	Monticello
$5	Lincoln	Lincoln Memorial
$10	Hamilton	United States Treasury
$20	Jackson	The White House
$50	Grant	United States Capitol
$100	Franklin	Independence Hall
$500	McKinley	Five Hundred
$1000	Cleveland	One Thousand
$5000	Madison	Five Thousand
$10,000	Chase	Ten Thousand
$100,000	Wilson	One Hundred Thousand

DATING U.S. CURRENCY

Unlike coins, the date is not changed each year on U.S. currency.

The date appearing on all notes, large or small, is that of the year in which the design was first approved or issued. For instance, Large Size $1 United States Notes of the Series 1880 were issued with the same date until the new Series 1917 was issued. There was no further date change until the Series 1923.

The same rule applies to Small Size Notes. However, in this case a letter is added after the date to designate or indicate a minor change in the main design or probably a change in one or both of the signatures. For example: the $1 Silver Certificate of 1935 was changed to 1935-A because of a change in the size of the tiny plate numbers appearing in the lower right corners of the face and back of the note. It was changed again from 1935-A to 1935-B in 1945 when the signatures of Julian/Morganthau were changed to Julian/Vinson. Subsequent changes in signatures continued in the 1935 Series to the year 1963 when the signatures of Smith/Dillon terminated the issue with the Series 1935-H. Therefore, these notes were issued for twenty-eight years bearing the date 1935.

THE TREASURY SEAL

FORMER DESIGN:
The former design had the Latin inscription *Thesaur. Amer. Septent. Sigil.*, which has several translations. It was the Seal of the North American Treasury.

NEW DESIGN:
This new design drops the Latin and states THE DEPARTMENT OF THE TREASURY, 1789. First used on the $100 Note of the Series 1966.

GRADES AND CONDITIONS
OF PAPER MONEY

CONDITION

The physical condition of a note or bill plays an important role in determining its value. There are many notes that have no premium value beyond face value in ordinary condition but are valuable or moderately valuable when uncirculated. Even in the case of scarce early specimens, the price given for an Average example is generally much less than that commanded by Fine or Very Fine condition.

Defects encountered in paper money include:

Creases, folds, wrinkles. Generally the characteristic that distinguishes uncirculated notes from those that almost—but not quite—qualify for such designation is a barely noticeable crease running approximately down the center vertically, resulting from the note being folded for insertion into a wallet or billfold. It may be possible, through manipulation or storage beneath a heavy weight, to remove evidence of the crease; but the knowledge that it once existed cannot be obliterated.

Discoloration. Discoloration is not as easy to recognize as most defects, but it must be classed as one. A distinction should be made between notes printed from underinked rollers and those which originally were normally colored but became "washed out." Sometimes washing is indeed the cause; a well-intentioned collector will bathe a note, attempting to clean it, with the result that its color is no longer strong. This should not happen if warm water is used, without strong cleanser. Atmospheric conditions may play some part in discoloration.

Foxing. Fox spots may sometimes be observed on old notes, especially those of the pre-1890 era, just as on old paper in general. They seem more common to foreign currency than American, but their presence on our notes is certainly not rare. These are tiny brownish-red dots, caused by an infestation of lice attacking the paper fibers.

Holes. Holes are more likely to be encountered in early paper money than specimens of recent origin. In early years it was customary for Federal Reserve Banks to use wire clips in making up bundles of notes for distribution to banking organizations, and these clips or staples often pierced the bills. Another common occurrence years ago was the practice of shop clerks and cashiers in general to impale notes upon holders consisting of nails mounted on stands.

Missing pieces. Missing pieces is a highly undesirable defect which, except in the case of rare specimens, renders the item valueless to collectors. Even if only a blank unprinted corner is torn away, this is called a missing-piece note and hardly anyone will give it a second glance.

Stains. Notes sometimes become stained with ink or other liquids. If the specimen is commonplace and easily obtainable in Very Fine or Uncirculated condition, it will be worthless with any kind of stain. In a note of moderate value, its price will be hurt to a greater or lesser degree depending on the stain's intensity, size, nature, and the area it touches. A stain in an outer margin or at a corner is not so objectionable as one occurring at the center or across a signature or serial number. Ink stains, because of their strong color, are generally deemed the worst, but bad staining can also be caused by oil, crayon, "magic marker," and food substances. Pencil markings, which frequently are found on bank notes, will yield to ordinary erasing with a piece of soft "artgum" worked gently over the surface and brushed away with an artist's camel-hair brush. Most other stains cannot be so easily removed. With ink there is no hope, as any caustic sufficiently strong to remove the ink will also injure the printing and possibly eat through the paper as well. Oil stains can sometimes be lightened, though not removed, by sprinkling the note on both sides (even if the stain shows only on one) with talcum powder or other absorbent powder, placing it between sheets of waxed kitchen paper, and leaving it beneath a heavy weight for several days in a room where the humidity is not unduly high.

Tears. Tears in notes are very common defects, which may be minute or run nearly the whole length of the bill. As a rule the paper on which American currency is printed is fairly rugged and will not tear as readily as most ordinary paper, but given careless or hurried handling anything is possible. An old worn note is more apt to tear in handling than a new one. Repaired tears are more common in the world of paper money collecting than may be generally supposed. A clean tear—one which does not involve loss of surface—can be patched so as to become virtually unnoticed, unless examined against a light or through a strong magnifying glass. X-ray examination will reveal repairs when all else fails.

CONDITION GRADES

The following condition standards have been used throughout this book and, with slight variations depending upon individual interpretation, are generally current in the trade.

Uncirculated—UNC. A specimen that for all appearances has not been handled or passed through general circulation; a crisp fresh note in "bank" condition. There may be minor blemishes, such as a finger smudge or pinhole, but if these are in any respect severe the condition merits description as "Almost Uncirculated." There is not much satisfaction to be taken in a note fresh and crisp that has gaping holes and fingerprints. Obviously, an 1870 Uncirculated note should not be expected to match a 1970 in appearance or feel.

*Uncirculated—*Unc. An uncirculated "Star Note."

Almost Uncirculated—A.U. In the case of modern or semimodern notes, this is generally taken to mean a specimen that shows no evidence of having passed through general circulation but, because of some detraction, fails to measure up to a rating of Uncirculated. The problem may be finger smudges, counting crinkles, a light crease, a fold along one or more of the corners, or pinholes. But if more than one of these impairments is present, the item would surely not deserve a classification of Almost Uncirculated.

Extremely Fine—X.F. A note exhibiting little evidence of wear from handling, but not so perfect or near-perfect as to qualify for a rating of Uncirculated or Almost Uncirculated.

On a used note issued before 1900 there may be clear evidence of circulation, but no disfiguring marks.

Very Fine—V.F. A Very Fine note has experienced some circulation but escaped without "being mangled." It is still clean and crisp, and its creases are not offensive.

Fine—F. Here the scale begins sliding down. It is obvious that, being the fifth in rank of condition grades, Fine notes are quite a good deal removed from Uncirculated. They have been handed around pretty thoroughly and suffered the normal consequences, but still are without serious blemishes such as tears, missing corners, serious stains, or holes.

Very Good—V.G. A well-circulated note bearing evidence of much folding, creasing, and wrinkling. It may possibly be lightly stained, smudged, or pin punctured, but major defects—such as a torn-off corner—would drop it into an even lower category.

Good—G. Heavily circulated, worn notes that are possibly stained or scribbled on, edges could be frayed or "dog-eared." There may be holes larger than pin punctures, but not on the central portion of design. This is the lowest grade of condition acceptable to a collector, and only when nothing better is available. Unless very rare, such specimens are considered space-fillers only.

Average Buying Prices—A.B.P. The Average Buying Prices given here are the approximate sums paid by retail dealers for specimens in Good condition. As selling prices vary, so do buying prices, and, in fact, they usually vary a bit more.

RECORD KEEPING

For your convenience, we suggest you use the following record-keeping system to note condition of your paper money in the checklist box:

⊠ FAIR	⊠ VERY GOOD	⊓ VERY FINE	⊠ ALMOST UNC
⊠ GOOD	⊟ FINE	⊠ EXTREMELY FINE	■ UNCIRCULATED

ABOUT THE PRICES
IN THIS BOOK

Prices are compiled from offerings made by dealers and from auction sale results. In all cases (except for the Average Buying Price) the prices are retail selling prices. While prices are current at the time of publication, the market can be influenced by buying or selling trends, causing prices to change. All prices, except in the case of seldom-offered rarities, are averages, calculated from numerous sales. The actual prices charged by any individual currency dealer may be slightly higher or lower than those indicated in this book. In any given sale various factors play a role, such as whether the seller is overstocked on notes of that type.

HOW TO USE THIS BOOK

The *Official Blackbook Price Guide to United States Paper Money* provides a convenient reference to prices of all standard U.S. currency, old and new, as well as many unusual issues.

Notes are divided into section by denomination. Within each section can be found the various series of notes for that denomination. The series are arranged chronologically and will vary slightly from section to section, as some notes were issued in one series and not in another. An index page is provided at the beginning of each section.

To familiarize yourself with the various currency terms, the following illustration might be helpful:

To price a note correctly, it is necessary that it be accurately identified and graded. The illustrations will aid in identification, and a grading guide has been provided. In the case of some notes, particularly very old ones, the value depends upon minor details. In all such cases these details have been clearly noted.

Listings include the following information:

Date. This is the "series date," as it appears on the note, and may bear no relation whatsoever to the year in which the note was actually issued. The date of actual issue is not of importance to collectors. If the series date on the note carries a suffix letter, such as 1935A, it will be so indicated in the listing.

Seal. The color of the Treasury Seal will be noted, along with other information if relevant. The following abbreviations are also used: Sm.—small, Lg.—large; w/r—with rays, w/s—with scallops.

Signatures. All U.S. notes carry two signatures, and the names of each signer are given for every note listed. If different signature combinations exist for your note, be sure you refer to the correct signature combination. The listings will show you whether there is just one set of signatures for that note or more than one.

Type. In a small minority of cases, notes were issued in more than one type. For example, a slight change was made in the paper or printing. All recorded types are identified in the listings.

Issuing Bank. This information is provided for Federal Reserve Notes and Federal Reserve Bank Notes only. Check the Federal Reserve seal on your note to identify the issuing bank. In some instances there is a difference in value depending on where the note originated. Space prevents us from listing the numerous local banks issuing National Bank Notes.

A.B.P. The first price column is the A.B.P. or Average Buying Price. This is the approximate sum being paid by dealers for a specimen in the lowest listed grade of condition. The lowest listed grade of condition is the column next to the A.B.P. If the next column is headed "Good," the A.B.P. is for a specimen in Good condition. In all cases the A.B.P. includes the face value of the note. This is an important consideration insofar as U.S. notes, regardless of their age or physical condition, can still be spent as legal tender.

Current Selling Prices. The current selling prices are given in two or three different grades of condition, as indicated at the top of each price column. Different groups of notes are priced in different condition grades, owing to market availability. Some are virtually unobtainable in Uncirculated condition, so it would be pointless to give such a price. Others are of no premium value in less than V.F., hence V.F. is the lowest grade shown.

ONE DOLLAR NOTES

ONE DOLLAR NOTES (1862) UNITED STATES NOTES
(ALSO KNOWN AS LEGAL TENDER NOTES)
(Large Size)

Face Design: Portrait of Salmon Portland Chase (1808–73), Secretary of the Treasury under Lincoln, red Treasury Seal, signatures of Chittenden and Spinner, lower right.

Back Design: Large circle center with legal tender obligation.

SERIES	SIGNATURES	SEAL	A.B.P.	GOOD	V. FINE	UNC.
1862	Chittenden-Spinner					
☐Type I, National Bank Note, American Bank						
Note without monogram		Red	175.00	250.00	1000.00	2400.00
☐Type II, National Bank Note, American Bank						
Note with monogram ABNCO		Red	85.00	135.00	625.00	1850.00
☐Type III, National Bank Note, National Bank						
Note without monogram		Red	80.00	140.00	725.00	1850.00
☐Type IV, National Bank Note, National Bank						
Note with monogram ABNCO		Red	80.00	140.00	625.00	1850.00

ONE DOLLAR NOTES (1869) UNITED STATES NOTES
(ALSO KNOWN AS LEGAL TENDER NOTES)
(Large Size)

Face Design: Portrait of President Washington in the center, large red seal to the right. Scene of Columbus in sight of land to left; also called "Rainbow Note" because of the many colors used in printing. Black ink for main design, red seal and serial numbers, green background for the serial number, green shading in upper-half and blue tint in paper left of portrait to deter counterfeiting.

Back Design: Green, ONE DOLLAR and ONE over "1" center, letters U.S. interwoven to left. Legal tender obligation to right of center.

SERIES	SIGNATURES	SEAL	A.B.P.	GOOD	V. FINE	UNC.
☐1869	Allison-Spinner	Red	70.00	130.00	800.00	2200.00
☐1869	Allison-Spinner Water Mark Paper		82.00	155.00	1275.00	2650.00

ONE DOLLAR NOTES (1874–1917)
UNITED STATES NOTES
(ALSO KNOWN AS LEGAL TENDER NOTES)
(Large Size)

Back Design: Large green "X" with UNITED STATES OF AMERICA in the center. Legal tender obligation and counterfeiting warning to right.

Face Design: No blue or green shading and tinting.

SERIES	SIGNATURES	SEAL	A.B.P.	GOOD	V. FINE	UNC.
☐ 1874	Allison-Spinner	Sm. Red	50.00	75.00	425.00	1450.00
☐ 1875	Allison-New	Sm. Red	50.00	75.00	350.00	1150.00
☐ 1875	Same Series A	Sm. Red	150.00	300.00	1000.00	2650.00
☐ 1875	Same Series B	Sm. Red	150.00	310.00	1000.00	2600.00
☐ 1875	Same Series C	Sm. Red	160.00	325.00	1250.00	2850.00
☐ 1875	Same Series D	Sm. Red	185.00	445.00	1045.00	2850.00
☐ 1875	Same Series E	Sm. Red	300.00	640.00	1350.00	3200.00
☐ 1875	Allison-Wyman	Sm. Red	45.00	75.00	250.00	1200.00
☐ 1878	Allison-Gilfillan	Sm. Red	45.00	80.00	250.00	1175.00
☐ 1878	Allison-Gilfillan	Water Marked Paper	55.00	115.00	450.00	1650.00
☐ 1880	Scofield-Gilfillan	Lg. Brown	40.00	80.00	300.00	1000.00
☐ 1880	Bruce-Gilfillan	Lg. Brown	40.00	80.00	300.00	1030.00
☐ 1880	Bruce-Wyman	Lg. Brown	40.00	80.00	300.00	1000.00
☐ 1880	Rosecrans-Huston	Lg. Red	115.00	250.00	975.00	4400.00
☐ 1880	Rosecrans-Huston	Lg. Brown	105.00	175.00	875.00	4200.00
☐ 1880	Rosecrans-Nebeker	Lg. Brown	105.00	175.00	875.00	4250.00
☐ 1880	Rosecrans-Nebeker	Sm. Red	38.00	60.00	260.00	875.00
☐ 1880	Tillman-Morgan	Sm. Red	38.00	60.00	260.00	875.00
☐ 1917	Tehee-Burke	Sm. Red	28.00	53.00	100.00	300.00

Sm.—Small Seal, Lg.—Large Seal

*This note with signatures of Burke and Elliott is an error issue. The regular procedure was to have the signature of the Register of the Treasury on the left, and that of the Treasurer to the right. The signatures were transposed in this instance.

SERIES	SIGNATURES	SEAL	A.B.P.	GOOD	V. FINE	UNC.
☐1917	Elliott-Burke	Sm. Red	22.00	27.00	90.00	300.00
☐1917	Burke-Elliott*	Sm. Red	75.00	100.00	500.00	1500.00
☐1917	Elliott-White	Sm. Red	22.00	27.00	85.00	325.00
☐1917	Speelman-White	Sm. Red	22.00	27.00	85.00	325.00

ONE DOLLAR NOTES (1923) UNITED STATES NOTES (ALSO KNOWN AS LEGAL TENDER NOTES)

(Large Size)

Face Design: Portrait of President Washington in center. Red seal to left, red "1" to the right, red serial numbers.

Back Design: UNITED STATES OF AMERICA and ONE DOLLAR in center. Figures "1" to right and left. This was the last issue of Large Size ONE DOLLAR United States Notes. The last series of Large Size Notes was kept in use until 1929 when the first issue of Small Size Notes was released.

SERIES	SIGNATURES	SEAL	A.B.P.	GOOD	V. FINE	UNC.
☐1923	Speelman-White	Red	26.00	37.00	145.00	650.00

ONE DOLLAR NOTES (1928) UNITED STATES NOTES
(ALSO KNOWN AS LEGAL TENDER NOTES)
(Small Size)

Face Design: Red seal to left—red serial numbers, large ONE to right. This is the only issue of the $1 United States Note, Small Size. At the present time only the $100 United States Note is current.

Back Design: Large ONE in center with ONE DOLLAR overprint, back printed in green.

SERIES	SIGNATURES	SEAL	A.B.P.	GOOD	V. FINE	UNC.	★UNC.
☐1928	Woods-Woodin	Red	28.00	40.00	135.00	485.00	5500.00

*Star Notes: Damaged or unsatisfactory notes were replaced at the Bureau of Engraving with new notes bearing a star (★) in place of the first letter and preceding the serial no. Example: *12345678A

ONE DOLLAR NOTES (1863–1875)
NATIONAL BANK NOTES
FIRST CHARTER PERIOD (Large Size)

Face Design: Name of National Bank top center, maidens at altar below.

Back Design: Landing of Pilgrims center, State Seal of state issuing bank to left, eagle and flag.

SERIES	SIGNATURES	SEAL	A.B.P.	GOOD	V. FINE	UNC.
☐Original*	Colby-Spinner	Red w/r	80.00	125.00	750.00	3200.00
☐Original*	Jeffries-Spinner	Red w/r	145.00	470.00	1350.00	4600.00
☐Original*	Allison-Spinner	Red w/r	95.00	140.00	750.00	3100.00
☐1875	Allison-New	Red w/s	95.00	140.00	750.00	3100.00
☐1875	Allison-Wyman	Red w/s	95.00	140.00	750.00	3100.00
☐1875	Allison-Gilfillan	Red w/s	95.00	140.00	750.00	3100.00
☐1875	Scofield-Gilfillan	Red w/s	95.00	140.00	750.00	3100.00

w/r—with Rays, w/s—with Scallops
*Early notes of the First Charter Period did not have the series imprinted on them. They are known by the date on the bill which was usually the date of charter or organization, or as the Original Series. These notes had a seal with rays or small notches. In 1875 the series was imprinted in red, and the seal was changed to have scallops around the border. The charter number was added to later issues of notes of the original series and to all notes of the 1875 series.

ONE DOLLAR NOTES (1886) SILVER CERTIFICATES
(Large Size)

SERIES	SIGNATURES	SEAL	A.B.P.	GOOD	V. FINE	UNC.
☐1886	Rosecrans-Jordan	Sm. Red	75.00	110.00	475.00	1500.00
☐1886	Rosecrans-Hyatt	Sm. Red	75.00	110.00	475.00	1500.00
☐1886	Rosecrans-Hyatt	Lg. Red	75.00	110.00	475.00	1500.00
☐1886	Rosecrans-Huston	Lg. Red	75.00	110.00	475.00	1500.00
☐1886	Rosecrans-Huston	Lg. Brown	75.00	120.00	475.00	1600.00
☐1886	Rosecrans-Nebeker	Lg. Brown	75.00	120.00	475.00	1600.00
☐1886	Rosecrans-Nebeker	Sm. Red	75.00	120.00	475.00	1800.00

ONE DOLLAR NOTES (1891) SILVER CERTIFICATES
(Large Size)
Back Design
Face Design:
Same as 1886
note.

SERIES	SIGNATURES	SEAL	A.B.P.	GOOD	V. FINE	UNC.
☐1891	Rosecrans-Nebeker	Sm. Red	75.00	100.00	350.00	1400.00
☐1891	Tillman-Morgan	Sm. Red	75.00	100.00	340.00	1400.00

ONE DOLLAR NOTES (1896) SILVER CERTIFICATES
(Large Size)

Face Design: History instructing youth. To the right, panoramic view of the Capitol and Washington Monument. Constitution on tablet, names of famous Americans on top and side borders.

Back Design: Portrait of Martha Washington to left and President Washington to right with large numeral "1" in center.

There is a story that when this note was issued people objected to it because they said No. "1" (ONE) shouldn't stand between George and Martha Washington. The set consists of $1, $2, and $5 denominations. They all have very beautiful engravings, and they are truly the most beautiful notes ever issued by our government. They were first released in 1896 and replaced by a new issue in 1899. They were short-lived because of objections to the unclad female on the $5 Note.

SERIES	SIGNATURES	SEAL	A.B.P.	GOOD	V. FINE	UNC.
☐1896	Tillman-Morgan	Red	85.00	120.00	500.00	1750.00
☐1896	Bruce-Roberts	Red	85.00	120.00	500.00	1750.00

ONE DOLLAR NOTES (1899) SILVER CERTIFICATES
(Large Size)

Face Design: Eagle on flag and Capitol background over portraits of Presidents Lincoln and Grant.

Back Design

SERIES	SIGNATURES	SEAL	A.B.P.	GOOD	V. FINE	UNC.
	SERIES OF 1899 (above upper right serial number)					
☐1899	Lyons-Roberts	Blue	35.00	50.00	150.00	550.00
	SERIES OF 1899 (below upper right serial number)					
☐1899	Lyons-Roberts	Blue	25.00	37.00	135.00	500.00
☐1899	Lyons-Treat	Blue	28.00	37.00	135.00	500.00
☐1899	Vernon-Treat	Blue	28.00	37.00	135.00	500.00
☐1899	Vernon-McClung	Blue	28.00	37.00	135.00	500.00
	SERIES OF 1899 (vertical to right of blue seal)					
☐1899	Napier-McClung	Blue	27.00	35.00	110.00	475.00
☐1899	Napier-Thompson	Blue	40.00	60.00	285.00	1400.00
☐1899	Parker-Burke	Blue	27.00	37.00	105.00	475.00
☐1899	Teehee-Burke	Blue	27.00	37.00	105.00	475.00
☐1899	Elliott-Burke	Blue	23.00	37.00	105.00	475.00
☐1899	Elliott-White	Blue	23.00	37.00	105.00	475.00

SERIES	SIGNATURES	SEAL	A.B.P.	GOOD	V. FINE	UNC.
☐1899	Speelman-White	Blue	21.00	30.00	100.00	385.00

ONE DOLLAR NOTES (1923) SILVER CERTIFICATES
(Large Size)

Face Design: Portrait of President Washington in center, blue seal left, blue 1 DOLLAR right, blue numbers.

Back Design: Same as 1923 note.

SERIES	SIGNATURES	SEAL	A.B.P.	GOOD	V. FINE	UNC.
☐1923	Speelman-White	Blue	16.00	21.00	42.00	125.00
☐1923	Woods-White	Blue	16.00	24.00	44.00	125.00
☐1923	Woods-Tate	Blue	22.00	32.00	97.00	425.00

ONE DOLLAR NOTES (1928) SILVER CERTIFICATES
(Small Size)

Face Design: Portrait of President Washington, blue seal to the left, ONE to right, blue seal and numbers. ONE SILVER DOL-LAR under portrait.

Back Design

First issue of Series 1928. U.S. paper money was reduced in 1928 from the old Large Size to the size presently in use. This was mostly an economy measure. Unlike Large Size Notes, the Small Notes have a letter designation after the date to denote a minor change in design or change of one or both signatures.

SERIES	SIGNATURES	SEAL	A.B.P.	GOOD	V. FINE	UNC.	★UNC.
☐ 1928	Tate-Mellon	Blue	5.00	10.00	18.00	100.00	600.00
☐ 1928A	Woods-Mellon	Blue	5.00	10.00	18.00	100.00	500.00
☐ 1928B	Woods-Mills	Blue	5.00	10.00	18.00	100.00	1650.00
☐ 1928C	Woods-Woodin	Blue	27.00	60.00	300.00	750.00	30000.00
☐ 1928D	Julian-Woodin	Blue	21.00	40.00	100.00	450.00	20000.00
☐ 1928E	Julian-Morgenthau	Blue	80.00	200.00	625.00	2500.00	50000.00

ONE DOLLAR NOTES (1934) SILVER CERTIFICATES
(Small Size)

Face Design: Portrait of President Washington, blue "1" to left. ONE and blue seal to right. ONE DOLLAR IN SILVER under portrait.
Back Design: Same as 1928 note.

SERIES	SIGNATURES	SEAL	A.B.P.	GOOD	V. FINE	UNC.	★UNC.
☐1934	Julian-Morgenthau	Blue	6.50	13.00	25.00	145.00	1800.00

ONE DOLLAR NOTES (1935) SILVER CERTIFICATES
(Small Size)

Face Design: Portrait of President Washington in center. Gray "1" to left, blue seal right, and blue numbers. ONE DOLLAR IN SILVER under portrait.

The following notes are without IN GOD WE TRUST on back.

SERIES	SIGNATURES	SEAL	A.B.P.	GOOD	V. FINE	UNC.	★UNC.
☐1935	Julian-Morgenthau	Blue	3.00	4.50	10.00	37.00	600.00
☐1935A	Julian-Morgenthau	Blue	2.00	3.50	4.00	13.00	115.00
☐1935A	Julian-Morgenthau	Brown	6.00	9.00	25.00	175.00	2000.00

This note was a special issue for use in war zones in the Pacific area during World War II. Brown serial numbers and HAWAII stamped on front and back.

ONE DOLLAR NOTES (1935) SILVER CERTIFICATES
(Small Size)

SERIES	SIGNATURES	SEAL	A.B.P.	GOOD	V. FINE	UNC.	★UNC.
☐1935A	Julian-Morgenthau	Yellow	5.50	8.00	30.00	150.00	2250.00

The above note was a special issue for use in war zones in the North African and European areas during World War II. Blue serial numbers and yellow seal.

☐1935A	Julian-Morgenthau	Blue	11.00	30.00	75.00	400.00	8000.00

Red "R" between the Treasury Seal and signature of Morgenthau. This was an experimental issue to test wearing qualities of differently treated paper.

☐1935A	Julian-Morgenthau	Blue	10.00	27.00	65.00	350.00	7500.00

Above note with red "S" between Treasury Seal and signature of Morgenthau. Experimental issue "R" was for regular paper, "S" for special paper.

☐1935B	Julian-Vinson	Blue	2.50	3.00	5.50	18.00	275.00
☐1935C	Julian-Snyder	Blue	2.50	3.00	3.80	13.00	90.00
☐1935D	Clark-Snyder	Blue	2.50	3.00	3.80	15.00	75.00

Wide design on back. This and all notes of 1935 prior to this have the wide design. See Fig I.

☐1935D	Clark-Snyder	Blue	2.00	3.00	4.00	13.00	60.00

Narrow design on back. This and all $1 Notes following have narrow design. See Fig. II.

Figure I

Figure II

ONE DOLLAR NOTES (1935) SILVER CERTIFICATES
(Small Size)

SERIES	SIGNATURES	SEAL	A.B.P.	GOOD	V. FINE	UNC.	★UNC.
☐1935E	Priest-Humphrey	Blue	1.50	3.00	3.25	11.50	19.50
☐1935F	Priest-Anderson	Blue	1.50	3.00	3.50	11.50	19.50
☐1935G	Smith-Dillon	Blue	1.50	3.00	3.50	12.00	25.00

IN GOD WE TRUST added. All notes following have the motto.

☐1935G	Smith-Dillon	Blue	1.80	5.00	10.00	50.00	250.00
☐1935H	Granahan-Dillon	Blue	1.80	3.50	3.25	15.00	45.00

ONE DOLLAR NOTES (1957) SILVER CERTIFICATES
(Small Size)

The following three notes are the last issue of the $1 Silver Certificates. The reason for the change in series from 1935H to 1957 was due to printing improvements. The 1935 Series, up until the issue of Clark and Snyder, was printed in sheets of twelve subjects to a sheet. During the term of Clark and Snyder notes were printed eighteen subjects to a sheet. Starting with Series 1957, new high-speed rotary presses were installed and notes were printed thirty-two subjects to a sheet.

SERIES	SIGNATURES	SEAL	A.B.P.	GOOD	V. FINE	UNC.	★UNC.
☐1957	Priest-Anderson	Blue	1.80	2.00	2.25	6.50	15.50
☐1957A	Smith-Dillon	Blue	1.80	2.00	2.15	7.50	13.50
☐1957B	Granahan-Dillon	Blue	1.80	2.00	2.15	7.50	12.50

The redemption of Silver Certificates by the U.S. Treasury Department ended on June 24, 1968. These notes are now worth only their face value, plus the numismatic value to collectors. Notes in used condition are not regarded as collectors' items.

ONE DOLLAR NOTES (1890)
TREASURY OR COIN NOTES
(Large Size)

Face Design: Portrait of Stanton, Secretary of War during the Civil War.

Back Design: Green large ornate ONE. Entire back is beautifully engraved.

SERIES	SIGNATURES	SEAL	A.B.P.	GOOD	V. FINE	UNC.
☐1890	Rosecrans-Huston	Brown	90.00	135.00	900.00	3350.00
☐1890	Rosecrans-Nebeker	Brown	90.00	135.00	900.00	3350.00
☐1890	Rosecrans-Nebeker	Red	90.00	135.00	900.00	3350.00

ONE DOLLAR NOTES (1891)
TREASURY OR COIN NOTES

(Large Size)

Face Design: Is similar to 1890 note.

Back Design: More unengraved area, numerous ONES and "1"s.

SERIES	SIGNATURES	SEAL	A.B.P.	GOOD	V. FINE	UNC.
☐1891	Rosecrans-Nebeker	Red	65.00	100.00	275.00	1400.00
☐1891	Tillman-Morgan	Red	65.00	100.00	275.00	1400.00
☐1891	Bruce-Roberts	Red	65.00	100.00	275.00	1400.00

ONE DOLLAR NOTES (1918)
FEDERAL RESERVE BANK NOTES
(Large Size)

Face Design: Portrait of President Washington, signature to left of center. Bank and city center, blue seal to right. Signatures of government officials above. Signatures of bank officials below. Federal Reserve district letter and numbers in four corners.

Back Design: Flying eagle and flag in center. All are Series 1918 and have blue seals and blue numbers.

BANK	GOV'T SIGNATURES	BANK SIGNATURES	A.B.P.	GOOD	V. FINE	UNC.
☐ Boston	Teehee-Burke	Bullen-Morss				
			27.00	37.00	115.00	265.00
☐ Boston	Teehee-Burke	Willet-Morss				
			27.00	37.00	130.00	520.00
☐ Boston	Elliot-Burke	Willet-Morss				
			27.00	37.00	115.00	335.00

BANK	GOV'T SIGNATURES	BANK SIGNATURES	A.B.P.	GOOD	V. FINE	UNC.
☐ New York	Teehee-Burke	Sailer-Strong	27.00	35.00	110.00	265.00
☐ New York	Teehee-Burke	Hendricks-Strong	27.00	35.00	110.00	265.00
☐ New York	Elliott-Burke	Hendricks-Strong	27.00	35.00	110.00	265.00
☐ Philadelphia	Teehee-Burke	Hardt-Passmore	27.00	35.00	110.00	265.00
☐ Philadelphia	Teehee-Burke	Dyer-Passmore	27.00	35.00	110.00	265.00
☐ Philadelphia	Elliott-Burke	Dyer-Passmore	41.00	60.00	255.00	845.00
☐ Philadelphia	Elliott-Burke	Dyer-Norris	27.00	35.00	110.00	335.00
☐ Cleveland	Teehee-Burke	Baxter-Fancher	27.00	35.00	110.00	335.00
☐ Cleveland	Teehee-Burke	Davis-Fancher	27.00	35.00	110.00	335.00
☐ Cleveland	Elliott-Burke	Davis-Fancher	27.00	35.00	110.00	335.00
☐ Richmond	Teehee-Burke	Keesee-Seay	27.00	35.00	110.00	335.00
☐ Richmond	Elliott-Burke	Keesee-Seay	27.00	35.00	110.00	335.00
☐ Atlanta	Teehee-Burke	Pike-McCord	27.00	35.00	110.00	335.00
☐ Atlanta	Teehee-Burke	Bell-McCord	41.00	55.00	290.00	910.00
☐ Atlanta	Teehee-Burke	Bell-Wellborn	36.00	55.00	265.00	785.00
☐ Atlanta	Elliott-Burke	Bell-Wellborn	27.00	40.00	113.00	310.00
☐ Chicago	Teehee-Burke	McCloud-McDougal	27.00	35.00	110.00	310.00
☐ Chicago	Teehee-Burke	Cramer-McDougal	27.00	35.00	115.00	310.00
☐ Chicago	Elliott-Burke	Cramer-McDougal	27.00	35.00	110.00	310.00
☐ St. Louis	Teehee-Burke	Attebery-Wells	27.00	35.00	110.00	310.00
☐ St. Louis	Teehee-Burke	Attebery-Biggs	41.00	55.00	255.00	805.00

BANK	GOV'T SIGNATURES	BANK SIGNATURES	A.B.P.	GOOD	V. FINE	UNC.
☐ St. Louis	Elliott-Burke	Attebery-Biggs				
			41.00	55.00	260.00	760.00
☐ St. Louis	Elliott-Burke	White-Biggs				
			27.00	35.00	120.00	275.00
☐ Minneapolis	Teehee-Burke	Cook-Wold				
			31.00	35.00	120.00	275.00
☐ Minneapolis	Teehee-Burke	Cook-Young				
			106.00	207.00	485.00	1105.00
☐ Minneapolis	Elliott-Burke	Cook-Young				
			28.00	37.00	115.00	385.00
☐ Kansas City	Teehee-Burke	Anderson-Miller				
			27.00	35.00	115.00	385.00
☐ Kansas City	Elliott-Burke	Anderson-Miller				
			27.00	35.00	115.00	385.00
☐ Kansas City	Elliott-Burke	Helm-Miller				
			27.00	35.00	115.00	385.00
☐ Dallas	Teehee-Burke	Talley-VanZandt				
			27.00	35.00	115.00	385.00
☐ Dallas	Elliott-Burke	Talley-VanZandt				
			37.00	41.00	155.00	365.00
☐ Dallas	Elliott-Burke	Lawder-VanZandt				
			27.00	35.00	115.00	310.00
☐ San Francisco	Teehee-Burke	Clerk-Lynch				
			27.00	35.00	125.00	310.00
☐ San Francisco	Teehee-Burke	Clerk-Calkins				
			37.00	52.00	165.00	535.00
☐ San Francisco	Elliott-Burke	Clerk-Calkins				
			37.00	50.00	140.00	410.00
☐ San Francisco	Elliott-Burke	Ambrose-Calkins				
			27.00	35.00	115.00	265.00

ONE DOLLAR NOTES (1963)
FEDERAL RESERVE NOTES

(Small Size)

Face Design: Portrait of President Washington in center, black Federal Reserve seal with city and district letter to left, green Treasury Seal to right. Green serial numbers, Federal Reserve numbers in four corners.

Back Design: Same as all $1 Notes from 1935.

SERIES OF 1963, GRANAHAN-DILLON, GREEN SEAL

DISTRICT	A.B.P.	UNC.	★UNC.	DISTRICT	A.B.P.	UNC.	★UNC.
☐1A Boston	1.80	4.75	10.00	☐7G Chicago	1.80	4.75	8.00
☐2B New York	1.80	4.75	7.50	☐8H St. Louis	1.80	4.75	8.00
☐3C Philadelphia	1.80	4.75	8.50	☐9I Minneapolis	1.80	4.75	12.00
☐4D Cleveland	1.80	4.75	8.50	☐10J Kansas City	1.80	4.75	8.00
☐5E Richmond	1.80	4.75	8.00	☐11K Dallas	1.80	4.75	8.00
☐6F Atlanta	1.80	4.75	8.00	☐12L San Francisco	1.80	4.75	15.00
District Sets (12 notes)		60.00					

The Dallas note of this series as shown, with the letter "K" in the black seal and the number "11" in the four corners, does not have any more significance or value than any other notes with their respective district letter and corresponding number.

A false rumor was circulated several years ago that the "K" was for Kennedy, the "11" was for November (the month in which he was assassinated), and that the note was issued by the Dallas Bank to commemorate the occasion. The entire story is apocryphal.

This note is in no way associated with the late President Kennedy. The notes were authorized by the Act of June 4, 1963. This was five months before Kennedy was assassinated. The Federal Reserve district for Dallas is K-11.

SERIES OF 1963A, GRANAHAN-FOWLER, GREEN SEAL

DISTRICT	A.B.P.	UNC.	★UNC.	DISTRICT	A.B.P.	UNC.	★UNC.
☐1A Boston	1.75	4.50	8.00	☐7G Chicago	1.75	4.50	8.50
☐2B New York	1.75	4.50	8.00	☐8H St. Louis	1.75	4.50	8.50
☐3C Philadelphia	1.75	4.50	8.00	☐9I Minneapolis	1.75	4.50	8.50
☐4D Cleveland	1.75	4.50	8.00	☐10J Kansas City	1.75	4.50	8.50
☐5E Richmond	1.75	4.50	8.00	☐11K Dallas	1.75	4.50	8.50
☐6F Atlanta	1.75	4.50	8.00	☐12L San Francisco	1.75	4.50	8.50
District Sets (12 notes)		60.00					

ONE DOLLAR NOTES (1963-B) FEDERAL RESERVE (WITH SIGNATURE OF JOSEPH W. BARR)
(Small Size)

Joseph W. Barr served as Secretary of the Treasury from December 20, 1968, to January 20, 1969, filling the unexpired term of Henry H. Fowler. His signature appears on the $1 Federal Reserve Notes of the Series of 1963-B only.

During the one-month term of Joseph W. Barr, about 471 million notes were printed with his signature. These notes were for the following Federal Reserve Banks.

	REGULAR NUMBERS	A.B.P.	UNC.	★UNC.
☐2B New York	123,040,000	1.75	5.00	20.00
☐5E Richmond	93,600,000	1.75	5.00	20.00
☐7G Chicago	91,040,000	1.75	5.00	20.00
☐10J Kansas City	44,800,000	1.75	5.00	—
☐12L San Francisco	106,400,000	1.75	5.00	20.00
District Sets (5 notes)				27.50

ONE DOLLAR NOTES (1969)
FEDERAL RESERVE NOTES
(WORDING IN GREEN, TREASURY SEAL CHANGED FROM LATIN TO ENGLISH)

FORMER DESIGN:
The former design had the Latin inscription: *"Thesaur. Amer. Septent. Sigil.,"* which has several translations. It was the Seal of the North American Treasury.

NEW DESIGN:
This new design drops the Latin and states *"The Department of The Treasury, 1789."* First used on the $100 Note of the Series 1966.

ONE DOLLAR NOTES (1969)
FEDERAL RESERVE NOTES

(Small Size)

SERIES OF 1969, SIGNATURES OF ELSTON-KENNEDY, GREEN SEAL

BANK	A.B.P.	V.FINE	UNC.	★UNC.	BANK	A.B.P.	V.FINE	UNC.	★UNC.
☐ Boston	—	1.25	5.50	7.00	☐ Chicago	—	1.25	5.50	7.00
☐ New York	—	1.25	5.50	7.00	☐ St. Louis	—	1.25	5.50	7.00
☐ Philadelphia	—	1.25	5.50	7.00	☐ Minneapolis	—	1.25	5.50	7.00
☐ Cleveland	—	1.25	5.50	7.00	☐ Kansas City	—	1.25	5.50	7.00
☐ Richmond	—	1.25	5.50	7.00	☐ Dallas	—	1.25	5.50	7.00
☐ Atlanta	—	1.25	5.50	7.00	☐ San Francisco	—	1.25	5.50	7.00

SERIES OF 1969A, SIGNATURES OF KABIS-KENNEDY, GREEN SEAL

BANK	A.B.P.	V.FINE	UNC.	★UNC.	BANK	A.B.P.	V.FINE	UNC.	★UNC.
☐ Boston	—	1.25	5.00	9.00	☐ Chicago	—	1.25	5.00	9.00
☐ New York	—	1.25	5.00	9.00	☐ St. Louis	—	1.25	5.00	9.00
☐ Philadelphia	—	1.25	5.00	9.00	☐ Minneapolis	—	1.25	5.00	9.00
☐ Cleveland	—	1.25	5.00	9.00	☐ Kansas City	—	1.25	5.00	9.00
☐ Richmond	—	1.25	5.00	9.00	☐ Dallas	—	1.25	5.00	—
☐ Atlanta	—	1.25	5.00	9.00	☐ San Francisco	—	1.25	5.00	9.00

SERIES OF 1969B, SIGNATURES OF KABIS-CONNALLY, GREEN SEAL

BANK	A.B.P.	V.FINE	UNC.	★UNC.	BANK	A.B.P.	V.FINE	UNC.	★UNC.
☐ Boston	—	1.15	5.00	7.50	☐ Chicago	—	1.15	5.00	7.50
☐ New York	—	1.15	5.00	7.50	☐ St. Louis	—	1.15	5.00	7.50
☐ Philadelphia	—	1.15	5.00	7.50	☐ Minneapolis	—	1.15	5.00	7.50
☐ Cleveland	—	1.15	5.00	7.50	☐ Kansas City	—	1.15	5.00	7.50
☐ Richmond	—	1.15	5.00	7.50	☐ Dallas	—	1.15	5.00	7.50
☐ Atlanta	—	1.15	5.00	7.50	☐ San Francisco	—	1.15	5.00	7.50

SERIES OF 1969C, SIGNATURES OF BANUELOS-CONNALLY, GREEN SEAL

BANK	A.B.P.	V.FINE	UNC.	★UNC.	BANK	A.B.P.	V.FINE	UNC.	★UNC.
☐ New York	—	1.15	5.50	—	☐ Chicago	—	1.15	5.50	30.00
☐ Cleveland	—	1.15	5.50	40.00	☐ St. Louis	—	1.15	5.50	40.00
☐ Richmond	—	1.15	5.50	45.00	☐ Minneapolis	—	1.15	5.50	40.00
☐ Atlanta	—	1.15	5.50	30.00	☐ Kansas City	—	1.15	5.50	35.00
					☐ Dallas	—	1.15	5.50	40.00
					☐ San Francisco	—	1.15	5.50	30.00

SERIES OF 1969D, SIGNATURES OF BANUELOS-SHULTZ, GREEN SEAL

BANK	A.B.P.	V.FINE	UNC.	★UNC.	BANK	A.B.P.	V.FINE	UNC.	★UNC.
☐ Boston	—	1.15	5.00	10.00	☐ Chicago	—	1.15	5.00	10.00
☐ New York	—	1.15	5.00	10.00	☐ St. Louis	—	1.15	5.00	10.00
☐ Philadelphia	—	1.15	5.00	10.00	☐ Minneapolis	—	1.15	5.00	—
☐ Cleveland	—	1.15	5.00	10.00	☐ Kansas City	—	1.15	5.00	10.00
☐ Richmond	—	1.15	5.00	10.00	☐ Dallas	—	1.15	5.00	10.00
☐ Atlanta	—	1.15	5.00	10.00	☐ San Francisco	—	1.15	5.00	10.00

SERIES OF 1974, SIGNATURES OF NEFF-SIMON, GREEN SEAL

BANK	A.B.P.	V.FINE	UNC.	★UNC.	BANK	A.B.P.	V.FINE	UNC.	★UNC.
☐ Boston	—	1.15	4.50	10.00	☐ Chicago	—	1.15	4.50	6.00
☐ New York	—	1.15	4.50	6.00	☐ St. Louis	—	1.15	4.50	6.00
☐ Philadelphia	—	1.15	4.50	8.00	☐ Minneapolis	—	1.15	4.50	40.00
☐ Cleveland	—	1.15	4.50	20.00	☐ Kansas City	—	1.15	4.50	6.00
☐ Richmond	—	1.15	4.50	6.00	☐ Dallas	—	1.15	4.50	10.00
☐ Atlanta	—	1.15	4.50	6.00	☐ San Francisco	—	1.15	4.50	6.00

SERIES OF 1977, SIGNATURES OF MORTON-BLUMENTHAL, GREEN SEAL

BANK	A.B.P.	V.FINE	UNC.	★UNC.	BANK	A.B.P.	V.FINE	UNC.	★UNC.
☐ Boston	—	1.15	6.50	9.00	☐ Chicago	—	1.15	6.50	9.00
☐ New York	—	1.15	6.50	9.00	☐ St. Louis	—	1.15	6.50	9.00
☐ Philadelphia	—	1.15	6.50	9.00	☐ Minneapolis	—	1.15	6.50	9.00
☐ Cleveland	—	1.15	6.50	9.00	☐ Kansas City	—	1.15	6.50	9.00
☐ Richmond	—	1.15	6.50	9.00	☐ Dallas	—	1.15	6.50	9.00
☐ Atlanta	—	1.15	6.50	9.00	☐ San Francisco	—	1.15	6.50	9.00

SERIES OF 1977A, SIGNATURES OF MORTON-MILLER, GREEN SEAL

BANK	A.B.P.	V.FINE	UNC.	★UNC.	BANK	A.B.P.	V.FINE	UNC.	★UNC.
☐ Boston	—	1.10	6.00	7.00	☐ Chicago	—	1.10	6.00	7.00
☐ New York	—	1.10	6.00	7.00	☐ St. Louis	—	1.10	6.00	7.00
☐ Philadelphia	—	1.10	6.00	7.00	☐ Minneapolis	—	1.10	6.00	25.00
☐ Cleveland	—	1.10	6.00	7.00	☐ Kansas City	—	1.10	6.00	7.00
☐ Richmond	—	1.10	6.00	7.00	☐ Dallas	—	1.10	6.00	7.00
☐ Atlanta	—	1.10	6.00	7.00	☐ San Francisco	—	1.10	6.00	7.00

SERIES OF 1981, SIGNATURES OF BUCHANAN-REGAN, GREEN SEAL

BANK	A.B.P.	V.FINE	UNC.	★UNC.	BANK	A.B.P.	V.FINE	UNC.	★UNC.
☐ Boston	—	1.10	5.00	10.00	☐ Chicago	—	1.10	5.00	10.00
☐ New York	—	1.10	5.00	10.00	☐ St. Louis	—	1.10	5.00	15.00
☐ Philadelphia	—	1.10	5.00	50.00	☐ Minneapolis	—	1.10	5.00	15.00
☐ Cleveland	—	1.10	5.00	10.00	☐ Kansas City	—	1.10	5.00	10.00
☐ Richmond	—	1.10	5.00	10.00	☐ Dallas	—	1.10	5.00	15.00
☐ Atlanta	—	1.10	5.00	10.00	☐ San Francisco	—	1.10	5.00	10.00

SERIES OF 1981A, SIGNATURES OF ORTEGA-REGAN, GREEN SEAL

BANK	A.B.P.	V.FINE	UNC.	★UNC.	BANK	A.B.P.	V.FINE	UNC.	★UNC.
☐ Boston	—	—	5.00	10.00	☐ St. Louis	—	—	5.00	10.00
☐ New York	—	1.10	5.00	10.00	☐ Minneapolis	—	—	5.00	10.00
☐ Philadelphia	—	—	5.00	10.00	☐ Kansas City	—	—	5.00	10.00
☐ Cleveland	—	—	5.00	10.00	☐ Chicago	—	1.10	5.00	10.00
☐ Richmond	—	1.10	5.00	10.00	☐ Dallas	—	1.10	5.00	1100.00
☐ Atlanta	—	—	5.00	10.00	☐ San Francisco	—	1.10	5.00	10.00

SERIES OF 1981A or 1985 (REVERSE #129 LEFT), SIGNATURES OF ORTEGA-REGAN, GREEN SEAL

BANK	A.B.P.	V.FINE	UNC.	★UNC.	BANK	A.B.P.	V.FINE	UNC.	★UNC.
☐ Boston	—	25.00	41.00	—	☐ Chicago	—	25.00	41.00	—
☐ New York	—	25.00	41.00	—	☐ St. Louis	—	25.00	41.00	—
☐ Philadelphia	—	25.00	41.00	—	☐ Minneapolis	—	25.00	41.00	—
☐ Cleveland	—	25.00	41.00	—	☐ Kansas City	—	25.00	41.00	—
☐ Richmond	—	25.00	41.00	—	☐ Dallas	—	25.00	41.00	—
☐ Atlanta	—	25.00	41.00	—	☐ San Francisco	—	25.00	41.00	—

SERIES OF 1985, SIGNATURES OF ORTEGA-BAKER, GREEN SEAL

★Notes not issued for all banks

BANK	A.B.P.	V.FINE	UNC.	★UNC.	BANK	A.B.P.	V.FINE	UNC.	★UNC.
☐ Boston	—	1.10	5.00	—	☐ Chicago	—	1.10	5.00	10.00
☐ New York	—	1.10	5.00	—	☐ St. Louis	—	1.10	5.00	1100.00
☐ Philadelphia	—	1.10	5.00	—	☐ Minneapolis	—	1.10	5.00	10.00
☐ Cleveland	—	1.10	5.00	—	☐ Kansas City	—	1.10	5.00	—
☐ Richmond	—	1.10	5.00	10.00	☐ Dallas	—	1.10	5.00	10.00
☐ Atlanta	—	1.10	5.00	—	☐ San Francisco	—	1.10	5.00	10.00

SERIES OF 1985 (REVERSE #129 LEFT), SIGNATURES OF ORTEGA-BAKER, GREEN SEAL

BANK	A.B.P.	V.FINE	UNC.	★UNC.	BANK	A.B.P.	V.FINE	UNC.	★UNC.
☐ Boston	—	24.00	35.00	—	☐ Chicago	—	24.00	35.00	—
☐ New York	—	24.00	35.00	—	☐ St. Louis	—	24.00	35.00	—
☐ Philadelphia	—	24.00	35.00	—	☐ Minneapolis	—	24.00	35.00	—
☐ Cleveland	—	24.00	35.00	—	☐ Kansas City	—	24.00	35.00	—
☐ Richmond	—	24.00	35.00	—	☐ Dallas	—	24.00	35.00	—

SERIES OF 1988, SIGNATURES OF ORTEGA-BRADY, GREEN SEAL
★Notes not issued for all banks

BANK	A.B.P.	V.FINE	UNC.	★UNC.	BANK	A.B.P.	V.FINE	UNC.	★UNC.
☐ Boston	—	1.10	5.00	10.00	☐ Chicago	—	1.10	5.00	—
☐ New York	—	1.10	5.00	10.00	☐ St. Louis	—	1.10	5.00	
☐ Philadelphia	—	1.10	5.00	—	☐ Minneapolis	—	1.10	5.00	
☐ Cleveland	—	1.10	5.00	—	☐ Kansas City	—	1.10	5.00	10.00
☐ Richmond	—	1.10	5.00	10.00	☐ Dallas	—	1.10	5.00	10.00
☐ Atlanta	—	1.10	5.00	1200.00	☐ San Francisco	—	1.10	5.00	10.00

SERIES OF 1988A, SIGNATURES OF VILLALPANDO-BRADY, GREEN SEAL
★Notes not issued for all banks

BANK	A.B.P.	V.FINE	UNC.	★UNC.	BANK	A.B.P.	V.FINE	UNC.	★UNC.
☐ Boston	—	1.10	4.00	—	☐ Chicago	—	1.10	4.00	10.00
☐ New York	—	1.10	4.00	10.00	☐ St. Louis	—	1.10	4.00	10.00
☐ Philadelphia	—	1.10	4.00	—	☐ Minneapolis	—	1.10	4.00	10.00
☐ Cleveland	—	1.10	4.00	10.00	☐ Kansas City	—	1.10	4.00	—
☐ Richmond	—	1.10	4.00	10.00	☐ Dallas	—	1.10	4.00	10.00
☐ Atlanta	—	1.10	4.00	10.00	☐ San Francisco	—	1.10	4.00	10.00

SERIES OF 1993, SIGNATURES OF WITHROW-BENTSEN, GREEN SEAL
★Notes not issued for all banks

BANK	A.B.P.	V.FINE	UNC.	★UNC.	BANK	A.B.P.	V.FINE	UNC.	★UNC.
☐ Boston	—	1.10	2.00	—	☐ Chicago	—	1.10	2.00	4.00
☐ New York	—	1.10	2.00	4.00	☐ St. Louis	—	1.10	2.00	—
☐ Philadelphia	—	1.10	2.00	200.00	☐ Minneapolis	—	1.10	125.00	
☐ Cleveland	—	1.10	2.00	—	☐ Dallas	—	1.10	2.00	4.00
☐ Richmond	—	1.10	2.00	—	☐ San Francisco	—	1.10	2.00	
☐ Atlanta	—	1.10	2.00	4.00					

SERIES OF 1995, SIGNATURES OF WITHROW-RUBIN, GREEN SEAL
★Notes not issued for all banks

BANK	A.B.P.	V.FINE	UNC.	★UNC.	BANK	A.B.P.	V.FINE	UNC.	★UNC.
☐ Boston	—	1.10	2.00	6.00	☐ Chicago	—	1.10	2.00	6.00
☐ New York	—	1.10	2.00	6.00	☐ St. Louis	—	1.10	2.00	—
☐ Philadelphia	—	1.10	2.00	6.00	☐ Minneapolis	—	1.10	2.00	6.00
☐ Cleveland	—	1.10	2.00	6.00	☐ Kansas City	—	1.10	2.00	6.00
☐ Richmond	—	1.10	2.00	6.00	☐ Dallas	—	1.10	2.00	25.00
☐ Atlanta	—	1.10	2.00	6.00	☐ San Francisco	—	1.10	2.00	6.00

TWO DOLLAR NOTES

TWO DOLLAR NOTES (1862) UNITED STATES NOTES
(ALSO KNOWN AS LEGAL TENDER NOTES)
(Large Size)

Face Design: Portrait of Alexander Hamilton (1754–1804), cloverleaf "2"s in upper corners, medallion with "II" in lower left, medallion with "1, 2, 3" right of portrait.

Back Design: "2" in each corner, with "2" motif repeated in scallop circles around obligation; back is printed green.

SERIES	SIGNATURES	SEAL	A.B.P.	GOOD	V. FINE	UNC.
☐1862	Chittenden-Spinner					
	Type I, American Banknote Company vertical in left border	Red	135.00	185.00	1150.00	3000.00
☐1862	Chittenden-Spinner					
	Type II, National Banknote Company vertical in left border	Red	135.00	185.00	1175.00	3000.00

TWO DOLLAR NOTES (1869) UNITED STATES NOTES
(ALSO KNOWN AS LEGAL TENDER NOTES)
(Large Size)

Face Design: Portrait of President Jefferson to left, Capitol in center, large red seal to right.

Back Design: Roman "II" left, arabic "2" center, TWO right. This is the companion note to the $1 "Rainbow Note".

SERIES	SIGNATURES	SEAL	A.B.P.	GOOD	V. FINE	UNC.
☐1869	Allison-Spinner	Red	120.00	175.00	975.00	3800.00
☐1869	Allison-Spinner	Water Mark Paper	135.00	220.00	1425.00	4500.00

TWO DOLLAR NOTES (1874) UNITED STATES NOTES
(ALSO KNOWN AS LEGAL TENDER NOTES)
(Large Size)

Face Design: Portrait of President Jefferson; same as 1869 note.

Back Design: Completely revised.

SERIES	SIGNATURES	SEAL	A.B.P.	GOOD	V. FINE	UNC.
☐1874	Allison-Spinner	Red	95.00	150.00	750.00	2160.00
☐1875	Allison-New	Red	100.00	150.00	1025.00	2450.00
☐Series A	Allison-New	Red	195.00	335.00	3050.00	6050.00
☐Series B	Allison-New	Red	195.00	335.00	3050.00	5850.00
☐1875	Allison-Wyman	Red	105.00	160.00	800.00	2050.00
☐1878	Allison-Gilfillan	Red	100.00	135.00	725.00	1800.00
☐1878	Scofield-Gilfillan	Red	1000.00	1310.00	4950.00	20000.00
☐1880	Scofield-Gilfillan	Brown	55.00	75.00	325.00	1050.00
☐1880	Bruce-Gilfillan	Brown	55.00	75.00	320.00	1050.00
☐1880	Bruce-Wyman	Brown	55.00	75.00	320.00	1100.00
☐1880	Rosecrans-Huston	Red	305.00	660.00	1800.00	7000.00
☐1880	Rosecrans-Huston	Brown	680.00	1360.00	3550.00	25000.00
☐1880	Rosecrans-Nebeker	Red	90.00	135.00	550.00	1500.00
☐1880	Tillman-Morgan	Red	40.00	67.00	240.00	825.00

SERIES	SIGNATURES	SEAL	A.B.P.	GOOD	V. FINE	UNC.
☐1917	Teehee-Burke	Red	18.00	24.00	75.00	280.00
☐1917	Elliott-Burke	Red	18.00	24.00	75.00	280.00
☐1917	Elliott-Burke (error)	Red	75.00	100.00	300.00	1000.00
☐1917	Elliott-White	Red	18.00	24.00	75.00	280.00
☐1917	Speelman-White	Red	18.00	22.00	80.00	280.00

TWO DOLLAR NOTES (1928) UNITED STATES NOTES (ALSO KNOWN AS LEGAL TENDER NOTES)

(Small Size)

Face Design: Portrait of President Jefferson, red seal left, TWO right, red serial numbers.

Back Design: Jefferson Home—Monticello.

SERIES	SIGNATURES	SEAL	A.B.P.	GOOD	V. FINE	UNC.	★UNC.
☐1928	Tate-Mellon	Red	4.00	10.00	20.00	170.00	850.00
☐1928A	Woods-Mellon	Red	8.00	20.00	75.00	450.00	8000.00
☐1928B	Woods-Mills	Red	26.00	60.00	150.00	1500.00	50000.00
☐1928C	Julian-Morgenthau	Red	4.00	10.00	20.00	170.00	2500.00
☐1928D	Julian-Morgenthau	Red	3.50	6.00	15.00	65.00	500.00
☐1928E	Julian-Vinson	Red	3.50	9.00	20.00	110.00	7500.00
☐1928F	Julian-Snyder	Red	3.50	5.00	11.00	60.00	550.00
☐1928G	Clark-Snyder	Red	3.50	5.00	10.00	50.00	450.00

TWO DOLLAR NOTES (1953) UNITED STATES NOTES
(ALSO KNOWN AS LEGAL TENDER NOTES)
(Small Size)

Face Design: Portrait of President Jefferson, gray "2" to left, red seal to right over TWO.
Back Design: Same as 1928 note.

SERIES	SIGNATURES	SEAL	A.B.P.	GOOD	V. FINE	UNC.	★UNC.
☐1953	Priest-Humphrey	Red	2.75	3.50	4.50	22.00	45.00
☐1953A	Priest-Anderson	Red	2.75	3.50	4.50	18.00	75.00
☐1953B	Smith-Dillon	Red	2.75	3.50	4.50	17.00	50.00
☐1953C	Granahan-Dillon	Red	2.75	3.50	4.50	18.00	85.00

Back Design: IN GOD WE TRUST on back.
Face Design: Same as previous note.

SERIES	SIGNATURES	SEAL	A.B.P.	GOOD	V. FINE	UNC.	★UNC.
☐1963	Granahan-Dillon	Red	2.50	2.75	3.50	14.00	30.00
☐1963A	Granahan-Fowler	Red	2.50	2.75	3.50	17.00	50.00

Production of $2 United States Notes was discontinued on August 10, 1966.

TWO DOLLAR NOTES (1875) NATIONAL BANK NOTES
FIRST CHARTER PERIOD (Large Size)

Face Design: This note is known as the "Lazy Two Note" due to the unusual "lying down" shape of the "2" shown on the face. Liberty with flag and red seal.

Back Design: Sir Walter Raleigh in England, 1585, exhibiting corn and smoking tobacco from America, State Seal, and eagle.

SERIES	SIGNATURES	SEAL	A.B.P.	GOOD	V. FINE	UNC.
☐ Original	Colby-Spinner	Red	325.00	575.00	2250.00	7000.00
☐ Original	Jeffries-Spinner	Red	350.00	1025.00	2400.00	7050.00
☐ Original	Allison-Spinner	Red	325.00	575.00	2250.00	7000.00
☐ 1875	Allison-New	Red	325.00	575.00	2250.00	7000.00
☐ 1875	Allison-Wyman	Red	325.00	575.00	2250.00	7000.00
☐ 1875	Allison-Gilfillan	Red	325.00	575.00	2250.00	7000.00
☐ 1875	Scofield-Gilfillan	Red	325.00	575.00	2250.00	7000.00

TWO DOLLAR NOTES (1886) SILVER CERTIFICATES
(Large Size)

Face Design: General Hancock portrait left. Treasury Seal to the right of center.

Back Design: "2" left and right, very ornate engraving, obligation in center of note. Note is printed in green.

SERIES	SIGNATURES	SEAL	A.B.P.	GOOD	V. FINE	UNC.
☐1886	Rosecrans-Jordan	Red	120.00	165.00	900.00	2200.00
☐1886	Rosecrans-Hyatt	Sm.Red	120.00	165.00	900.00	2200.00
☐1886	Rosecrans-Hyatt	Lg.Red	120.00	165.00	900.00	2200.00
☐1886	Rosecrans-Huston	Red	120.00	165.00	900.00	2200.00
☐1886	Rosecrans-Huston	Brown	120.00	165.00	925.00	2200.00

TWO DOLLAR NOTES (1891) SILVER CERTIFICATES
(Large Size)

Face Design: Portrait of William Windom, Secretary of the Treasury 1881–84 and 1889–91, red seal right.

Back Design: "2" left and right, scalloped design center with obligation, printed in green.

SERIES	SIGNATURES	SEAL	A.B.P.	GOOD	V. FINE	UNC.
☐1891	Rosecrans-Nebeker	Red	125.00	170.00	825.00	3350.00
☐1891	Tillman-Morgan	Red	125.00	170.00	825.00	3350.00

TWO DOLLAR NOTES (1896) SILVER CERTIFICATES
(Large Size)

Face Design: Science presenting Steam and Electricity to Industry and Commerce.

Back Design: Portraits of Robert Fulton and Samuel F.B. Morse.

This is the second note of the popular Educational Series.

SERIES	SIGNATURES	SEAL	A.B.P.	GOOD	V. FINE	UNC.
☐1896	Tillman-Morgan	Red	160.00	200.00	1275.00	3500.00
☐1896	Bruce-Roberts	Red	160.00	200.00	1275.00	3500.00

TWO DOLLAR NOTES (1899) SILVER CERTIFICATES
(Large Size)

Face Design: Portrait of President Washington between figures of Trade and Agriculture, blue "2" left, blue seal right.

Back Design

SERIES	SIGNATURES	SEAL	A.B.P.	GOOD	V. FINE	UNC.
☐1899	Lyons-Roberts	Blue	90.00	125.00	290.00	1700.00
☐1899	Lyons-Treat	Blue	90.00	125.00	290.00	1700.00
☐1899	Vernon-Treat	Blue	90.00	125.00	290.00	1700.00
☐1899	Vernon-McClung	Blue	90.00	125.00	290.00	1700.00
☐1899	Napier-McClung	Blue	90.00	125.00	290.00	1700.00
☐1899	Napier-Thompson	Blue	105.00	165.00	440.00	2300.00
☐1899	Parker-Burke	Blue	90.00	125.00	290.00	1700.00
☐1899	Teehee-Burke	Blue	90.00	125.00	290.00	1700.00
☐1899	Elliott-Burke	Blue	90.00	125.00	290.00	1700.00
☐1899	Speelman-White	Blue	90.00	125.00	290.00	1700.00

TWO DOLLAR NOTES (1890-1891)
TREASURY OR COIN NOTES
(Large Size)

Face Design: Portrait of General James McPherson.

Back Design: Large TWO center, over obligation. Large "2" on engraved background right. Intricate engraving, printed green.

SERIES	SIGNATURES	SEAL	A.B.P.	GOOD	V. FINE	UNC.
☐1890	Rosecrans-Huston	Brown	190.00	250.00	2250.00	6300.00
☐1890	Rosecrans-Nebeker	Brown	190.00	250.00	2250.00	6300.00
☐1890	Rosecrans-Nebeker	Red	190.00	250.00	2250.00	6300.00

TWO DOLLAR NOTES (1890-1891)
TREASURY OR COIN NOTES

(Large Size)   **NOTE NO. 30**

Face Design: Similar to 1890–1891 note.
Back Design: Revised.

SERIES	SIGNATURES	SEAL	A.B.P.	GOOD	V. FINE	UNC.
☐1891	Rosecrans-Nebeker	Red	90.00	135.00	725.00	2500.00
☐1891	Tillman-Morgan	Red	90.00	135.00	725.00	2500.00
☐1891	Bruce-Roberts	Red	90.00	135.00	725.00	2500.00

TWO DOLLAR NOTES (1918)
FEDERAL RESERVE BANK NOTES
(Large Size)

Face Design: Portrait of President Jefferson to left, name of bank in center, blue seal to the right, blue numbers, Federal Reserve district letter and number in four corners.

Back Design: American battleship of World War I.

TWO DOLLAR NOTES (1918)
FEDERAL RESERVE BANK NOTES
(Large Size)

BANK	GOV'T SIGNATURES	BANK SIGNATURES	A.B.P.	GOOD	V. FINE	UNC.
☐ Boston	Teehee-Burke	Bullen-Morss	100.00	150.00	450.00	1700.00
☐ Boston	Teehee-Burke	Willet-Morss	100.00	150.00	450.00	1800.00
☐ Boston	Elliot-Burke	Willet-Morss	100.00	150.00	450.00	1700.00
☐ New York	Teehee-Burke	Sailer-Strong	100.00	150.00	450.00	1700.00
☐ New York	Teehee-Burke	Hendricks-Strong	100.00	150.00	450.00	1700.00
☐ New York	Elliott-Burke	Hendricks-Strong	100.00	150.00	450.00	1700.00
☐ Philadelphia	Teehee-Burke	Hardt-Passmore	100.00	150.00	450.00	1700.00
☐ Philadelphia	Teehee-Burke	Dyer-Passmore	100.00	150.00	500.00	1800.00
☐ Philadelphia	Elliott-Burke	Dyer-Passmore	100.00	150.00	940.00	2675.00
☐ Philadelphia	Elliott-Burke	Dyer-Norris	100.00	150.00	450.00	1700.00
☐ Cleveland	Teehee-Burke	Baxter-Francher	100.00	150.00	450.00	1700.00
☐ Cleveland	Teehee-Burke	Davis-Francher	100.00	150.00	450.00	1700.00
☐ Cleveland	Elliott-Burke	Davis-Francher	100.00	150.00	450.00	1700.00
☐ Richmond	Teehee-Burke	Keesee-Seay	100.00	150.00	450.00	1700.00
☐ Richmond	Elliott-Burke	Keesee-Seay	100.00	150.00	515.00	1925.00
☐ Atlanta	Teehee-Burke	Pike-McCord	100.00	150.00	500.00	1700.00
☐ Atlanta	Teehee-Burke	Bell-McCord	100.00	150.00	940.00	2675.00
☐ Atlanta	Elliott-Burke	Bell-Wellborn	100.00	150.00	895.00	2575.00
☐ Chicago	Teehee-Burke	McCloud-McDougal	100.00	150.00	450.00	1700.00

BANK	GOV'T SIGNATURES	BANK SIGNATURES	A.B.P.	GOOD	V. FINE	UNC.
☐ Chicago	Teehee-Burke	Cramer-McDougal	100.00	150.00	540.00	1700.00
☐ Chicago	Elliott-Burke	Cramer-McDougal	100.00	150.00	515.00	1600.00
☐ St. Louis	Teehee-Burke	Attebery-Wells	100.00	150.00	515.00	1600.00
☐ St. Louis	Teehee-Burke	Attebery-Biggs	100.00	150.00	690.00	2150.00
☐ St. Louis	Elliott-Burke	Attebery-Biggs	100.00	150.00	690.00	2150.00
☐ St. Louis	Elliott-Burke	White-Biggs	100.00	150.00	765.00	2100.00
☐ Minneapolis	Teehee-Burke	Cook-Wold	100.00	150.00	480.00	1650.00
☐ Minneapolis	Elliott-Burke	Cook-Young	100.00	150.00	590.00	1875.00
☐ Kansas City	Teehee-Burke	Anderson-Miller	100.00	150.00	450.00	1750.00
☐ Kansas City	Elliott-Burke	Helm-Miller	100.00	150.00	515.00	1775.00
☐ Dallas	Teehee-Burke	Talley-VanZandt	100.00	150.00	590.00	1650.00
☐ Dallas	Elliott-Burke	Talley-VanZandt	100.00	150.00	590.00	1775.00
☐ San Francisco	Teehee-Burke	Clerk-Lynch	100.00	150.00	515.00	1775.00
☐ San Francisco	Elliott-Burke	Clerk-Calkins	100.00	150.00	515.00	1775.00
☐ San Francisco	Elliott-Burke	Ambrose-Calkins	100.00	150.00	515.00	1775.00

TWO DOLLAR NOTES (1976)
FEDERAL RESERVE NOTES

(Small Size)

Face Design: Portrait of President Jefferson.

Back Design: Signing of the Declaration of Independence.

SERIES OF 1976, NEFF-SIMON, GREEN SEAL

DISTRICT	A.B.P.	UNC.	★UNC.	DISTRICT	A.B.P.	UNC.	★UNC.
☐1A Boston	3.00	6.50	15.00	☐7G Chicago	3.00	6.50	50.00
☐2B New York	3.00	6.00	20.00	☐8H St. Louis	3.00	5.50	15.00
☐3C Philadelphia	3.00	6.00	15.00	☐9I Minneapolis	3.00	10.00	250.00
☐4D Cleveland	3.00	7.00	30.00	☐10J Kansas City	3.00	25.00	275.00
☐5E Richmond	3.00	6.00	40.00	☐11K Dallas	3.00	8.00	20.00
☐6F Atlanta	3.00	6.50	15.00	☐12L San Francisco	3.00	6.00	20.00

SERIES OF 1995, GREEN SEAL

DISTRICT	A.B.P.	UNC.	★UNC.
☐6F Atlanta	2.15	4.00	10.00

FIVE DOLLAR NOTES

ORDER OF ISSUE

FIVE DOLLAR NOTES (1861) DEMAND NOTES
(Large Size)

Face Design: Left, Statue of America by Crawford atop United States Capitol. Center, numeral "5" in green. Right, portrait of Alexander Hamilton, statesman, first Secretary of the Treasury.

Back Design: Numerous small "5"s in ovals. This note has no Treasury Seal. The signatures are those of Treasury Department employees who signed for officials.

CITY	A.B.P.	GOOD	V. GOOD
☐Boston (I)	925.00	1675.00	3500.00
☐New York (I)	925.00	1675.00	3500.00
☐Philadelphia (I)	925.00	1675.00	3500.00
☐Cincinnati (I)	2575.00	8075.00	16800.00
☐St. Louis (I)	2575.00	8075.00	16800.00
☐Boston (II)	525.00	675.00	1400.00
☐New York (II)	525.00	675.00	1400.00
☐Philadelphia (II)	525.00	675.00	1400.00
☐Cincinnati (II)	3075.00	6075.00	12300.00
☐St. Louis (II)	3075.00	6075.00	12300.00

FIVE DOLLAR NOTES (1875–1907)
UNITED STATES NOTES
(ALSO KNOWN AS LEGAL TENDER NOTES)

(Large Size)

Back Design: First Obligation.

Back Design: Second Obligation

SERIES	SIGNATURES	SEAL	A.B.P.	GOOD	V. FINE	UNC.
☐1862	Crittenden-Spinner*	Red	90.00	135.00	750.00	1800.00
☐1862	Crittenden-Spinner**	Red	90.00	135.00	750.00	1800.00
☐1863	Crittenden-Spinner**	Red	90.00	135.00	750.00	1800.00

*First Obligation
**Second Obligation

FIVE DOLLAR NOTES (1869) UNITED STATES NOTES (ALSO KNOWN AS LEGAL TENDER NOTES)
(Large Size)

Face Design: Portrait of President Jackson on left. Pioneer and family in center.

Back Design: Color, green. This is a companion note to the $1 and $2 Notes of 1869 "Rainbow Notes."

SERIES	SIGNATURES	SEAL	A.B.P.	GOOD	V. FINE	UNC.
☐1869	Allison-Spinner	Red	100.00	135.00	550.00	1550.00
☐1869	Allison-Spinner	Water Marked Paper	105.00	160.00	1100.00	2250.00

FIVE DOLLAR NOTES (1875–1907)
UNITED STATES NOTES
(ALSO KNOWN AS LEGAL TENDER NOTES)
(Large Size)

Back Design: Revised.
Face Design: Similar to 1869 note.

SERIES	SIGNATURES	SEAL	A.B.P.	GOOD	V. FINE	UNC.
☐1875	Allison-New	Red	70.00	115.00	310.00	1060.00
☐1875A	Allison-New	Red	90.00	155.00	660.00	1960.00
☐1875B	Allison-New	Red	70.00	110.00	385.00	1035.00
☐1875	Allison-Wyman	Red	75.00	110.00	360.00	1135.00
☐1878	Allison-Gilfillan	Red	65.00	100.00	405.00	1110.00
☐1880	Scofield-Gilfillan	Brown	315.00	720.00	3510.00	7110.00
☐1880	Bruce-Gilfillan	Brown	100.00	165.00	785.00	2210.00
☐1880	Bruce-Wyman	Brown	70.00	115.00	370.00	1010.00
☐1880	Bruce-Wyman	Red	75.00	125.00	435.00	1710.00
☐1880	Rosecrans-Jordan	Red	70.00	120.00	425.00	1310.00
☐1880	Rosecrans-Hyatt	Red	330.00	740.00	3440.00	7160.00
☐1880	Rosecrans-Huston	Red	75.00	140.00	640.00	1750.00
☐1880	Rosecrans-Huston	Brown	103.00	190.00	685.00	1960.00
☐1880	Rosecrans-Nebeker	Brown	55.00	140.00	485.00	1460.00
☐1880	Rosecrans-Nebeker	Red	45.00	80.00	260.00	960.00
☐1880	Tillman-Morgan	Red	45.00	80.00	245.00	785.00
☐1880	Bruce-Roberts	Red	35.00	65.00	210.00	860.00
☐1880	Lyons-Roberts	Red	55.00	100.00	840.00	2110.00
☐1907	Vernon-Treat	Red	35.00	60.00	215.00	915.00
☐1907	Vernon-McClung	Red	35.00	60.00	215.00	915.00
☐1907	Napier-McClung	Red	35.00	50.00	165.00	650.00
☐1907	Napier-Thompson	Red	55.00	120.00	320.00	795.00
☐1907	Parker-Burke	Red	35.00	60.00	165.00	600.00
☐1907	Teehee-Burke	Red	35.00	60.00	185.00	600.00
☐1907	Elliott-Burke	Red	35.00	60.00	185.00	625.00

SERIES	SIGNATURES	SEAL	A.B.P.	GOOD	V. FINE	UNC.
☐1907	Elliott-White	Red	41.00	55.00	185.00	550.00
☐1907	Speelman-White	Red	41.00	53.00	145.00	510.00
☐1907	Woods-White	Red	41.00	55.00	185.00	560.00

FIVE DOLLAR NOTES (1928) UNITED STATES NOTES
(ALSO KNOWN AS LEGAL TENDER NOTES)
(Small Size)

Face Design: Portrait of President Lincoln center. Red seal to left, red serial numbers.

Back Design: Lincoln Memorial in Washington, D.C.

SERIES	SIGNATURES	SEAL	A.B.P	GOOD	V. FINE	UNC.	★UNC.
☐1928	Woods-Mellon	Red	6.50	9.00	15.00	100.00	2000.00
☐1928A	Woods-Mills	Red	6.50	9.00	25.00	160.00	5000.00
☐1928B	Julian-Morgenthau	Red	6.50	9.00	15.00	45.00	1250.00
☐1928C	Julian-Morgenthau	Red	6.50	9.00	15.00	60.00	650.00
☐1928D	Julian-Vinson	Red	6.50	9.00	35.00	450.00	3000.00
☐1928E	Julian-Snyder	Red	6.50	9.00	15.00	55.00	750.00
☐1928F	Clark-Snyder	Red	6.50	9.00	15.00	60.00	500.00

FIVE DOLLAR NOTES (1953–1963)
UNITED STATES NOTES

(Small Size)

Face Design: Similar to previous note. Portrait of President Lincoln center. Red seal is moved to the right, red numbers.
Back Design: Similar to 1928 note.

SERIES	SIGNATURES	SEAL	A.B.P.	GOOD	V. FINE	UNC.	★UNC.
☐1953	Priest-Humphrey	Red	6.00	7.50	11.00	45.00	275.00
☐1953A	Priest-Anderson	Red	6.00	7.50	13.00	30.00	200.00
☐1953B	Smith-Dillon	Red	6.00	7.50	11.00	25.00	175.00
☐1953C	Granahan-Dillon	Red	6.00	7.50	11.00	50.00	350.00

FIVE DOLLAR NOTES (1953-1963)
UNITED STATES NOTES
(ALSO KNOWN AS LEGAL TENDER NOTES)

(Small Size)

Back Design: The following notes have IN GOD WE TRUST on the back.
Face Design: Similar to 1953–1963 note.

SERIES	SIGNATURES	SEAL	A.B.P.	GOOD	V. FINE	UNC.	★UNC.
☐1963	Granahan-Dillon	Red	6.00	7.50	12.00	25.00	90.00

Production of $5 United States Notes ended in 1967.

FIVE DOLLAR NOTES (1863-1875)
NATIONAL BANK NOTES
FIRST CHARTER PERIOD (Large Size)

Face Design: The Columbus Note. The face shows Columbus in sight of land and Columbus with an Indian princess.

Back Design: Christopher Columbus landing at San Salvador, 1492. Also the State Seal left, and American eagle right.

SERIES	SIGNATURES	SEAL	A.B.P.	GOOD	V. FINE	UNC.
☐Original	Chittenden-Spinner	Red	125.00	175.00	1200.00	8800.00
☐Original	Colby-Spinner	Red	125.00	175.00	1200.00	8700.00
☐Original	Jeffries-Spinner	Red	245.00	590.00	2300.00	10800.00
☐Original	Allison-Spinner	Red	125.00	175.00	1200.00	8800.00
☐1875	Allison-New	Red	125.00	175.00	1200.00	8750.00
☐1875	Allison-Wyman	Red	125.00	175.00	1200.00	8750.00
☐1875	Allison-Gilfillan	Red	125.00	175.00	1200.00	8750.00
☐1875	Scofield-Gilfillan	Red	125.00	175.00	1200.00	8750.00
☐1875	Bruce-Gilfillan	Red	125.00	175.00	1200.00	8750.00
☐1875	Bruce-Wyman	Red	125.00	175.00	1200.00	8750.00
☐1875	Bruce-Jordan	Red		EXTREMELY RARE		
☐1875	Rosecrans-Huston	Red	125.00	175.00	1200.00	8750.00
☐1875	Rosecrans-Jordan	Red	125.00	175.00	1200.00	8750.00

FIVE DOLLAR NOTES (1882) NATIONAL BANK NOTES
SECOND CHARTER PERIOD (Large Size)

First Issue (Brown seal and brown backs.)
Face Design: Portrait of President Garfield left. Name of bank
and city center, brown seal to right. Brown charter number.

Back Design: Brown border design similar to previous note.
Center oval now has the bank's charter number in green.
The top signatures are those of the Treasury officials.
Bottom signatures, usually handwritten or probably rubber-
stamped, are bank officials.

SERIES	SIGNATURES	SEAL	A.B.P.	GOOD	V. FINE	UNC.
☐1882	Bruce-Gilfillan	Brown	80.00	110.00	600.00	2800.00
☐1882	Bruce-Wyman	Brown	80.00	110.00	600.00	2800.00
☐1882	Bruce-Jordan	Brown	80.00	110.00	600.00	2800.00
☐1882	Rosecrans-Jordan	Brown	80.00	110.00	600.00	2800.00
☐1882	Rosecrans-Hyatt	Brown	80.00	110.00	600.00	2800.00
☐1882	Rosecrans-Huston	Brown	80.00	110.00	600.00	2800.00
☐1882	Rosecrans-Nebeker	Brown	80.00	110.00	600.00	2800.00
☐1882	Rosecrans-Morgan	Brown	80.00	208.00	725.00	3150.00
☐1882	Tillman-Morgan	Brown	80.00	110.00	600.00	2800.00
☐1882	Tillman-Roberts	Brown	80.00	110.00	600.00	2800.00
☐1882	Bruce-Roberts	Brown	80.00	110.00	600.00	2800.00
☐1882	Lyons-Roberts	Brown	80.00	110.00	600.00	2800.00
☐1882	Lyons-Treat			(Unknown in any collection)		
☐1882	Vernon-Treat	Brown	80.00	125.00	600.00	2800.00

FIVE DOLLAR NOTES (1882) NATIONAL BANK NOTES
SECOND CHARTER PERIOD, Second Issue (Large Size)

Face Design: Similar to preceding portrait of President Garfield.

Back Design: Back is now green with date "1882–1908" in center.

SERIES	SIGNATURES	SEAL	A.B.P.	GOOD	V. FINE	UNC.
☐1882	Rosecrans-Huston	Blue	70.00	110.00	450.00	2350.00
☐1882	Rosecrans-Nebeker	Blue	70.00	110.00	450.00	2350.00
☐1882	Rosecrans-Morgan	Blue	130.00	250.00	980.00	3415.00
☐1882	Tillman-Morgan	Blue	70.00	110.00	450.00	2350.00
☐1882	Tillman-Roberts	Blue	70.00	110.00	450.00	2350.00
☐1882	Bruce-Roberts	Blue	70.00	110.00	450.00	2350.00
☐1882	Lyons-Roberts	Blue	70.00	110.00	450.00	2350.00
☐1882	Vernon-Treat	Blue	70.00	110.00	450.00	3150.00
☐1882	Vernon-McClung	Blue				RARE
☐1882	Napier-McClung	Blue	105.00	315.00	1100.00	3350.00

FIVE DOLLAR NOTES (1882) NATIONAL BANK NOTES
SECOND CHARTER PERIOD, Third Issue (Large Size)

Face Design: Same as 1882 note. Blue seal.

Back Design: Similar to 1882 Second Issue note. FIVE DOL-
LARS replaces "1882–1908."

SERIES	SIGNATURES	SEAL	A.B.P.	GOOD	V. FINE	UNC.
☐1882	Tillman-Morgan	Blue	85.00	115.00	650.00	3000.00
☐1882	Tillman-Roberts	Blue	85.00	115.00	650.00	3100.00
☐1882	Bruce-Roberts	Blue	85.00	115.00	650.00	3000.00
☐1882	Lyons-Roberts	Blue	85.00	115.00	650.00	3100.00
☐1882	Vernon-Treat	Blue	85.00	115.00	650.00	3000.00
☐1882	Napier-McClung	Blue	85.00	115.00	650.00	3000.00
☐1882	Teehee-Burke	Blue			EXTREMELY RARE	

FIVE DOLLAR NOTES (1902) NATIONAL BANK NOTES
THIRD CHARTER PERIOD (Large Size)

First Issue (Red seal and charter numbers.)
Face Design: Portrait of President Harrison left, name of bank and city center, Treasury Seal to right, red seal and charter number.

Back Design: Landing of Pilgrims.

SERIES	SIGNATURES	SEAL	A.B.P.	GOOD	V. FINE	UNC.
☐1902	Lyons-Roberts	Red	80.00	120.00	675.00	5500.00
☐1902	Lyons-Treat	Red	80.00	120.00	675.00	5500.00
☐1902	Vernon-Treat	Red	80.00	120.00	675.00	5500.00

FIVE DOLLAR NOTES (1902) NATIONAL BANK NOTES
THIRD CHARTER PERIOD (Large Size)
SECOND ISSUE

SERIES	SIGNATURES	SEAL	A.B.P.	GOOD	V. FINE	UNC.
☐1902	Lyons-Roberts	Blue	35.00	50.00	375.00	1175.00
☐1902	Lyons-Treat	Blue	35.00	50.00	375.00	1175.00
☐1902	Vernon-Treat	Blue	35.00	50.00	375.00	1175.00
☐1902	Vernon-McClung	Blue	35.00	50.00	375.00	1175.00
☐1902	Napier-McClung	Blue	35.00	50.00	375.00	1175.00
☐1902	Napier-Thompson	Blue	42.00	60.00	385.00	1275.00
☐1902	Napier-Burke	Blue	35.00	50.00	375.00	1175.00
☐1902	Parker-Burke	Blue	35.00	50.00	375.00	1175.00
☐1902	Teehee-Burke	Blue	35.00	50.00	1390.00	1175.00

FIVE DOLLAR NOTES (1902) NATIONAL BANK NOTES
THIRD CHARTER PERIOD (Large Size)
Third Issue (Blue seal and numbers.)
The following notes do not have date of "1902–1908" on the back.

SERIES	SIGNATURES	SEAL	A.B.P.	GOOD	V. FINE	UNC.
☐1902	Lyons-Roberts	Blue	30.00	45.00	275.00	900.00
☐1902	Lyons-Treat	Blue	30.00	45.00	275.00	900.00
☐1902	Vernon-Treat	Blue	30.00	45.00	275.00	900.00
☐1902	Vernon-McClung	Blue	30.00	45.00	275.00	900.00
☐1902	Napier-McClung	Blue	30.00	45.00	275.00	900.00
☐1902	Napier-Thompson	Blue	30.00	45.00	275.00	900.00
☐1902	Napier-Burke	Blue	30.00	45.00	275.00	900.00
☐1902	Parker-Burke	Blue	30.00	45.00	275.00	900.00
☐1902	Teehee-Burke	Blue	30.00	45.00	275.00	900.00
☐1902	Elliott-Burke	Blue	30.00	45.00	275.00	900.00
☐1902	Elliott-White	Blue	30.00	45.00	275.00	900.00
☐1902	Speelman-White	Blue	30.00	45.00	275.00	900.00
☐1902	Woods-White	Blue	30.00	45.00	275.00	900.00
☐1902	Woods-Tate	Blue	30.00	45.00	275.00	900.00
☐1902	Jones-Woods	Blue	76.00	106.00	395.00	1125.00

FIVE DOLLAR NOTES (1929) NATIONAL BANK NOTES
(Small Size)

TYPE I

TYPE II

Face Design: Portrait of President Lincoln in center, name of bank to left, brown seal to the right. Type I—charter number in black. Type II—similar; charter number added in brown.

Back Design: Lincoln Memorial.

SERIES	SIGNATURES	SEAL	A.B.P.	GOOD	V. FINE	UNC.
□1929	Type I Jones-Woods	Brown	20.00	30.00	75.00	340.00
□1929	Type II Jones-Woods	Brown	20.00	35.00	105.00	345.00

FIVE DOLLAR NOTES (1870)
NATIONAL GOLD BANK NOTES
(Large Size)

Face Design: Vignettes of Columbus sighting land. Presentation of an Indian princess. Red seal. Signatures, Allison-Spinner.

Back Design: California State Seal left, gold coins center, American eagle right.

DATE	BANK	CITY	A.B.P.	GOOD	V. GOOD
☐1870 First National Gold Bank		San Francisco	900.00	1275.00	2950.00
☐1872 National Gold Bank and Trust Co.		San Francisco	900.00	1275.00	2950.00
☐1872 National Gold Bank of D.O. Mills and Co.		Sacramento	1020.00	1450.00	3350.00
☐1873 First National Gold Bank		Santa Barbara	1020.00	1450.00	3350.00
☐1873 First National Gold Bank		Stockton	1020.00	1450.00	3750.00
☐1874 Farmers National Gold Bank		San Jose	1020.00	1450.00	3750.00

FIVE DOLLAR NOTES (1886–1891)
SILVER CERTIFICATES

(Large Size)

Face Design: Portrait of President Grant.

Back Design: Five silver dollars.

SERIES	SIGNATURES	SEAL	A.B.P.	GOOD	V. FINE	UNC.
☐1886	Rosecrans-Jordan	Red	195.00	275.00	1950.00	4650.00
☐1886	Rosecrans-Hyatt	Sm. Red	195.00	275.00	1950.00	4650.00
☐1886	Rosecrans-Hyatt	Lg. Red	195.00	275.00	1950.00	4650.00
☐1886	Rosecrans-Huston	Lg. Red	195.00	275.00	1950.00	4650.00
☐1886	Rosecrans-Huston	Brown	195.00	275.00	1950.00	4650.00
☐1886	Rosecrans-Nebeker	Brown	195.00	275.00	1950.00	4650.00
☐1886	Rosecrans-Nebeker	Sm. Red	215.00	290.00	1875.00	5150.00

FIVE DOLLAR NOTES (1891) SILVER CERTIFICATES
(Large Size)

Face Design: Similar to previous note.

Back Design: Revised.

SERIES	SIGNATURES	SEAL	A.B.P.	GOOD	V. FINE	UNC.
☐1891	Rosecrans-Nebeker	Red	110.00	160.00	925.00	3650.00
☐1891	Tillman-Morgan	Red	110.00	160.00	925.00	3450.00

FIVE DOLLAR NOTES (1896) SILVER CERTIFICATES
(Large Size)

Face Design: Portraits of General Grant and General Sheridan.

Back Design: Five females representing Electricity as the dominant force in the world.

This was the last note of the popular Education Series.

SERIES	SIGNATURES	SEAL	A.B.P.	GOOD	V. FINE	UNC.
☐1896	Tillman-Morgan	Red	275.00	345.00	1750.00	7700.00
☐1896	Bruce-Roberts	Red	275.00	345.00	1750.00	7700.00
☐1896	Lyons-Roberts	Red	275.00	345.00	1750.00	7700.00

FIVE DOLLAR NOTES (1899) SILVER CERTIFICATES
(Large Size)

Face Design: Portrait of Indian chief.

Back Design: Green "V" and "5."

SERIES	SIGNATURES	SEAL	A.B.P.	GOOD	V. FINE	UNC.
☐1899	Lyons-Roberts	Blue	190.00	250.00	750.00	2300.00
☐1899	Lyons-Treat	Blue	190.00	250.00	750.00	2300.00
☐1899	Vernon-Treat	Blue	190.00	250.00	750.00	2300.00
☐1899	Vernon-McClung	Blue	190.00	250.00	750.00	2300.00
☐1899	Napier-McClung	Blue	190.00	250.00	750.00	2300.00
☐1899	Napier-Thompson	Blue	190.00	250.00	1045.00	3175.00
☐1899	Parker-Burke	Blue	190.00	250.00	750.00	2300.00
☐1899	Teehee-Burke	Blue	190.00	250.00	750.00	2300.00
☐1899	Elliott-Burke	Blue	190.00	250.00	750.00	2300.00
☐1899	Elliott-White	Blue	190.00	250.00	750.00	2300.00
☐1899	Speelman-White	Blue	190.00	250.00	750.00	2300.00

FIVE DOLLAR NOTES (1923) SILVER CERTIFICATES
(Large Size)

Face Design: Portrait of President Lincoln in oval, nick-
name "Porthole Note," blue seal left, blue "5" right.

Back Design: Obverse of Great Seal of the United States.

SERIES	SIGNATURES	SEAL	A.B.P.	GOOD	V. FINE	UNC.
☐1923	Speelman-White	Blue	175.00	225.00	800.00	2700.00

FIVE DOLLAR NOTES (1934) SILVER CERTIFICATES
(Small Size)

First Issue (Small size of $5 Silver Certificates 1934.)
Face Design: Portrait of President Lincoln, blue "5" to left, blue seal to right.

Back Design: All Small Size $5 Notes have the same back design.

SERIES	SIGNATURES	SEAL	A.B.P.	GOOD	V. FINE	UNC.	★UNC.
☐1934	Julian-Morgenthau	Blue	6.00	8.00	13.00	42.00	450.00
☐1934A	Julian-Morgenthau	Blue	6.00	8.00	10.00	35.00	350.00
☐1934A	Julian-Morgenthau	Yellow	6.50	15.00	40.00	300.00	750.00

This note, with yellow Treasury Seal, was a Special Issue during World War II for military use in combat areas of North Africa and Europe.

SERIES	SIGNATURES	SEAL	A.B.P.	GOOD	V. FINE	UNC.	★UNC.
☐1934B	Julian-Vinson	Blue	6.00	8.00	21.00	65.00	450.00
☐1934C	Julian-Synder	Blue	6.00	8.00	11.00	32.00	250.00
☐1934D	Clark-Snyder	Blue	6.00	8.00	11.00	30.00	300.00

FIVE DOLLAR NOTES (1953) SILVER CERTIFICATES
(Small Size)

Face Design: The following notes are similar to the previous note. The face design has been revised. Gray "5" replaces blue "5" to left of Lincoln. Blue seal is slightly smaller.

Back Design: Same as previous note.

SERIES	SIGNATURES	SEAL	A.B.P.	GOOD	V. FINE	UNC.	★UNC.
☐1953	Priest-Humphrey	Blue	6.25	7.25	10.00	30.00	55.00
☐1953A	Priest-Anderson	Blue	6.25	7.25	10.00	25.00	30.00
☐1953B	Smith-Dillon	Blue	6.25	7.25	10.00	25.00	5000.00

Production of $5 Silver Certificates ended in 1962.

FIVE DOLLAR NOTES (1890) TREASURY OR COIN NOTES
(Large Size)

Face Design: Portrait of General George Henry Thomas (1816–70), the "Rock of Chickamauga."

Back Design:

SERIES	SIGNATURES	SEAL	A.B.P.	GOOD	V. FINE	UNC.
☐1890	Rosecrans-Huston	Brown	130.00	190.00	1150.00	4100.00
☐1890	Rosecrans-Nebeker	Brown	130.00	190.00	1150.00	4300.00
☐1890	Rosecrans-Nebeker	Red	130.00	190.00	1150.00	4100.00

Back Design: Second Issue

SERIES	SIGNATURES	SEAL	A.B.P.	GOOD	V.FINE	UNC.
☐1891	Rosecrans-Nebeker	Red	100.00	140.00	575.00	2350.00
☐1891	Tillman-Morgan	Red	100.00	140.00	575.00	2350.00
☐1891	Bruce-Roberts	Red	100.00	140.00	575.00	2350.00
☐1891	Lyons-Roberts	Red	100.00	140.00	575.00	2350.00

FIVE DOLLAR NOTES (1914)
FEDERAL RESERVE NOTES

(Large Size)

Face Design: Portrait of President Lincoln center, Federal Reserve Seal left, Treasury Seal right.

Back Design: Scene of Columbus in sight of land left, landing of Pilgrims right.

SERIES OF 1914, RED TREASURY SEAL AND RED NUMBERS

SERIES BANK	SIGNATURES	SEAL	A.B.P.	GOOD	V. FINE	UNC.
☐1914 Boston	Burke-McAdoo	Red	65.00	100.00	575.00	2100.00
☐1914 New York	Burke-McAdoo	Red	65.00	100.00	470.00	2025.00
☐1914 Philadelphia	Burke-McAdoo	Red	65.00	100.00	480.00	2075.00
☐1914 Cleveland	Burke-McAdoo	Red	65.00	100.00	500.00	2025.00
☐1914 Richmond	Burke-McAdoo	Red	65.00	100.00	520.00	2100.00
☐1914 Atlanta	Burke-McAdoo	Red	65.00	100.00	480.00	2050.00
☐1914 Chicago	Burke-McAdoo	Red	65.00	100.00	625.00	2025.00
☐1914 St. Louis	Burke-McAdoo	Red	65.00	100.00	520.00	2050.00
☐1914 Minneapolis	Burke-McAdoo	Red	65.00	100.00	565.00	2300.00
☐1914 Kansas City	Burke-McAdoo	Red	65.00	100.00	475.00	2050.00
☐1914 Dallas	Burke-McAdoo	Red	65.00	100.00	575.00	2125.00
☐1914 San Francisco	Burke-McAdoo	Red	65.00	100.00	575.00	2200.00

FIVE DOLLAR NOTES (1914)
FEDERAL RESERVE NOTES

SERIES OF 1914, BLUE TREASURY SEAL AND BLUE NUMBERS

SERIES BANK	SIGNATURES	SEAL	A.B.P.	GOOD	V. FINE	UNC.
☐1914 Boston	Burke-McAdoo	Blue	18.00	25.00	135.00	365.00
☐1914 Boston	Burke-Glass	Blue	18.00	25.00	150.00	410.00
☐1914 Boston	Burke-Huston	Blue	18.00	25.00	125.00	330.00
☐1914 Boston	White-Mellon	Blue	18.00	25.00	125.00	320.00
☐1914 New York	Burke-McAdoo	Blue	18.00	25.00	125.00	330.00
☐1914 New York	Burke-Glass	Blue	18.00	25.00	135.00	365.00
☐1914 New York	Burke-Huston	Blue	18.00	25.00	125.00	325.00
☐1914 New York	White-Mellon	Blue	18.00	25.00	125.00	320.00
☐1914 Philadelphia	Burke-McAdoo	Blue	18.00	25.00	150.00	410.00
☐1914 Philadelphia	Burke-Glass	Blue	18.00	25.00	150.00	410.00
☐1914 Philadelphia	Burke-Huston	Blue	18.00	25.00	125.00	330.00

SERIES BANK	SIGNATURES	SEAL	A.B.P.	GOOD	V. FINE	UNC.
☐1914 Philadelphia	White-Mellon	Blue	16.00	25.00	125.00	210.00
☐1914 Cleveland	Burke-McAdoo	Blue	16.00	25.00	135.00	265.00
☐1914 Cleveland	Burke-Glass	Blue	16.00	25.00	175.00	365.00
☐1914 Cleveland	Burke-Huston	Blue	16.00	25.00	125.00	225.00
☐1914 Cleveland	White-Mellon	Blue	16.00	25.00	125.00	220.00
☐1914 Richmond	Burke-McAdoo	Blue	16.00	25.00	125.00	225.00
☐1914 Richmond	Burke-Glass	Blue	16.00	25.00	175.00	380.00
☐1914 Richmond	Burke-Huston	Blue	16.00	25.00	125.00	340.00
☐1914 Richmond	White-Mellon	Blue	16.00	25.00	125.00	315.00
☐1914 Atlanta	Burke-McAdoo	Blue	16.00	25.00	175.00	380.00
☐1914 Atlanta	Burke-Glass	Blue	16.00	25.00	335.00	630.00
☐1914 Atlanta	Burke-Huston	Blue	16.00	25.00	145.00	310.00
☐1914 Atlanta	White-Mellon	Blue	16.00	25.00	125.00	225.00
☐1914 Chicago	Burke-McAdoo	Blue	16.00	25.00	175.00	375.00
☐1914 Chicago	Burke-Glass	Blue	16.00	25.00	125.00	220.00
☐1914 Chicago	Burke-Huston	Blue	16.00	25.00	125.00	220.00
☐1914 Chicago	White-Mellon	Blue	16.00	25.00	125.00	220.00
☐1914 St. Louis	Burke-McAdoo	Blue	16.00	25.00	145.00	220.00
☐1914 St. Louis	Burke-Glass	Blue	16.00	26.50	127.00	235.00
☐1914 St. Louis	Burke-Huston	Blue	16.00	25.00	123.00	230.00
☐1914 St. Louis	White-Mellon	Blue	16.00	25.00	125.00	225.00
☐1914 Minneapolis	Burke-McAdoo	Blue	16.00	26.50	145.00	310.00
☐1914 Minneapolis	Burke-Glass	Blue	16.00	26.50	175.00	340.00
☐1914 Minneapolis	Burke-Huston	Blue	16.00	25.00	135.00	270.00
☐1914 Minneapolis	White-Mellon	Blue	16.00	25.00	125.00	235.00
☐1914 Kansas City	Burke-McAdoo	Blue	16.00	25.00	135.00	260.00
☐1914 Kansas City	Burke-Glass	Blue	16.00	26.50	145.00	310.00
☐1914 Kansas City	Burke-Huston	Blue	16.00	25.00	125.00	260.00
☐1914 Kansas City	White-Mellon	Blue	16.00	25.00	125.00	220.00
☐1914 Dallas	Burke-McAdoo	Blue	16.00	25.00	180.00	350.00
☐1914 Dallas	Burke-Glass	Blue	16.00	27.50	175.00	320.00
☐1914 Dallas	Burke-Huston	Blue	16.00	25.00	175.00	315.00
☐1914 Dallas	White-Mellon	Blue	16.00	25.00	130.00	235.00
☐1914 San Francisco	Burke-McAdoo	Blue	16.00	25.00	185.00	360.00
☐1914 San Francisco	Burke-Glass	Blue	16.00	26.50	235.00	430.00
☐1914 San Francisco	Burke-Huston	Blue	16.00	25.00	165.00	350.00
☐1914 San Francisco	White-Mellon	Blue	16.00	25.00	125.00	230.00

FIVE DOLLAR NOTES (1928)
FEDERAL RESERVE NOTES
(Small Size)

Face Design: Portrait of President Lincoln center, black Federal Reserve Seal with numeral for district in center. City of issuing bank in seal circle. Green Treasury Seal to right.
Back Design: Similar to 1935 note. Lincoln Memorial in Washington, D.C.

SERIES OF 1928,
SIGNATURES OF TATE AND MELLON, GREEN SEAL

BANK	A.B.P.	GOOD	V.FINE	UNC.	★UNC.	BANK	A.B.P.	GOOD	V.FINE	UNC.	★UNC.
Boston	10.00	14.00	50.00	380.00	1500.00	Chicago	8.50	12.00	30.00	160.00	975.00
New York	10.00	14.00	30.00	180.00	850.00	St. Louis	8.50	12.00	30.00	230.00	1500.00
Philadelphia	10.00	14.00	30.00	180.00	850.00	Minneapolis	8.50	12.00	125.00	805.00	2500.00
Cleveland	10.00	14.00	30.00	180.00	950.00	Kansas City	8.50	12.00	40.00	230.00	1800.00
Richmond	10.00	14.00	30.00	180.00	1250.00	Dallas	8.50	12.00	30.00	180.00	2000.00
Atlanta	10.00	14.00	30.00	180.00	1500.00	San Francisco	8.50	12.00	30.00	280.00	1500.00

SERIES OF 1928A,
SIGNATURES OF WOODS-MELLON, GREEN SEAL

BANK	A.B.P.	GOOD	V.FINE	UNC.	★UNC.	BANK	A.B.P.	GOOD	V.FINE	UNC.	★UNC.
Boston	8.00	13.00	25.00	265.00	1500.00	Chicago	8.00	12.00	26.00	165.00	900.00
New York	8.00	13.00	25.00	140.00	1000.00	St. Louis	8.00	12.00	26.00	165.00	2500.00
Philadelphia	8.00	13.00	25.00	165.00	1000.00	Minneapolis	8.00	12.00	30.00	2015.00	5000.00
Cleveland	8.00	13.00	25.00	165.00	1500.00	Kansas City	8.00	12.00	28.00	215.00	5000.00
Richmond	8.00	13.00	52.00	165.00	1500.00	Dallas	8.00	12.00	54.00	265.00	2000.00
Atlanta	8.00	13.00	25.00	365.00	2500.00	San Francisco	8.00	12.00	28.00	265.00	1500.00

SERIES OF 1928B,
SIGNATURES OF WOODS-MELLON, GREEN SEAL

The black Federal Reserve Seal now has a letter for district in place of the numeral.

BANK	A.B.P.	GOOD	V.FINE	UNC.	★UNC.	BANK	A.B.P.	GOOD	V.FINE	UNC.	★UNC.
☐ Boston	7.00	11.00	22.00	90.00	750.00	☐ Chicago	7.00	11.00	22.00	90.00	750.00
☐ New York	7.00	11.00	22.00	90.00	750.00	☐ St. Louis	7.00	11.00	22.00	90.00	750.00
☐ Philadelphia	7.00	11.00	22.00	90.00	750.00	☐ Minneapolis	7.00	11.00	22.00	205.00	1000.00
☐ Cleveland	7.00	11.00	22.00	90.00	750.00	☐ Kansas City	7.00	11.00	22.00	90.00	1000.00
☐ Richmond	7.00	11.00	22.00	90.00	750.00	☐ Dallas	7.00	11.00	22.00	155.00	1000.00
☐ Atlanta	7.00	11.00	22.00	90.00	750.00	☐ San Francisco	7.00	11.00	22.00	90.00	1000.00

SERIES OF 1928C,
SIGNATURES OF WOODS-WOODIN, GREEN SEAL

BANK	A.B.P.	GOOD	V.FINE	UNC.	★UNC.
☐ Atlanta	80.00	110.00	600.00	3000.00	RARE

SERIES OF 1928D,
SIGNATURES OF WOODS-MILLS, GREEN SEAL

BANK	A.B.P.	GOOD	V.FINE	UNC.	★UNC.
☐ Atlanta	255.00	410.00	1500.00	6500.00	RARE

FIVE DOLLAR NOTES (1934)
FEDERAL RESERVE NOTES
SERIES OF 1934,
JULIAN-MORGENTHAU, GREEN SEAL

"Redeemable in Gold" was removed from obligation over Federal Reserve Seal. Also, the green Treasury Seal on this note is known in a light and dark color. The light seal is worth about 10–20 percent more in most cases.

BANK	A.B.P.	V.FINE	UNC.	★UNC.	BANK	A.B.P.	V.FINE	UNC.	★UNC.
☐ Boston	8.00	13.00	65.00	180.00	☐ St. Louis	8.00	13.00	45.00	180.00
☐ New York	8.00	13.00	45.00	180.00	☐ Minneapolis	8.00	13.00	55.00	180.00
☐ Philadelphia	8.00	13.00	55.00	180.00	☐ Kansas City	8.00	13.00	45.00	180.00
☐ Cleveland	8.00	13.00	45.00	180.00	☐ Dallas	8.00	13.00	75.00	180.00
☐ Richmond	8.00	13.00	65.00	180.00	☐ San Francisco	8.00	13.00	45.00	180.00
☐ Atlanta	8.00	13.00	55.00	180.00	☐ San Francisco*	20.00	100.00	695.00	6000.00
☐ Chicago	8.00	13.00	45.00	180.00					

*This note has brown Treasury Seal and is surprinted HAWAII. For use in Pacific area of operations during World War II.

(Small Size)

Note—1934A (Julian-Morgenthau) is surprinted HAWAII. It was used in the Pacific area during World War II.

SERIES OF 1934A, JULIAN-MORGENTHAU, GREEN SEAL

BANK	A.B.P.	V.FINE	UNC.	★UNC.	BANK	A.B.P.	V.FINE	UNC.	★UNC.
☐ Boston	7.00	13.00	40.00	280.00	☐ Atlanta	7.00	13.00	40.00	600.00
☐ New York	7.00	13.00	40.00	280.00	☐ Chicago	7.00	13.00	40.00	280.00
☐ Philadelphia	7.00	13.00	40.00	280.00	☐ St. Louis	7.00	13.00	40.00	280.00
☐ Cleveland	7.00	13.00	40.00	500.00	☐ San Francisco	7.00	13.00	40.00	280.00
☐ Richmond	7.00	13.00	40.00	400.00	☐ Hawaii*	20.00	75.00	640.00	15000.00

*This note has brown Treasury Seal and is surprinted HAWAII. For use in Pacific area of operations during World War II.

(Small Size)

SERIES OF 1934B,
SIGNATURES OF JULIAN-VINSON, GREEN SEAL

BANK	A.B.P.	V.FINE	UNC.	★UNC.	BANK	A.B.P.	V.FINE	UNC.	★UNC.
☐ Boston	7.00	12.00	50.00	500.00	☐ Chicago	6.00	11.00	50.00	500.00
☐ New York	7.00	12.00	50.00	500.00	☐ St. Louis	6.00	11.00	50.00	500.00
☐ Philadelphia	7.00	12.00	50.00	500.00	☐ Minneapolis	6.00	11.00	50.00	500.00
☐ Cleveland	7.00	12.00	50.00	500.00	☐ Kansas City	75.00	1000.00	2500.00	8000.00
☐ Richmond	7.00	12.00	50.00	500.00	☐ Dallas			NOT ISSUED	
☐ Atlanta	7.00	12.00	50.00	500.00	☐ San Francisco	6.00	11.00	55.00	500.00

SERIES OF 1934C,
SIGNATURES OF JULIAN-SNYDER, GREEN SEAL

BANK	A.B.P.	V.FINE	UNC.	★UNC.	BANK	A.B.P.	V.FINE	UNC.	★UNC.
☐ Boston	7.00	11.00	60.00	750.00	☐ Chicago	7.00	10.00	60.00	600.00
☐ New York	7.00	11.00	60.00	600.00	☐ St. Louis	7.00	10.00	60.00	600.00
☐ Philadelphia	7.00	11.00	60.00	700.00	☐ Minneapolis	7.00	10.00	60.00	1250.00
☐ Cleveland	7.00	11.00	60.00	500.00	☐ Kansas City	7.00	10.00	60.00	700.00
☐ Richmond	7.00	11.00	60.00	650.00	☐ Dallas	7.00	10.00	60.00	1500.00
☐ Atlanta	7.00	11.00	60.00	750.00	☐ San Francisco	7.00	10.00	60.00	750.00

SERIES OF 1934D,
SIGNATURES OF CLARK-SNYDER, GREEN SEAL

BANK	A.B.P.	V.FINE	UNC.	★UNC.	BANK	A.B.P.	V.FINE	UNC.	★UNC.
☐ Boston	6.50	9.00	80.00	650.00	☐ Chicago	6.50	9.00	65.00	500.00
☐ New York	6.50	9.00	70.00	500.00	☐ St. Louis	6.50	9.00	70.00	750.00
☐ Philadelphia	6.50	9.00	75.00	700.00	☐ Minneapolis	6.50	9.00	75.00	1250.00
☐ Cleveland	6.50	9.00	75.00	750.00	☐ Kansas City	6.50	9.00	80.00	750.00
☐ Richmond	6.50	9.00	115.00	750.00	☐ Dallas	6.50	9.00	135.00	750.00
☐ Atlanta	100.00	400.00	2245.00	4500.00	☐ San Francisco	6.50	9.00	80.00	750.00

FIVE DOLLAR NOTES (1950)
FEDERAL RESERVE NOTES
BLACK FEDERAL RESERVE SEAL AND
GREEN TREASURY SEALS ARE NOW SMALLER
(Small Size)

SERIES OF 1950, SIGNATURES OF CLARK-SNYDER, GREEN SEAL

BANK	A.B.P.	V.FINE	UNC.	★UNC.	BANK	A.B.P.	V.FINE	UNC.	★UNC.
☐ Boston	6.00	10.00	45.00	500.00	☐ Chicago	6.00	10.00	25.00	400.00
☐ New York	6.00	10.00	35.00	300.00	☐ St. Louis	6.00	10.00	45.00	400.00
☐ Philadelphia	6.00	10.00	35.00	400.00	☐ Minneapolis	6.00	10.00	70.00	750.00
☐ Cleveland	6.00	10.00	30.00	400.00	☐ Kansas City	6.00	10.00	70.00	400.00
☐ Richmond	6.00	10.00	45.00	500.00	☐ Dallas	6.00	10.00	60.00	600.00
☐ Atlanta	6.00	10.00	45.00	500.00	☐ San Francisco	6.00	10.00	45.00	500.00

SERIES OF 1950A, SIGNATURES OF PRIEST-HUMPHREY, GREEN SEAL

BANK	A.B.P.	V.FINE	UNC.	★UNC.	BANK	A.B.P.	V.FINE	UNC.	★UNC.
☐ Boston	6.00	10.00	20.00	75.00	☐ Chicago	6.00	10.00	20.00	65.00
☐ New York	6.00	10.00	20.00	65.00	☐ St. Louis	6.00	10.00	20.00	125.00
☐ Philadelphia	6.00	10.00	20.00	75.00	☐ Minneapolis	6.00	10.00	20.00	175.00
☐ Cleveland	6.00	10.00	20.00	75.00	☐ Kansas City	6.00	10.00	20.00	100.00
☐ Richmond	6.00	10.00	20.00	75.00	☐ Dallas	6.00	10.00	20.00	150.00
☐ Atlanta	6.00	10.00	20.00	75.00	☐ San Francisco	6.00	10.00	20.00	75.00

SERIES OF 1950B, SIGNATURES OF PRIEST-ANDERSON, GREEN SEAL

BANK	A.B.P.	V.FINE	UNC.	★UNC.	BANK	A.B.P.	V.FINE	UNC.	★UNC.
☐ Boston	6.00	9.00	20.00	55.00	☐ Chicago	6.00	9.00	20.00	55.00
☐ New York	6.00	9.00	20.00	55.00	☐ St. Louis	6.00	9.00	20.00	55.00
☐ Philadelphia	6.00	9.00	20.00	55.00	☐ Minneapolis	6.00	10.00	20.00	55.00
☐ Cleveland	6.00	9.00	20.00	55.00	☐ Kansas City	6.00	10.00	20.00	55.00
☐ Richmond	6.00	9.00	20.00	55.00	☐ Dallas	6.00	9.00	20.00	55.00
☐ Atlanta	6.00	9.00	20.00	55.00	☐ San Francisco	6.00	9.00	20.00	55.00

SERIES OF 1950C, SIGNATURES OF SMITH-DILLON, GREEN SEAL

BANK	A.B.P.	V.FINE	UNC.	★UNC.	BANK	A.B.P.	V.FINE	UNC.	★UNC.
☐ Boston	5.75	8.00	20.00	100.00	☐ Chicago	5.75	8.00	20.00	50.00
☐ New York	5.75	8.00	20.00	60.00	☐ St. Louis	5.75	8.00	20.00	150.00
☐ Philadelphia	5.75	8.00	20.00	100.00	☐ Minneapolis	5.75	9.00	20.00	200.00
☐ Cleveland	5.75	8.00	20.00	75.00	☐ Kansas City	5.75	9.00	20.00	100.00
☐ Richmond	5.75	8.00	20.00	100.00	☐ Dallas	5.75	8.00	20.00	250.00
☐ Atlanta	5.75	8.00	20.00	75.00	☐ San Francisco	5.75	8.00	20.00	150.00

SERIES OF 1950D, SIGNATURES OF GRANAHAN-DILLON, GREEN SEAL

BANK	A.B.P.	V.FINE	UNC.	★UNC.	BANK	A.B.P.	V.FINE	UNC.	★UNC.
☐ Boston	5.75	8.00	26.00	95.00	☐ Chicago	5.75	8.00	16.00	60.00
☐ New York	5.75	8.00	16.00	65.00	☐ St. Louis	5.75	8.00	24.00	100.00
☐ Philadelphia	5.75	8.00	26.00	90.00	☐ Minneapolis	5.75	9.00	28.00	155.00
☐ Cleveland	5.75	8.00	18.00	80.00	☐ Kansas City	5.75	8.00	18.00	105.00
☐ Richmond	5.75	8.00	23.00	80.00	☐ Dallas	5.75	8.00	23.00	175.00
☐ Atlanta	5.75	8.00	23.00	100.00	☐ San Francisco	5.75	8.00	16.00	95.00

SERIES OF 1950E, SIGNATURES OF GRANAHAN-FOWLER, GREEN SEAL

BANK	A.B.P.	V.FINE	UNC.	★UNC.	BANK	A.B.P.	V.FINE	UNC.	★UNC.
					☐ Chicago	6.00	9.00	60.00	175.00
☐ New York	6.00	9.00	40.00	85.00					
					☐ San Francisco	6.00	9.00	50.00	225.00

FIVE DOLLAR NOTES (1963)
FEDERAL RESERVE NOTES
(IN GOD WE TRUST IS ADDED ON BACK)
SERIES OF 1963, SIGNATURES OF GRANAHAN-DILLON, GREEN SEAL

BANK	A.B.P.	V.FINE	UNC.	★UNC.	BANK	A.B.P.	V.FINE	UNC.	★UNC.
☐ Boston	5.25	8.00	23.00	50.00	☐ Chicago	5.25	8.00	14.00	50.00
☐ New York	5.25	8.00	14.00	50.00	☐ St. Louis	5.25	8.00	18.00	42.00
☐ Philadelphia	5.25	8.00	16.00	50.00	☐ Minneapolis	5.25	8.00	18.00	50.00
☐ Cleveland	5.25	8.00	14.00	50.00	☐ Kansas City	5.25	8.00	18.00	40.00
☐ Richmond	5.25	8.00	14.00	50.00	☐ Dallas	5.25	8.00	18.00	50.00
☐ Atlanta	5.25	8.00	16.00	50.00	☐ San Francisco	5.25	8.00	18.00	50.00

SERIES OF 1963A, SIGNATURES OF GRANAHAN-FOWLER, GREEN SEAL

BANK	A.B.P.	V.FINE	UNC.	★UNC.	BANK	A.B.P.	V.FINE	UNC.	★UNC.
☐ Boston	5.25	7.00	15.00	30.00	☐ Chicago	5.25	7.00	15.00	30.00
☐ New York	5.25	7.00	15.00	30.00	☐ St. Louis	5.25	7.00	15.00	30.00
☐ Philadelphia	5.25	7.00	15.00	30.00	☐ Minneapolis	5.25	7.00	15.00	30.00
☐ Cleveland	5.25	7.00	15.00	30.00	☐ Kansas City	5.25	7.00	15.00	30.00
☐ Richmond	5.25	7.00	15.00	30.00	☐ Dallas	5.25	7.00	15.00	30.00
☐ Atlanta	5.25	7.00	15.00	30.00	☐ San Francisco	5.25	7.00	15.00	30.00

FIVE DOLLAR NOTES (1969)
FEDERAL RESERVE NOTES
(WORDING IN GREEN TREASURY SEAL IS CHANGED FROM LATIN TO ENGLISH)

SERIES OF 1969, SIGNATURES OF ELSTON-KENNEDY, GREEN SEAL

BANK	A.B.P.	V.FINE	UNC.	★UNC.	BANK	A.B.P.	V.FINE	UNC.	★UNC.
☐ Boston	5.00	6.00	15.00	33.00	☐ Chicago	5.00	6.00	15.00	33.00
☐ New York	5.00	6.00	15.00	33.00	☐ St. Louis	5.00	6.00	15.00	33.00
☐ Philadelphia	5.00	6.00	15.00	33.00	☐ Minneapolis	5.00	6.00	15.00	33.00
☐ Cleveland	5.00	6.00	15.00	33.00	☐ Kansas City	5.00	6.00	15.00	33.00
☐ Richmond	5.00	6.00	15.00	33.00	☐ Dallas	5.00	6.00	15.00	33.00
☐ Atlanta	5.00	6.00	15.00	33.00	☐ San Francisco	5.00	6.00	15.00	33.00

SERIES OF 1969A, SIGNATURES OF KABIS-CONNALLY, GREEN SEAL

BANK	A.B.P.	V.FINE	UNC.	★UNC.	BANK	A.B.P.	V.FINE	UNC.	★UNC.
☐ Boston	5.00	6.00	20.00	45.00	☐ Chicago	5.00	6.00	22.00	41.00
☐ New York	5.00	6.00	20.00	40.00	☐ St. Louis	5.00	6.00	22.00	55.00
☐ Philadelphia	5.00	6.00	20.00	40.00	☐ Minneapolis	5.00	6.00	22.00	45.00
☐ Cleveland	5.00	6.00	20.00	45.00	☐ Kansas City	5.00	6.00	22.00	45.00
☐ Richmond	5.00	6.00	20.00	45.00	☐ Dallas	5.00	6.00	22.00	47.00
☐ Atlanta	5.00	6.00	20.00	45.00	☐ San Francisco	5.00	6.00	22.00	50.00

SERIES OF 1969B, SIGNATURES OF BANUELOS-CONNALLY, GREEN SEAL

BANK	A.B.P.	V.FINE	UNC.	★UNC.	BANK	A.B.P.	V.FINE	UNC.	★UNC.
☐ Boston	5.00	12.00	65.00	—	☐ Chicago	5.00	12.00	40.00	150.00
☐ New York	5.00	8.00	40.00	130.00	☐ St. Louis	5.00	12.00	70.00	—
☐ Philadelphia	5.00	12.00	40.00	—	☐ Minneapolis	5.00	12.00	80.00	—
☐ Cleveland	5.00	12.00	40.00	—	☐ Kansas City	5.00	12.00	70.00	140.00
☐ Richmond	5.00	12.00	40.00	150.00	☐ Dallas	5.00	12.00	40.00	—
☐ Atlanta	5.00	12.00	40.00	175.00	☐ San Francisco	5.00	12.00	40.00	150.00

SERIES OF 1969C, SIGNATURES OF BANUELOS-SHULTZ, GREEN SEAL

BANK	A.B.P.	V.FINE	UNC.	★UNC.	BANK	A.B.P.	V.FINE	UNC.	★UNC.
☐ Boston	5.00	6.00	13.00	40.00	☐ Chicago	5.00	6.00	13.00	—
☐ New York	5.00	6.00	13.00	40.00	☐ St. Louis	5.00	6.00	13.00	40.00
☐ Philadelphia	5.00	6.00	13.00	40.00	☐ Minneapolis	5.00	6.00	13.00	—
☐ Cleveland	5.00	6.00	13.00	40.00	☐ Kansas City	5.00	6.00	13.00	40.00
☐ Richmond	5.00	6.00	13.00	40.00	☐ Dallas	5.00	6.00	13.00	40.00
☐ Atlanta	5.00	6.00	13.00	40.00	☐ San Francisco	5.00	6.00	13.00	40.00

FIVE DOLLAR NOTES (1974)
FEDERAL RESERVE NOTES
SERIES OF 1974, SIGNATURES OF NEFF-SIMON, GREEN SEAL

BANK	A.B.P.	V.FINE	UNC.	★UNC.	BANK	A.B.P.	V.FINE	UNC.	★UNC.
☐ Boston	—	6.00	10.00	25.00	☐ Chicago	—	6.00	10.00	25.00
☐ New York	—	6.00	10.00	25.00	☐ St. Louis	—	6.00	10.00	25.00
☐ Philadelphia	—	6.00	10.00	25.00	☐ Minneapolis	—	7.00	12.00	25.00
☐ Cleveland	—	6.00	10.00	25.00	☐ Kansas City	—	7.00	12.00	25.00
☐ Richmond	—	6.00	10.00	25.00	☐ Dallas	—	7.00	12.00	25.00
☐ Atlanta	—	6.00	10.00	25.00	☐ San Francisco	—	6.00	10.00	25.00

FIVE DOLLAR NOTES (1977)
FEDERAL RESERVE NOTES
SERIES OF 1977, SIGNATURES OF MORTON-BLUMENTHAL, GREEN SEAL

★Notes not issued for all banks

BANK	A.B.P.	V.FINE	UNC.	★UNC.	BANK	A.B.P.	V.FINE	UNC.	★UNC.
☐ Boston	—	6.00	10.00	50.00	☐ Chicago	—	6.00	10.00	26.00
☐ New York	—	6.00	10.00	26.00	☐ St. Louis	—	6.00	10.00	70.00
☐ Philadelphia	—	6.00	10.00	32.00	☐ Kansas City	—	7.00	10.00	35.00
☐ Cleveland	—	6.00	10.00	32.00	☐ Dallas	—	7.00	10.00	35.00
☐ Richmond	—	6.00	10.00	32.00	☐ San Francisco	—	6.00	10.00	35.00
☐ Atlanta	—	6.00	10.00	32.00					

SERIES OF 1977A, SIGNATURES OF MORTON-BLUMENTHAL, GREEN SEAL

BANK	A.B.P.	V.FINE	UNC.	★UNC.	BANK	A.B.P.	V.FINE	UNC.	★UNC.
☐ Boston	—	6.00	8.00	55.00	☐ Chicago	—	6.00	8.00	35.00
☐ New York	—	6.00	8.00	30.00	☐ St. Louis	—	6.00	8.00	60.00
☐ Philadelphia	—	6.00	8.00	30.00	☐ Minneapolis	—	6.00	8.00	75.00
☐ Cleveland	—	6.00	8.00	45.00	☐ Kansas City	—	6.00	8.00	50.00
☐ Richmond	—	6.00	8.00	85.00	☐ Dallas	—	6.00	8.00	45.00
☐ Atlanta	—	6.00	8.00	35.00	☐ San Francisco	—	6.00	8.00	35.00

FIVE DOLLAR NOTES (1981)
FEDERAL RESERVE NOTES
SERIES OF 1981, SIGNATURES OF BUCHANAN-REGAN, GREEN SEAL
★Notes not issued for all banks

BANK	A.B.P.	V.FINE	UNC.	★UNC.	BANK	A.B.P.	V.FINE	UNC.	★UNC.
☐ Boston	—	6.00	15.00	—	☐ Chicago	—	6.00	15.00	45.00
☐ New York	—	6.00	15.00	45.00	☐ St. Louis	—	6.00	15.00	45.00
☐ Philadelphia	—	6.00	15.00	45.00	☐ Minneapolis	—	7.00	15.00	45.00
☐ Cleveland	—	6.00	15.00	45.00	☐ Kansas City	—	7.00	15.00	45.00
☐ Richmond	—	6.00	15.00	45.00	☐ Dallas	—	7.00	15.00	45.00
☐ Atlanta	—	6.00	15.00	45.00	☐ San Francisco	—	6.00	15.00	45.00

SERIES OF 1981A, SIGNATURES OF ORTEGA-REGAN, GREEN SEAL
★Notes not issued for all banks

BANK	A.B.P.	V.FINE	UNC.	★UNC.	BANK	A.B.P.	V.FINE	UNC.	★UNC.
☐ Boston	—	6.00	20.00	—	☐ Chicago	—	6.00	20.00	—
☐ New York	—	6.00	20.00	40.00	☐ St. Louis	—	6.00	20.00	—
☐ Philadelphia	—	6.00	20.00	—	☐ Minneapolis	—	7.00	20.00	—
☐ Cleveland	—	6.00	20.00	—	☐ Kansas City	—	6.00	20.00	—
☐ Richmond	—	6.00	20.00	—	☐ Dallas	—	6.00	20.00	—
☐ Atlanta	—	6.00	20.00	—	☐ San Francisco	—	6.00	20.00	40.00

FIVE DOLLAR NOTES (1985)
FEDERAL RESERVE NOTES
SERIES OF 1985, SIGNATURES OF ORTEGA-BAKER, GREEN SEAL
★Notes not issued for all banks

BANK	A.B.P.	V.FINE	UNC.	★UNC.	BANK	A.B.P.	V.FINE	UNC.	★UNC.
☐ Boston	—	6.00	10.00	30.00	☐ Chicago	—	6.00	10.00	30.00
☐ New York	—	6.00	10.00	30.00	☐ St. Louis	—	6.00	10.00	30.00
☐ Philadelphia	—	6.00	10.00	30.00	☐ Minneapolis	—	6.00	10.00	30.00
☐ Cleveland	—	6.00	10.00	30.00	☐ Kansas City	—	6.00	10.00	30.00
☐ Richmond	—	6.00	10.00	30.00	☐ Dallas	—	6.00	10.00	30.00
☐ Atlanta	—	6.00	10.00	30.00	☐ San Francisco	—	6.00	10.00	30.00

FIVE DOLLAR NOTES (1988)
FEDERAL RESERVE NOTES
SERIES OF 1988, SIGNATURES OF ORTEGA-BRADY, GREEN SEAL

★Notes not issued for all banks

BANK	A.B.P.	V.FINE	UNC.	★UNC.	BANK	A.B.P.	V.FINE	UNC.	★UNC.
☐ Boston	—	6.00	10.00	20.00	☐ Chicago	—	6.00	10.00	20.00
☐ New York	—	6.00	10.00	20.00	☐ St. Louis	—	6.00	10.00	20.00
☐ Philadelphia	—	6.00	10.00	20.00	☐ Minneapolis	—	6.00	10.00	20.00
☐ Cleveland	—	6.00	10.00	20.00	☐ Kansas City	—	6.00	10.00	20.00
☐ Richmond	—	6.00	10.00	20.00	☐ Dallas	—	6.00	10.00	20.00
☐ Atlanta	—	6.00	10.00	20.00	☐ San Francisco	—	6.00	10.00	20.00

SERIES OF 1988A, SIGNATURES OF VILLALPANDO-BRADY, GREEN SEAL

★Notes not issued for all banks

BANK	A.B.P.	V.FINE	UNC.	★UNC.	BANK	A.B.P.	V.FINE	UNC.	★UNC.
☐ Boston	—	6.00	10.00	20.00	☐ Chicago	—	6.00	10.00	20.00
☐ New York	—	6.00	10.00	20.00	☐ St. Louis	—	6.00	10.00	20.00
☐ Philadelphia	—	6.00	10.00	20.00	☐ Minneapolis	—	6.00	10.00	20.00
☐ Cleveland	—	6.00	10.00	20.00	☐ Kansas City	—	6.00	10.00	20.00
☐ Richmond	—	6.00	10.00	20.00	☐ Dallas	—	6.00	10.00	20.00
☐ Atlanta	—	6.00	10.00	20.00	☐ San Francisco	—	6.00	10.00	20.00

FIVE DOLLAR NOTES (1993)
FEDERAL RESERVE NOTES
SERIES OF 1993, SIGNATURES OF WITHROW-BENTSEN, GREEN SEAL

★Notes not issued for all banks

BANK	A.B.P.	V.FINE	UNC.	★UNC.	BANK	A.B.P.	V.FINE	UNC.	★UNC.
☐ Boston	—	6.00	10.00	20.00	☐ Chicago	—	6.00	10.00	20.00
☐ New York	—	6.00	10.00	20.00	☐ St. Louis	—	6.00	10.00	20.00
☐ Philadelphia	—	6.00	10.00	20.00	☐ Minneapolis	—	6.00	10.00	20.00
☐ Cleveland	—	—	—	—	☐ Kansas City	—	6.00	10.00	20.00
☐ Richmond	—	6.00	10.00	20.00	☐ Dallas	—	6.00	10.00	20.00
☐ Atlanta	—	6.00	10.00	20.00	☐ San Francisco	—	6.00	10.00	20.00

FIVE DOLLAR NOTES (1995)
FEDERAL RESERVE NOTES
SERIES OF 1995, SIGNATURES OF WITHROW-RUBIN, GREEN SEAL
★Notes not issued for all banks

BANK	A.B.P.	V.FINE	UNC.	★UNC.	BANK	A.B.P.	V.FINE	UNC.	★UNC.
☐ Boston	—	6.00	8.00	15.00	☐ Chicago	—	6.00	8.00	15.00
☐ New York	—	6.00	8.00	15.00	☐ St. Louis	—	6.00	8.00	15.00
☐ Philadelphia	—	6.00	8.00	15.00	☐ Minneapolis	—	6.00	8.00	15.00
☐ Cleveland	—	6.00	8.00	15.00	☐ Kansas City	—	6.00	8.00	15.00
☐ Richmond	—	6.00	8.00	15.00	☐ Dallas	—	6.00	8.00	15.00
☐ Atlanta	—	6.00	8.00	15.00	☐ San Francisco	—	6.00	8.00	15.00

FIVE DOLLAR NOTES (1918)
FEDERAL RESERVE BANK NOTES
(ALL WITH BLUE SEAL AND BLUE SERIAL NUMBERS)
(Large Size)

Face Design: Portrait of President Lincoln with Reserve City in center.

Back Design: Same as 1914 note.

BANK	SERIES	GOV'T SIGNATURES	BANK SIGNATURES	A.B.P.	GOOD	V. FINE	UNC.
☐Boston	1918	Teehee-Burke	Bullen-Morse	50.00	70.00	1325.00	3500.00
☐New York	1918	Teehee-Burke	Hendricks-Strong	50.00	70.00	275.00	1675.00
☐Philadelphia	1918	Teehee-Burke	Hardt-Passmore	50.00	70.00	325.00	1725.00
☐Philadelphia	1918	Teehee-Burke	Dyer-Passmore	50.00	70.00	325.00	1725.00
☐Cleveland	1918	Teehee-Burke	Dyer-Fancher	50.00	70.00	275.00	1700.00
☐Cleveland	1918	Teehee-Burke	Davis-Fancher	50.00	70.00	325.00	1600.00
☐Cleveland	1918	Elliott-Burke	Davis-Fancher	50.00	70.00	270.00	1525.00
☐Atlanta	1915	Teehee-Burke	Bell-Wellborn	50.00	70.00	1200.00	3000.00
☐Atlanta	1915	Teehee-Burke	Pike-McCord	50.00	70.00	325.00	1695.00
☐Atlanta	1918	Teehee-Burke	Pike-McCord	50.00	70.00	355.00	1700.00
☐Atlanta	1918	Teehee-Burke	Bell-Wellborn	50.00	70.00	355.00	1775.00

BANK	SERIES	GOV'T SIGNATURES	BANK SIGNATURES	A.B.P.	GOOD	V. FINE	UNC.
☐Atlanta	1918	Elliott-Burke	Bell-Wellborn	54.00	70.00	275.00	1250.00
☐Chicago	1915	Teehee-Burke	McLallen-McDougal	54.00	70.00	235.00	1175.00
☐Chicago	1918	Teehee-Burke	McCloud-McDougal	50.00	70.00	205.00	1175.00
☐Chicago	1918	Teehee-Burke	Cramer-McDougal	50.00	70.00	285.00	1250.00
☐St. Louis	1918	Teehee-Burke	Attebery-Wells	50.00	70.00	205.00	1175.00
☐St. Louis	1918	Teehee-Burke	Attebery-Biggs	50.00	70.00	205.00	1175.00
☐St. Louis	1918	Elliott-Burke	White-Biggs	50.00	70.00	205.00	1175.00
☐Minneapolis	1918	Teehee-Burke	Cook-Wold	50.00	70.00	245.00	1175.00
☐Kansas City	1915	Teehee-Burke	Anderson-Miller	52.00	73.00	245.00	1175.00
☐Kansas City	1915	Teehee-Burke	Cross-Miller	52.00	73.00	255.00	1175.00
☐Kansas City	1915	Teehee-Burke	Helm-Miller	52.00	73.00	1275.00	2750.00
☐Kansas City	1918	Teehee-Burke	Anderson-Miller	52.00	73.00	205.00	1175.00
☐Kansas City	1918	Elliott-Burke	Helm-Miller	52.00	73.00	250.00	1175.00
☐Dallas	1915	Teehee-Burke	Hoopes-VanZandt	52.00	63.00	235.00	1175.00
☐Dallas	1915	Teehee-Burke	Talley-VanZandt	52.00	63.00	305.00	1250.00
☐Dallas	1918	Teehee-Burke	Talley-VanZandt	52.00	63.00	1245.00	3000.00
☐San Francisco	1915	Teehee-Burke	Clerk-Lynch	52.00	63.00	1000.00	2750.00
☐San Francisco	1918	Teehee-Burke	Clerk-Lynch	52.00	63.00	1700.00	3500.00

FIVE DOLLAR NOTES (1929)
FEDERAL RESERVE BANK NOTES

(Small Size)
Face Design: Portrait of President Lincoln.
SERIES 1929, BROWN SEAL

BANK & CITY	SIGNATURES	A.B.P.	GOOD	V.FINE	UNC.	*UNC.
☐Boston	Jones-Woods	8.00	13.00	35.00	180.00	3500.00
☐New York	Jones-Woods	8.00	13.00	34.00	155.00	3200.00
☐Philadelphia	Jones-Woods	8.00	13.00	35.00	155.00	3000.00
☐Cleveland	Jones-Woods	8.00	13.00	35.00	145.00	3000.00
☐Atlanta	Jones-Woods	8.00	13.00	33.00	330.00	3500.00
☐Chicago	Jones-Woods	8.00	13.00	33.00	130.00	3200.00
☐St. Louis	Jones-Woods	8.00	13.00	215.00	3000.00	3500.00
☐Minneapolis	Jones-Woods	8.00	13.00	73.00	1000.00	3300.00
☐Kansas City	Jones-Woods	8.00	13.00	34.00	180.00	3000.00
☐Dallas	Jones-Woods	8.00	13.00	38.00	130.00	5000.00
☐San Francisco	Jones-Woods	150.00	235.00	835.00	8500.00	15000.00

TEN DOLLAR NOTES

ORDER OF ISSUE

TEN DOLLAR NOTES (1861) DEMAND NOTES
(NO TREASURY SEAL)

(Large Size)

Face Design: Portrait of President Lincoln left, female figure with sword and shield.

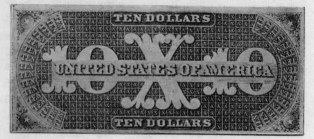

Back Design: Ornate designs of TEN.

PAYABLE AT	A.B.P.	GOOD	V. GOOD	FINE
☐ Boston (I)	1300.00	2825.00	8500.00	RARE
☐ New York (I)	1300.00	2825.00	8500.00	RARE
☐ Philadelphia (I)	1300.00	2825.00	8500.00	RARE
☐ Cincinnati (I)	1740.00	3800.00	RARE	RARE
☐ St. Louis (I)	1540.00	3800.00	RARE	RARE
☐ Boston (II)	765.00	1250.00	1800.00	3400.00
☐ New York (II)	740.00	1300.00	1800.00	3400.00
☐ Philadelphia (II)	740.00	1300.00	1800.00	3400.00
☐ Cincinnati (II)	4200.00	7800.00	18000.00	RARE
☐ St. Louis (II)	4500.00	8200.00	25000.00	RARE

TEN DOLLAR NOTES (1862–1863)
UNITED STATES NOTES
(ALSO KNOWN AS LEGAL TENDER NOTES)
(Large Size)

Back Design
Face Design: Similar to 1861 note.

SERIES	SIGNATURES	SEAL	A.B.P.	GOOD	V.FINE	UNC.
☐1862	Chittenden-Spinner*	Red	275.00	375.00	1450.00	3500.00
☐1862	Chittenden-Spinner**	Red	275.00	375.00	1450.00	3500.00
☐1863	Chittenden-Spinner**	Red	275.00	375.00	1450.00	3500.00

* First Obligation: Similar to 1875–1907 $5 note.
** Second Obligation: Shown above.

TEN DOLLAR NOTES (1869) UNITED STATES NOTES
(Large Size)

Face Design: Portrait of Daniel Webster left, presentation of Indian princess right. (This note is nicknamed "Jackass Note," because the EAGLE between the signatures resembles a donkey when it is held upside down.)

SERIES	SIGNATURES	SEAL	A.B.P.	GOOD	V.FINE	UNC.
☐1869	Allison-Spinner	Red	150.00	220.00	1000.00	3900.00

TEN DOLLAR NOTES (1875–1880)
UNITED STATES NOTES

(Large Size)

Face Design: Similar to 1869 note.

Back Design: Revised.

SERIES	SIGNATURES	SEAL	A.B.P.	GOOD	V.FINE	UNC.
☐1875	Allison-New	Red	170.00	215.00	825.00	4400.00
☐Same as above, Series A		Red	175.00	235.00	1225.00	4700.00
☐1878	Allison-Gilfillan	Red	170.00	215.00	1350.00	4800.00
☐1880	Scofield-Gilfillan	Brown	170.00	215.00	875.00	1850.00
☐1880	Bruce-Gilfillan	Brown	125.00	215.00	875.00	2000.00
☐1880	Bruce-Wyman	Brown	125.00	215.00	875.00	2000.00
☐1880	Bruce-Wyman	Red Plain	125.00	215.00	925.00	2050.00
☐1880	Rosecrans-Jordan	Red Plain	125.00	215.00	875.00	2700.00
☐1880	Rosecrans-Hyatt	Red Plain	125.00	215.00	875.00	2400.00
☐1880	Rosecrans-Hyatt	Red Spikes	125.00	215.00	875.00	2200.00
☐1880	Rosecrans-Huston	Red Spikes	125.00	215.00	825.00	2200.00
☐1880	Rosecrans-Huston	Brown	170.00	215.00	875.00	2600.00
☐1880	Rosecrans-Nebeker	Brown	650.00	2100.00	4500.00	8000.00
☐1880	Rosecrans-Nebeker	Red	120.00	1760.00	575.00	1600.00
☐1880	Tillman-Morgan	Red	120.00	1760.00	575.00	1600.00

SERIES	SIGNATURES	SEAL	A.B.P.	GOOD	V.FINE	UNC.
☐1880 Bruce-Roberts		Red	120.00	160.00	600.00	1700.00
☐1880 Lyons-Roberts		Red	120.00	160.00	600.00	1700.00

TEN DOLLAR NOTES (1901) UNITED STATES NOTES
(Large Size)

Face Design: American bison (buffalo) center, portrait of Lewis left, portrait of Clark right.

Back Design: Female allegorical figure in arch.

SERIES	SIGNATURES	SEAL	A.B.P.	GOOD	V.FINE	UNC.
☐1901	Lyons-Roberts	Red	235.00	335.00	850.00	3500.00
☐1901	Lyons-Treat	Red	235.00	335.00	850.00	3500.00
☐1901	Vernon-Treat	Red	235.00	335.00	825.00	3500.00
☐1901	Vernon-McClung	Red	235.00	335.00	825.00	3500.00
☐1901	Napier-McClung	Red	235.00	335.00	825.00	3500.00
☐1901	Parker-Burke	Red	235.00	335.00	825.00	3500.00
☐1901	Teehee-Burke	Red	235.00	335.00	825.00	3500.00
☐1901	Elliott-White	Red	235.00	335.00	825.00	3500.00
☐1901	Speelman-White	Red	235.00	335.00	825.00	3500.00

TEN DOLLAR NOTES (1923) UNITED STATES NOTES
(Large Size)

Face Design: Portrait of President Jackson center, red seal left, red "X" to right.

Back Design

SERIES	SIGNATURES	SEAL	A.B.P.	GOOD	V.FINE	UNC.
☐1923	Speelman-White	Red	180.00	250.00	1600.00	5200.00

TEN DOLLAR NOTES (1863–1875)
NATIONAL BANK NOTES
FIRST CHARTER PERIOD (Large Size)

Face Design: Benjamin Franklin and kite left, name of bank and city center. Effigy of Liberty and eagle right.

Back Design: Border green, center black. DeSoto on horseback at Mississippi River.

SERIES	SIGNATURES	SEAL	A.B.P.	GOOD	V.FINE	UNC.
☐Original	Chittenden-Spinner	Red	190.00	250.00	1100.00	4200.00
☐Original	Colby-Spinner	Red	190.00	250.00	1100.00	4200.00
☐Original	Jeffries-Spinner	Red	450.00	600.00	1600.00	4700.00
☐Original	Allison-Spinner	Red	190.00	250.00	1100.00	4250.00
☐1875	Allison-New	Red	190.00	250.00	1100.00	4000.00
☐1875	Allison-Wyman	Red	190.00	250.00	1250.00	4100.00
☐1875	Allison-Gilfillan	Red	190.00	250.00	1200.00	3900.00
☐1875	Scofield-Gilfillan	Red	190.00	250.00	1200.00	3900.00
☐1875	Bruce-Gilfillan	Red	190.00	250.00	1200.00	4000.00
☐1875	Bruce-Wyman	Red	190.00	250.00	1200.00	4000.00
☐1875	Rosecrans-Huston	Red	190.00	250.00	1200.00	4000.00
☐1875	Rosecrans-Nebeker	Red	190.00	250.00	1200.00	4000.00

TEN DOLLAR NOTES (1882) NATIONAL BANK NOTES
SECOND CHARTER PERIOD (Large Size)

First Issue (Brown seal and brown backs)
Face Design: Similar to 1863–1875 note.
Back Design: Similar to 1882 $5 note. Border in brown with green Charter Number.

SERIES	SIGNATURES	SEAL	A.B.P.	GOOD	V.FINE	UNC.
☐1882	Bruce-Gilfillan	Brown	100.00	125.00	550.00	2750.00
☐1882	Bruce-Wyman	Brown	100.00	125.00	550.00	2750.00
☐1882	Bruce-Jordan	Brown	100.00	125.00	550.00	2750.00
☐1882	Rosecrans-Jordan	Brown	100.00	125.00	550.00	2750.00
☐1882	Rosecrans-Hyatt	Brown	100.00	125.00	550.00	2750.00
☐1882	Rosecrans-Huston	Brown	100.00	125.00	550.00	2750.00
☐1882	Rosecrans-Nebeker	Brown	100.00	125.00	550.00	2750.00
☐1882	Rosecrans-Morgan	Brown	180.00	305.00	945.00	2900.00
☐1882	Tillman-Morgan	Brown	100.00	125.00	550.00	2750.00
☐1882	Tillman-Roberts	Brown	100.00	125.00	550.00	2750.00

SERIES	SIGNATURES	SEAL	A.B.P.	GOOD	V.FINE	UNC.
□1882	Bruce-Roberts	Brown	90.00	125.00	505.00	2750.00
□1882	Lyons-Roberts	Brown	90.00	125.00	505.00	2750.00
□1882	Lyons-Treat	Brown	90.00	125.00	505.00	2750.00
□1882	Vernon-Treat	Brown	90.00	125.00	505.00	2750.00

Second Issue (Blue seal, green back with date "1882–1908")
Face Design: Similar to 1863–1875 note.
Back Design: Similar to 1882 $5 Second Issue note.
(Large Size)

SERIES	SIGNATURES	SEAL	A.B.P.	GOOD	V.FINE	UNC.
□1882	Rosecrans-Huston	Blue	70.00	100.00	400.00	2400.00
□1882	Rosecrans-Nebeker	Blue	70.00	100.00	400.00	2400.00
□1882	Rosecrans-Morgan	Blue	135.00	225.00	610.00	2750.00
□1882	Tillman-Morgan	Blue	70.00	100.00	400.00	2750.00
□1882	Tillman-Roberts	Blue	70.00	100.00	400.00	2750.00
□1882	Bruce-Roberts	Blue	70.00	100.00	400.00	2750.00
□1882	Lyons-Roberts	Blue	70.00	100.00	400.00	2750.00
□1882	Vernon-Treat	Blue	70.00	100.00	400.00	2750.00
□1882	Vernon-McClung	Blue	70.00	100.00	400.00	2750.00
□1882	Napier-McClung	Blue	70.00	100.00	400.00	2750.00

TEN DOLLAR NOTES (1882) NATIONAL BANK NOTES
(Large Size)

Third Issue (Blue seal, green back with value in block letters)
Face Design: Similar to previous notes. (*see* 1863–1875 note).
Back Design: Similar to 1882 $500 Third Issue note.

SERIES	SIGNATURES	SEAL	A.B.P.	GOOD	V. FINE	UNC.
□1882	Tillman-Roberts	Blue	110.00	160.00	600.00	3500.00
□1882	Lyons-Roberts	Blue	110.00	160.00	600.00	3500.00
□1882	Vernon-Treat	Blue	110.00	160.00	600.00	3500.00
□1882	Napier-McClung	Blue	110.00	160.00	600.00	3300.00

These notes may exist with other signatures, but are very rare.

TEN DOLLAR NOTES (1902) NATIONAL BANK NOTES
THIRD CHARTER PERIOD (Large Size)

First Issue (Red seal and red Charter Numbers)
Face Design: Portrait of President McKinley left, name of
bank and city in center.

SERIES	SIGNATURES	SEAL	A.B.P.	GOOD	V.FINE	UNC.
☐1902	Lyons-Roberts	Red	100.00	145.00	550.00	2700.00
☐1902	Lyons-Treat	Red	100.00	145.00	550.00	2700.00
☐1902	Vernon-Treat	Red	100.00	145.00	550.00	2700.00

TEN DOLLAR NOTES (1902) NATIONAL BANK NOTES
THIRD CHARTER PERIOD (Large Size)

Second Issue (Blue seal and numbers, "1902–1908" on the
back)
Back Design: Same as 1882 Second Issue note. Date
1902–1908.
Face Design: Same as 1882 Third Issue note.

SERIES	SIGNATURES	SEAL	A.B.P.	GOOD	V.FINE	UNC.
☐1902	Lyons-Roberts	Blue	45.00	60.00	155.00	1325.00
☐1902	Lyons-Treat	Blue	45.00	60.00	155.00	1325.00
☐1902	Vernon-Treat	Blue	45.00	60.00	155.00	1325.00
☐1902	Vernon-McClung	Blue	45.00	60.00	155.00	1325.00

☐1902	Napier-McClung	Blue	45.00	60.00	150.00	1285.00

SERIES	SIGNATURES	SEAL	A.B.P.	GOOD	V.FINE	UNC.
☐1902	Napier-Thompson	Blue	50.00	70.00	235.00	1675.00
☐1902	Napier-Burke	Blue	45.00	60.00	150.00	1315.00
☐1902	Parker-Burke	Blue	45.00	60.00	150.00	1315.00
☐1902	Teehee-Burke	Blue	45.00	60.00	150.00	1315.00

Third Issue (Blue seal and numbers, without date on back.)

SERIES	SIGNATURES	SEAL	A.B.P.	GOOD	V.FINE	UNC.
☐1902	Lyons-Roberts	Blue	40.00	55.00	135.00	1265.00
☐1902	Lyons-Treat	Blue	40.00	55.00	140.00	1265.00
☐1902	Vernon-Treat	Blue	40.00	55.00	140.00	1265.00
☐1902	Vernon-McClung	Blue	40.00	55.00	140.00	1265.00
☐1902	Napier-McClung	Blue	40.00	55.00	140.00	1265.00
☐1902	Napier-Thompson	Blue	40.00	55.00	155.00	1575.00
☐1902	Napier-Burke	Blue	40.00	55.00	145.00	1265.00
☐1902	Parker-Burke	Blue	40.00	55.00	145.00	1265.00
☐1902	Teehee-Burke	Blue	40.00	55.00	145.00	1265.00
☐1902	Elliott-Burke	Blue	40.00	55.00	145.00	1265.00
☐1902	Elliott-White	Blue	40.00	55.00	145.00	1265.00
☐1902	Speelman-White	Blue	40.00	55.00	145.00	1265.00
☐1902	Woods-White	Blue	40.00	55.00	145.00	1265.00
☐1902	Woods-Tate	Blue	40.00	55.00	145.00	1265.00
☐1902	Jones-Woods	Blue	40.00	107.00	350.00	2030.00

TEN DOLLAR NOTES (1929) NATIONAL BANK NOTES
(Small Size)

Face Design, Type I: Portrait of Hamilton center, name of bank left, brown seal right, Charter Number black.

Face Design, Type II: Charter Number added in brown.

Back Design: United States Treasury Building.

SERIES	SIGNATURES	SEAL	A.B.P.	GOOD	V.FINE	UNC.
☐1929, Type I Jones-Woods		Brown	25.00	40.00	85.00	235.00
☐1929, Type II Jones-Woods		Brown	25.00	45.00	85.00	235.00

TEN DOLLAR NOTES (1870-1875)
NATIONAL GOLD BANK NOTES
(Large Size)

Face Design: Similar to 1863–1875 First Charter Period note.

Back Design: State Seal left, gold coins center, American eagle right.

The following have signatures of Allison-Spinner and a red Treasury Seal.

DATE	BANK	CITY	A.B.P.	GOOD	V. GOOD
☐1870	First National Gold Bank	San Francisco	1350.00	1600.00	2800.00
☐1872	National Gold Bank and Trust Co.	San Francisco	1400.00	1650.00	2550.00
☐1872	National Gold Bank of D.O. Mills and Co.	Sacramento	1550.00	2400.00	4250.00
☐1873	First National Gold Bank	Santa Barbara	1700.00	2400.00	4250.00
☐1873	First National Gold Bank	Stockton	1650.00	2700.00	4250.00
☐1874	Farmers Nat'l Gold Bank	San Jose	1650.00	2700.00	4250.00
☐1874	First National Gold Bank	Petaluma	1650.00	2700.00	7350.00
☐1875	First National Gold Bank	Oakland	1650.00	2700.00	7350.00

TEN DOLLAR NOTES (1880) SILVER CERTIFICATES
(Large Size)

Face Design: Portrait of Robert Morris left.

Back Design: Printed in black ink, SILVER in large letters.

SERIES	SIGNATURES	SEAL	A.B.P.	GOOD	V.FINE	UNC.
☐1880	Scofield-Gilfillan	Brown	500.00	650.00	2800.00	8000.00
☐1880	Bruce-Gilfillan	Brown	500.00	650.00	2800.00	8000.00
☐1880	Bruce-Wyman	Brown	500.00	650.00	2800.00	8000.00
☐1880	Bruce-Wyman	Red	550.00	650.00	4250.00	8700.00

TEN DOLLAR NOTES (1886) SILVER CERTIFICATES
(Large Size)

SERIES	SIGNATURES	SEAL	A.B.P.	GOOD	V.FINE	UNC.
☐1886	Rosencrans-Jordan	Sm. Red	285.00	480.00	2250.00	7900.00
☐1886	Rosecrans-Hyatt	Sm. Red	200.00	325.00	1750.00	6900.00
☐1886	Rosecrans-Hyatt	Lg. Red	175.00	325.00	1750.00	6900.00
☐1886	Rosecrans-Huston	Lg. Red	195.00	325.00	1750.00	6900.00
☐1886	Rosecrans-Huston	Lg. Brown	200.00	325.00	1750.00	6900.00
☐1886	Rosecrans-Nebeker	Lg. Brown	195.00	325.00	1750.00	6900.00
☐1886	Rosecrans-Nebeker	Sm. Red	335.00	500.00	2450.00	8400.00

TEN DOLLAR NOTES (1891–1908)
SILVER CERTIFICATES
(Large Size)

Face Design:
Same as 1886
note.
Back Design

SERIES	SIGNATURES	SEAL	A.B.P.	GOOD	V.FINE	UNC.
☐1891	Rosecrans-Nebeker	Red	115.00	175.00	1000.00	3400.00
☐1891	Tillman-Morgan	Red	115.00	150.00	950.00	3400.00
☐1891	Bruce-Roberts	Red	115.00	175.00	1000.00	3400.00
☐1891	Lyons-Roberts	Red	115.00	160.00	1080.00	3400.00
☐1891	Vernon-Treat	Blue	115.00	160.00	1080.00	3400.00
☐1891	Vernon-McClung	Blue	115.00	165.00	1080.00	3365.00
☐1891	Parker-Burke	Blue	115.00	150.00	1080.00	3280.00

TEN DOLLAR NOTES (1933) SILVER CERTIFICATES
(Small Size)

Face Design: Portrait of Alexander Hamilton center. Blue
seal to left, blue numbers.

Back Design: Green United States Treasury Building.

SERIES	SIGNATURES	SEAL	A.B.P.	GOOD	V.FINE	UNC.
☐1933	Julian-Woodin	Blue	1500.00	2000.00	6600.00	15000.00

TEN DOLLAR NOTES (1934) SILVER CERTIFICATES
(Small Size)

Face Design: Blue "10" to left of portrait, Treasury Seal is
now to right.
Back Design: Similar to 1933 issue.

TEN DOLLAR NOTES (1934) SILVER CERTIFICATES
(Small Size)

SERIES	SIGNATURES	SEAL	A.B.P.	GOOD	V.FINE	UNC.	★UNC.
☐1934	Julian-Morgenthau	Blue	13.00	17.00	30.00	175.00	1500.00
☐1934	Julian-Morgenthau	*Yellow	500.00	750.00	4000.00	25000.00	RARE
☐1934A	Julian-Morgenthau	Blue	13.00	18.00	30.00	200.00	1800.00
☐1934A	Julian-Morgenthau	*Yellow	15.00	25.00	40.00	300.00	1800.00
☐1934B	Julian-Vinson	Blue	20.00	31.00	200.00	5000.00	12000.00
☐1934C	Julian-Snyder	Blue	13.00	17.00	31.00	150.00	500.00
☐1934D	Clark-Snyder	Blue	13.00	17.00	31.00	175.00	3000.00

* Silver Certificates with a yellow seal were a special issue for use in combat areas of North Africa and Europe during World War II.

TEN DOLLAR NOTES (1953) SILVER CERTIFICATES
(Small Size)

Face Design: Gray "10" to left of portrait. Treasury Seal is smaller.
Back Design: Back similar to previous note.

SERIES	SIGNATURES	SEAL	A.B.P.	GOOD	V.FINE	UNC.	★UNC.
☐1953	Priest-Humphrey	Blue	13.00	16.00	35.00	200.00	700.00
☐1953A	Priest-Anderson	Blue	13.00	19.00	39.00	350.00	1400.00
☐1953B	Smith-Dillon	Blue	13.00	18.00	36.00	130.00	NONE

Regarding the 1953 note, there were 720,000 issued. This was the last issue of $10 Silver Certificates. These were not issued with IN GOD WE TRUST on the back. Production ended in 1962.

TEN DOLLAR (1879) REFUNDING CERTIFICATES

Face Design: Portrait of Benjamin Franklin.

Back Design: Large TEN, ornate cornucopia border.

SERIES	SIGNATURES	SEAL	A.B.P.	GOOD	V.FINE	UNC.
☐1879	Scofield-Gilfillan					
	PAY TO ORDER	Red	900.00		VERY RARE	
☐1879	Scofield-Gilfillan					
	PAY TO BEARER	Red	700.00	1000.00	2400.00	11000.00

TEN DOLLAR NOTES (1907) GOLD CERTIFICATES
(Large Size)

Face Design: Portrait of Hillegas center, yellow x left, yellow seal right, yellow numbers.

Back Design: The backs are a bright yellow color.

SERIES	SIGNATURES	SEAL	A.B.P.	GOOD	V.FINE	UNC.
☐ 1907	Vernon-Treat	Gold	50.00	70.00	235.00	1125.00
☐ 1907	Vernon-McClung	Gold	50.00	70.00	235.00	1500.00
☐ 1907	Napier-McClung (1882)	Gold	50.00	70.00	235.00	950.00
☐ 1907	Napier-McClung (1907)	Gold	50.00	75.00	290.00	1600.00
☐ 1907	Napier-Thompson (1882)	Gold	57.00	93.00	310.00	1500.00
☐ 1907	Napier-Thompson (1907)	Gold	50.00	85.00	340.00	1800.00
☐ 1907	Parker-Burke (1882)	Gold	57.00	70.00	235.00	1125.00
☐ 1907	Teehee-Burke	Gold	57.00	70.00	235.00	1125.00
☐ 1922	Speelman-White	Gold	57.00	70.00	235.00	850.00

TEN DOLLAR NOTES (1928) GOLD CERTIFICATES
(Small Size)

Face Design: Portrait of Alexander Hamilton center, yellow
seal to left, yellow numbers.

Back Design: Printed in green ink.

SERIES	SIGNATURES	SEAL	A.B.P.	GOOD	V.FINE	UNC.
☐1928	Woods-Mellon	Gold	19.00	37.50	100.00	600.00

TEN DOLLAR NOTES (1890) TREASURY OR COIN NOTES
(Large Size)

Face Design: Portrait of General Philip Sheridan.

Back Design:
Very ornate
large TEN.

SERIES	SIGNATURES	SEAL	A.B.P.	GOOD	V.FINE	UNC.
☐1890	Rosecrans-Huston	Lg. Brown	300.00	400.00	1800.00	6000.00
☐1890	Rosecrans-Nebeker	Lg. Brown	300.00	400.00	1800.00	6000.00
☐1890	Rosecrans-Nebeker	Sm. Red	300.00	400.00	1800.00	6000.00

TEN DOLLAR NOTES (1891) TREASURY OR COIN NOTES
(Large Size)

Face Design:
Same as 1890 note.
Back Design:
Ornate small
TEN.

SERIES	SIGNATURES	SEAL	A.B.P.	GOOD	V.FINE	UNC.
☐1891	Rosecrans-Nebeker	Sm. Red	140.00	190.00	900.00	3800.00
☐1891	Tillman-Morgan	Sm. Red	140.00	190.00	900.00	3800.00
☐1891	Bruce-Roberts	Sm. Red	140.00	190.00	900.00	4450.00

TEN DOLLAR NOTES (1914)
FEDERAL RESERVE NOTES

(Large Size)

Face Design: Portrait of President Jackson center, Federal Reserve Seal left, Treasury Seal right.

Back Design: Scenes of farming and industry.

The following have signatures of Burke-McAdoo, red seals and red serial numbers.

SERIES	BANK	SEAL	A.B.P.	GOOD	V.FINE	UNC.
☐1914	Boston	Red	120.00	185.00	950.00	2650.00
☐1914	New York	Red	120.00	185.00	875.00	2350.00
☐1914	Philadelphia	Red	120.00	185.00	930.00	2500.00
☐1914	Cleveland	Red	120.00	175.00	950.00	2650.00
☐1914	Richmond	Red	120.00	175.00	950.00	2650.00
☐1914	Atlanta	Red	120.00	175.00	950.00	2650.00
☐1914	Chicago	Red	120.00	175.00	925.00	2450.00
☐1914	St. Louis	Red	120.00	175.00	930.00	2450.00
☐1914	Minneapolis	Red	120.00	175.00	930.00	2450.00
☐1914	Kansas City	Red	120.00	175.00	1050.00	2650.00
☐1914	Dallas	Red	120.00	175.00	930.00	2450.00
☐1914	San Francisco	Red	120.00	175.00	950.00	2650.00

TEN DOLLAR NOTES (1914)
FEDERAL RESERVE NOTES
(Large Size)

BANK	SIGNATURES	SEAL	A.B.P.	V.FINE	UNC.
☐ Boston	Burke-McAdoo	Blue	26.00	105.00	565.00
☐ Boston	Burke-Glass	Blue	26.00	210.00	690.00
☐ Boston	Burke-Huston	Blue	26.00	90.00	500.00
☐ Boston	White-Mellon	Blue	26.00	90.00	500.00
☐ New York	Burke-McAdoo	Blue	26.00	85.00	600.00
☐ New York	Burke-Glass	Blue	26.00	85.00	600.00
☐ New York	Burke-Huston	Blue	26.00	85.00	500.00
☐ New York	White-Mellon	Blue	26.00	85.00	500.00
☐ Philadelphia	Burke-McAdoo	Blue	75.00	405.00	1750.00
☐ Philadelphia	Burke-Glass	Blue	75.00	405.00	1750.00
☐ Philadelphia	Burke-Huston	Blue	26.00	90.00	500.00
☐ Philadelphia	White-Mellon	Blue	26.00	90.00	500.00
☐ Cleveland	Burke-McAdoo	Blue	75.00	305.00	1500.00
☐ Cleveland	Burke-Glass	Blue	75.00	410.00	1800.00
☐ Cleveland	Burke-Huston	Blue	26.00	85.00	500.00
☐ Cleveland	White-Mellon	Blue	26.00	85.00	500.00
☐ Richmond	Burke-McAdoo	Blue	75.00	630.00	1100.00
☐ Richmond	Burke-Glass	Blue	75.00	630.00	1000.00
☐ Richmond	Burke-Huston	Blue	26.00	90.00	600.00
☐ Richmond	White-Mellon	Blue	26.00	90.00	600.00
☐ Atlanta	Burke-McAdoo	Blue	26.00	140.00	1750.00
☐ Atlanta	Burke-Glass	Blue	100.00	795.00	2200.00
☐ Atlanta	Burke-Huston	Blue	75.00	515.00	1500.00
☐ Atlanta	White-Mellon	Blue	26.00	90.00	900.00
☐ Chicago	Burke-McAdoo	Blue	26.00	85.00	600.00
☐ Chicago	Burke-Glass	Blue	26.00	85.00	600.00
☐ Chicago	Burke-Huston	Blue	26.00	85.00	500.00
☐ Chicago	White-Mellon	Blue	26.00	85.00	500.00
☐ St. Louis	Burke-McAdoo	Blue	75.00	300.00	1000.00
☐ St. Louis	Burke-Glass	Blue	75.00	415.00	1100.00
☐ St. Louis	Burke-Huston	Blue	26.00	85.00	600.00
☐ St. Louis	White-Mellon	Blue	26.00	85.00	600.00
☐ Minneapolis	Burke-McAdoo	Blue	65.00	345.00	1200.00
☐ Minneapolis	Burke-Glass	Blue	26.00	280.00	1000.00
☐ Minneapolis	Burke-Huston	Blue	26.00	280.00	1000.00
☐ Minneapolis	White-Mellon	Blue	26.00	85.00	650.00
☐ Kansas City	Burke-McAdoo	Blue	26.00	87.00	1400.00
☐ Kansas City	Burke-Glass	Blue	75.00	400.00	1750.00

BANK	SIGNATURES	SEAL	A.B.P.	V.FINE	UNC.
☐ Kansas City	Burke-Huston	Blue	26.00	87.00	550.00
☐ Kansas City	White-Mellon	Blue	26.00	87.00	550.00
☐ Dallas	Burke-McAdoo	Blue	26.00	87.00	575.00
☐ Dallas	Burke-Glass	Blue	26.00	600.00	1850.00
☐ Dallas	Burke-Huston	Blue	26.00	115.00	1000.00
☐ Dallas	White-Mellon	Blue	26.00	130.00	1300.00
☐ San Francisco	Burke-McAdoo	Blue	26.00	300.00	1500.00
☐ San Francisco	Burke-Glass	Blue	26.00	250.00	1350.00
☐ San Francisco	Burke-Huston	Blue	26.00	300.00	1500.00
☐ San Francisco	White Mellon	Blue	26.00	87.00	555.00

TEN DOLLAR NOTES (1928–1928A)
FEDERAL RESERVE NOTES

(Small Size)

Face Design: Portrait of Alexander Hamilton center, black Federal Reserve Seal left, with number over green Treasury Seal to the right.

Back Design: United States Treasury Building.

SERIES OF 1928, SIGNATURES OF TATE-MELLON, GREEN SEAL

BANK	A.B.P.	V.FINE	UNC.	★UNC.	BANK	A.B.P.	V.FINE	UNC.	★UNC.
☐ Boston	17.00	46.00	365.00	1500.00	☐ Chicago	18.00	40.00	240.00	1500.00
☐ New York	17.00	36.00	235.00	1200.00	☐ St. Louis	18.00	55.00	215.00	1200.00
☐ Philadelphia	17.00	41.00	235.00	1200.00	☐ Minneapolis	18.00	85.00	415.00	2500.00
☐ Cleveland	17.00	41.00	235.00	1200.00	☐ Kansas City	18.00	50.00	265.00	1500.00

BANK	A.B.P.	V.FINE	UNC.	★UNC.	BANK	A.B.P.	V.FINE	UNC.	★UNC.
☐ Richmond	35.00	70.00	355.00	2000.00	☐ Dallas	33.00	70.00	305.00	5000.00
☐ Atlanta	35.00	70.00	255.00	2000.00	☐ San Francisco	38.00	50.00	280.00	4500.00

SERIES OF 1928A,
SIGNATURES OF WOODS-MELLON, GREEN SEAL

BANK	A.B.P.	V.FINE	UNC.	★UNC.	BANK	A.B.P.	V.FINE	UNC.	★UNC.
☐ Boston	55.00	85.00	550.00	1500.00	☐ Chicago	50.00	100.00	275.00	1100.00
☐ New York	55.00	85.00	350.00	1100.00	☐ St. Louis	50.00	100.00	250.00	1100.00
☐ Philadelphia	55.00	85.00	350.00	1600.00	☐ Minneapolis	100.00	170.00	2000.00	5000.00
☐ Cleveland	55.00	85.00	275.00	1100.00	☐ Kansas City	75.00	130.00	350.00	5000.00
☐ Richmond	80.00	130.00	700.00	2000.00	☐ Dallas	75.00	130.00	600.00	5000.00
☐ Atlanta	55.00	85.00	400.00	1600.00	☐ San Francisco	75.00	130.00	425.00	2000.00

TEN DOLLAR NOTES (1928B-1928C)
FEDERAL RESERVE NOTES

(Small Size)

Face Design: Alexander Hamilton; black Federal Reserve Seal left, has letter instead of number.
Back Design: Same as 1928–1928A note.

SERIES OF 1928B,
SIGNATURES OF WOODS-MELLON, GREEN SEAL

BANK	A.B.P.	V.FINE	UNC.	★UNC.	BANK	A.B.P.	V.FINE	UNC.	★UNC.
☐ Boston	17.00	36.00	135.00	835.00	☐ Chicago	17.00	30.00	130.00	835.00
☐ New York	14.00	26.00	120.00	835.00	☐ St. Louis	17.00	30.00	130.00	835.00
☐ Philadelphia	17.00	36.00	145.00	835.00	☐ Minneapolis	27.00	50.00	170.00	835.00
☐ Cleveland	17.00	36.00	150.00	835.00	☐ Kansas City	17.00	30.00	125.00	835.00
☐ Richmond	22.00	40.00	155.00	835.00	☐ Dallas	27.00	50.00	180.00	835.00
☐ Atlanta	24.00	40.00	170.00	835.00	☐ San Francisco	24.00	45.00	170.00	835.00

SERIES OF 1928C,
SIGNATURES OF WOOD-MILLS, GREEN SEAL

BANK	A.B.P.	V.FINE	UNC.	★UNC.
☐New York	45.00	80.00	410.00	—
☐Cleveland	85.00	525.00	4100.00	15000.00
☐Richmond	260.00	2500.00	10000.00	—
☐Chicago	50.00	90.00	435.00	—

TEN DOLLAR NOTES (1934)
FEDERAL RESERVE NOTES

(Small Size)

SERIES OF 1934,
SIGNATURES OF JULIAN-MORGENTHAU, GREEN SEAL

BANK	A.B.P.	V.FINE	UNC.	★UNC.	BANK	A.B.P.	V.FINE	UNC.	★UNC.
☐ Boston	13.00	15.00	45.00	450.00	☐ Chicago	13.00	20.00	60.00	350.00
☐ New York	13.00	20.00	50.00	350.00	☐ St. Louis	13.00	20.00	65.00	450.00
☐ Philadelphia	13.00	20.00	65.00	450.00	☐ Minneapolis	13.00	20.00	65.00	450.00
☐ Cleveland	13.00	20.00	65.00	450.00	☐ Kansas City	13.00	20.00	65.00	450.00
☐ Richmond	13.00	20.00	65.00	450.00	☐ Dallas	13.00	20.00	65.00	450.00
☐ Atlanta	13.00	20.00	65.00	450.00	☐ San Francisco	13.00	20.00	65.00	450.00

The green Treasury Seal on this note is known in a light and dark color. The light seal is worth about 10–20 percent more in most cases. REDEEMABLE IN GOLD removed from obligation over Federal Reserve Seal.

TEN DOLLAR NOTES (1934)
FEDERAL RESERVE NOTES

(Small Size)

SERIES OF 1934A,
SIGNATURES OF JULIAN-MORGENTHAU, GREEN SEAL

BANK	A.B.P.	V.FINE	UNC.	★UNC.	BANK	A.B.P.	V.FINE	UNC.	★UNC.
☐ Boston	12.00	15.00	40.00	325.00	☐ Chicago	12.00	15.50	40.00	325.00
☐ New York	12.00	15.00	40.00	325.00	☐ St. Louis	12.00	15.50	40.00	325.00
☐ Philadelphia	12.00	15.00	40.00	325.00	☐ Minneapolis	12.00	15.50	60.00	325.00
☐ Cleveland	12.00	15.00	40.00	325.00	☐ Kansas City	12.00	15.50	47.00	325.00
☐ Richmond	12.00	15.00	40.00	325.00	☐ Dallas	12.00	15.50	47.00	375.00
☐ Atlanta	12.00	15.00	40.00	345.00	☐ San Francisco*	12.00	15.50	37.00	375.00

* San Francisco, 1934A, with brown seal and overprinted HAWAII on face and back. Special issue for use in combat areas during World War II. Value in V. FINE $100, value in UNC. $1000. ★UNC $10000.00

SERIES OF 1934B,
SIGNATURES OF JULIAN-VINSON, GREEN SEAL

BANK	A.B.P.	V.FINE	UNC.	★UNC.	BANK	A.B.P.	V.FINE	UNC.	★UNC.
☐ Boston	12.00	18.00	95.00	575.00	☐ Chicago	12.00	18.00	45.00	575.00
☐ New York	12.00	18.00	55.00	575.00	☐ St. Louis	12.00	18.00	55.00	575.00
☐ Philadelphia	12.00	18.00	55.00	575.00	☐ Minneapolis	12.00	18.00	120.00	2000.00
☐ Cleveland	12.00	18.00	95.00	575.00	☐ Kansas City	12.00	18.00	55.00	575.00
☐ Richmond	12.00	18.00	65.00	575.00	☐ Dallas	12.00	18.00	85.00	1500.00
☐ Atlanta	12.00	18.00	65.00	575.00	☐ San Francisco	12.00	18.00	65.00	575.00

SERIES OF 1934C,
SIGNATURES OF JULIAN-SNYDER, GREEN SEAL

BANK	A.B.P.	V.FINE	UNC.	★UNC.	BANK	A.B.P.	V.FINE	UNC.	★UNC.
☐ Boston	12.00	18.00	50.00	450.00	☐ Chicago	12.00	18.00	50.00	400.00
☐ New York	12.00	18.00	50.00	425.00	☐ St. Louis	12.00	18.00	50.00	450.00
☐ Philadelphia	12.00	18.00	50.00	450.00	☐ Minneapolis	12.00	18.00	50.00	1000.00
☐ Cleveland	12.00	18.00	50.00	450.00	☐ Kansas City	12.00	18.00	50.00	450.00
☐ Richmond	12.00	18.00	50.00	450.00	☐ Dallas	12.00	18.00	50.00	500.00
☐ Atlanta	12.00	18.00	50.00	450.00	☐ San Francisco	12.00	18.00	50.00	450.00

SERIES OF 1934D,
SIGNATURES OF CLARK-SNYDER, GREEN SEAL

BANK	A.B.P.	V.FINE	UNC.	★UNC.	BANK	A.B.P.	V.FINE	UNC.	★UNC.
☐ Boston	12.00	18.00	45.00	500.00	☐ Chicago	12.00	18.00	45.00	500.00
☐ New York	12.00	18.00	45.00	500.00	☐ St. Louis	12.00	18.00	80.00	625.00
☐ Philadelphia	12.00	18.00	45.00	500.00	☐ Minneapolis	12.00	18.00	80.00	750.00
☐ Cleveland	12.00	18.00	45.00	500.00	☐ Kansas City	12.00	18.00	80.00	750.00
☐ Richmond	12.00	18.00	45.00	900.00	☐ Dallas	12.00	18.00	80.00	1000.00
☐ Atlanta	12.00	18.00	45.00	500.00	☐ San Francisco	12.00	18.00	80.00	1000.00

TEN DOLLAR NOTES (1950)
FEDERAL RESERVE NOTES
SERIES OF 1950, SIGNATURES OF CLARK-SNYDER, GREEN SEAL

BANK	A.B.P.	V.FINE	UNC.	★UNC.	BANK	A.B.P.	V.FINE	UNC.	★UNC.
☐ Boston	12.00	25.00	65.00	500.00	☐ Chicago	12.00	25.00	65.00	500.00
☐ New York	12.00	25.00	65.00	500.00	☐ St. Louis	12.00	25.00	65.00	500.00
☐ Philadelphia	12.00	25.00	65.00	500.00	☐ Minneapolis	12.00	25.00	65.00	500.00
☐ Cleveland	12.00	25.00	65.00	500.00	☐ Kansas City	12.00	25.00	65.00	500.00
☐ Richmond	12.00	25.00	65.00	500.00	☐ Dallas	12.00	25.00	65.00	500.00
☐ Atlanta	12.00	25.00	65.00	500.00	☐ San Francisco	12.00	25.00	65.00	500.00

(Small Size)

SERIES OF 1950A, SIGNATURES OF PRIEST-HUMPHERY, GREEN SEAL

BANK	A.B.P.	V.FINE	UNC.	★UNC.	BANK	A.B.P.	V.FINE	UNC.	★UNC.
☐ Boston	12.00	23.00	45.00	225.00	☐ Chicago	12.00	23.00	45.00	325.00
☐ New York	12.00	23.00	45.00	225.00	☐ St. Louis	12.00	23.00	45.00	325.00
☐ Philadelphia	12.00	23.00	45.00	325.00	☐ Minneapolis	12.00	25.00	105.00	500.00
☐ Cleveland	12.00	23.00	45.00	325.00	☐ Kansas City	12.00	25.00	45.00	400.00
☐ Richmond	12.00	23.00	45.00	500.00	☐ Dallas	12.00	25.00	45.00	300.00
☐ Atlanta	12.00	23.00	45.00	325.00	☐ San Francisco	12.00	23.00	45.00	225.00

SERIES OF 1950B, SIGNATURES OF PRIEST-ANDERSON, GREEN SEAL

BANK	A.B.P.	V.FINE	UNC.	★UNC.	BANK	A.B.P.	V.FINE	UNC.	★UNC.
☐ Boston	12.00	20.00	35.00	150.00	☐ Chicago	12.00	20.00	35.00	150.00
☐ New York	12.00	20.00	35.00	150.00	☐ St. Louis	12.00	20.00	35.00	150.00
☐ Philadelphia	12.00	20.00	35.00	150.00	☐ Minneapolis	12.00	23.00	35.00	400.00
☐ Cleveland	12.00	20.00	35.00	150.00	☐ Kansas City	12.00	23.00	35.00	150.00
☐ Richmond	12.00	20.00	35.00	150.00	☐ Dallas	12.00	23.00	35.00	450.00
☐ Atlanta	12.00	20.00	35.00	150.00	☐ San Francisco	12.00	20.00	35.00	150.00

SERIES OF 1950C, SIGNATURES OF SMITH-DILLON, GREEN SEAL

BANK	A.B.P.	V.FINE	UNC.	★UNC.	BANK	A.B.P.	V.FINE	UNC.	★UNC.
☐ Boston	12.00	20.00	45.00	350.00	☐ Chicago	12.00	20.00	45.00	350.00
☐ New York	12.00	20.00	45.00	350.00	☐ St. Louis	12.00	20.00	55.00	350.00
☐ Philadelphia	12.00	20.00	45.00	350.00	☐ Minneapolis	15.00	25.00	85.00	350.00
☐ Cleveland	12.00	20.00	45.00	350.00	☐ Kansas City	15.00	25.00	85.00	350.00
☐ Richmond	12.00	20.00	45.00	350.00	☐ Dallas	15.00	25.00	75.00	350.00
☐ Atlanta	12.00	20.00	45.00	350.00	☐ San Francisco	12.00	20.00	75.00	350.00

SERIES OF 1950D, SIGNATURES OF GRANAHAN-DILLON, GREEN SEAL

BANK	A.B.P.	V.FINE	UNC.	★UNC.	BANK	A.B.P.	V.FINE	UNC.	★UNC.
☐ Boston	12.00	20.00	45.00	250.00	☐ Chicago	12.00	20.00	45.00	250.00
☐ New York	12.00	20.00	45.00	250.00	☐ St. Louis	12.00	20.00	45.00	250.00
☐ Philadelphia	12.00	20.00	45.00	250.00	☐ Minneapolis	15.00	25.00	45.00	250.00
☐ Cleveland	12.00	20.00	45.00	250.00	☐ Kansas City	15.00	25.00	45.00	250.00
☐ Richmond	12.00	20.00	45.00	250.00	☐ Dallas	15.00	25.00	45.00	250.00
☐ Atlanta	12.00	20.00	45.00	250.00	☐ San Francisco	12.00	20.00	45.00	250.00

SERIES OF 1950E, SIGNATURES OF GRANAHAN-FOWLER, GREEN SEAL

BANK	A.B.P.	V.FINE	UNC.	★UNC.	BANK	A.B.P.	V.FINE	UNC.	★UNC.
☐ New York	14.00	23.00	90.00	350.00	☐ Chicago	14.00	23.00	90.00	300.00
					☐ San Francisco	14.00	23.00	130.00	500.00

TEN DOLLAR NOTES (1963)
FEDERAL RESERVE NOTES
(IN GOD WE TRUST IS ADDED ON BACK)
SERIES OF 1963, SIGNATURES OF GRANAHAN-DILLON, GREEN SEAL

BANK	A.B.P.	V.FINE	UNC.	★UNC.	BANK	A.B.P.	V.FINE	UNC.	★UNC.
☐ Boston	—	12.00	40.00	100.00	☐ Chicago	—	12.00	40.00	100.00
☐ New York	—	12.00	40.00	100.00	☐ St. Louis	—	12.00	40.00	100.00
☐ Philadelphia	—	12.00	40.00	100.00	☐ Minneapolis	—	12.00	40.00	100.00
☐ Cleveland	—	12.00	40.00	100.00	☐ Kansas City	—	12.00	40.00	100.00
☐ Richmond	—	12.00	40.00	100.00	☐ Dallas	—	12.00	40.00	100.00
☐ Atlanta	—	12.00	40.00	100.00	☐ San Francisco	—	12.00	40.00	100.00

SERIES OF 1963A, SIGNATURES OF GRANAHAN-FOWLER, GREEN SEAL

BANK	A.B.P.	V.FINE	UNC.	★UNC.	BANK	A.B.P.	V.FINE	UNC.	★UNC.
☐ Boston	—	12.00	33.00	80.00	☐ Chicago	—	12.00	33.00	80.00
☐ New York	—	12.00	33.00	80.00	☐ St. Louis	—	12.00	33.00	80.00
☐ Philadelphia	—	12.00	33.00	80.00	☐ Minneapolis	—	12.00	33.00	80.00
☐ Cleveland	—	12.00	33.00	80.00	☐ Kansas City	—	12.00	33.00	80.00
☐ Richmond	—	12.00	33.00	80.00	☐ Dallas	—	12.00	33.00	80.00
☐ Atlanta	—	12.00	33.00	80.00	☐ San Francisco	—	12.00	33.00	80.00

TEN DOLLAR NOTES (1969)
FEDERAL RESERVE NOTES
(WORDING IN GREEN TREASURY SEAL IS CHANGED FROM LATIN TO ENGLISH)

SERIES OF 1969, SIGNATURES OF ELSTON-KENNEDY, GREEN SEAL

BANK	A.B.P.	V.FINE	UNC.	★UNC.	BANK	A.B.P.	V.FINE	UNC.	★UNC.
☐ Boston	—	12.00	30.00	70.00	☐ Chicago	—	12.00	30.00	70.00
☐ New York	—	12.00	30.00	70.00	☐ St. Louis	—	12.00	30.00	70.00
☐ Philadelphia	—	12.00	30.00	70.00	☐ Minneapolis	—	12.00	30.00	70.00
☐ Cleveland	—	12.00	30.00	70.00	☐ Kansas City	—	12.00	30.00	70.00
☐ Richmond	—	12.00	30.00	70.00	☐ Dallas	—	12.00	30.00	70.00
☐ Atlanta	—	12.00	30.00	70.00	☐ San Francisco	—	12.00	30.00	70.00

SERIES OF 1969A, SIGNATURES OF KABIS-CONNALLY, GREEN SEAL

BANK	A.B.P.	V.FINE	UNC.	★UNC.	BANK	A.B.P.	V.FINE	UNC.	★UNC.
☐ Boston	—	12.00	27.00	60.00	☐ Chicago	—	12.00	27.00	60.00
☐ New York	—	12.00	27.00	60.00	☐ St. Louis	—	12.00	27.00	60.00
☐ Philadelphia	—	12.00	27.00	60.00	☐ Minneapolis	—	15.00	27.00	60.00
☐ Cleveland	—	12.00	27.00	60.00	☐ Kansas City	—	12.00	27.00	60.00
☐ Richmond	—	12.00	27.00	60.00	☐ Dallas	—	12.00	27.00	60.00
☐ Atlanta	—	12.00	27.00	60.00	☐ San Francisco	—	12.00	27.00	60.00

SERIES OF 1969B, SIGNATURES OF BANUELOS-CONNALLY, GREEN SEAL

BANK	A.B.P.	V.FINE	UNC.	★UNC.	BANK	A.B.P.	V.FINE	UNC.	★UNC.
☐ Boston	—	20.00	150.00	—	☐ Chicago	—	20.00	150.00	250.00
☐ New York	—	20.00	150.00	300.00	☐ St. Louis	—	20.00	150.00	250.00
☐ Philadelphia	—	20.00	150.00	—	☐ Minneapolis	—	20.00	150.00	—
☐ Cleveland	—	20.00	150.00	—	☐ Kansas City	—	20.00	150.00	300.00
☐ Richmond	—	20.00	150.00	350.00	☐ Dallas	—	20.00	150.00	—
☐ Atlanta	—	20.00	150.00	300.00	☐ San Francisco	—	20.00	150.00	300.00

SERIES OF 1969C, SIGNATURES OF BANUELOS-SHULTZ, GREEN SEAL

BANK	A.B.P.	V.FINE	UNC.	★UNC.	BANK	A.B.P.	V.FINE	UNC.	★UNC.
☐ Boston	—	—	30.00	80.00	☐ Chicago	—	—	30.00	80.00
☐ New York	—	—	30.00	80.00	☐ St. Louis	—	—	30.00	80.00
☐ Philadelphia	—	—	30.00	80.00	☐ Minneapolis	—	—	30.00	80.00
☐ Cleveland	—	—	30.00	80.00	☐ Kansas City	—	—	30.00	80.00
☐ Richmond	—	—	30.00	80.00	☐ Dallas	—	—	30.00	80.00
☐ Atlanta	—	—	30.00	80.00	☐ San Francisco	—	—	30.00	80.00

TEN DOLLAR NOTES (1974)
FEDERAL RESERVE NOTES
SERIES OF 1974, SIGNATURES OF NEFF-SIMON, GREEN SEAL

BANK	A.B.P.	V.FINE	UNC.	★UNC.	BANK	A.B.P.	V.FINE	UNC.	★UNC.
☐ Boston	—	—	25.00	70.00	☐ Chicago	—	—	25.00	70.00
☐ New York	—	—	25.00	70.00	☐ St. Louis	—	—	25.00	70.00
☐ Philadelphia	—	—	25.00	70.00	☐ Minneapolis	—	—	25.00	70.00
☐ Cleveland	—	—	25.00	70.00	☐ Kansas City	—	—	25.00	70.00
☐ Richmond	—	—	25.00	70.00	☐ Dallas	—	—	25.00	70.00
☐ Atlanta	—	—	25.00	70.00	☐ San Francisco	—	—	25.00	70.00

TEN DOLLAR NOTES (1977)
FEDERAL RESERVE NOTES
SERIES OF 1977, SIGNATURES OF MORTON-BLUMENTHAL, GREEN SEAL

BANK	A.B.P.	V.FINE	UNC.	★UNC.	BANK	A.B.P.	V.FINE	UNC.	★UNC.
☐ Boston	—	—	25.00	60.00	☐ Chicago	—	—	25.00	60.00
☐ New York	—	—	25.00	60.00	☐ St. Louis	—	—	25.00	60.00
☐ Philadelphia	—	—	25.00	60.00	☐ Minneapolis	—	—	25.00	90.00
☐ Cleveland	—	—	25.00	60.00	☐ Kansas City	—	—	25.00	60.00
☐ Richmond	—	—	25.00	60.00	☐ Dallas	—	—	25.00	60.00
☐ Atlanta	—	—	25.00	60.00	☐ San Francisco	—	—	25.00	60.00

TEN DOLLAR NOTES (1981)
FEDERAL RESERVE NOTES
SERIES OF 1981, SIGNATURES OF BUCHANAN-REGAN, GREEN SEAL
★Notes not issued for all banks

BANK	A.B.P.	V.FINE	UNC.	★UNC.	BANK	A.B.P.	V.FINE	UNC.	★UNC.
☐ Boston	—	—	25.00	60.00	☐ Chicago	—	—	25.00	60.00
☐ New York	—	—	25.00	60.00	☐ St. Louis	—	—	25.00	—
☐ Philadelphia	—	—	25.00	60.00	☐ Minneapolis	—	—	25.00	60.00
☐ Cleveland	—	—	25.00	60.00	☐ Kansas City	—	—	25.00	—
☐ Richmond	—	—	25.00	60.00	☐ Dallas	—	—	25.00	—
☐ Atlanta	—	—	25.00	60.00	☐ San Francisco	—	—	25.00	60.00

SERIES OF 1981A, SIGNATURES OF ORTEGA-REGAN, GREEN SEAL
★Notes not issued for all banks

BANK	A.B.P.	V.FINE	UNC.	★UNC.	BANK	A.B.P.	V.FINE	UNC.	★UNC.
☐ Boston	—	—	25.00	—	☐Chicago	—	—	25.00	—
☐ New York	—	—	25.00	100.00	☐St. Louis	—	—	25.00	—
☐ Philadelphia	—	—	25.00	—	☐Minneapolis	—	—	25.00	—
☐ Cleveland	—	—	25.00	—	☐Kansas City	—	—	25.00	—
☐ Richmond	—	—	25.00	—	☐Dallas	—	—	25.00	—
☐ Atlanta	—	—	25.00	80.00	☐San Francisco	—	—	25.00	—

TEN DOLLAR NOTES (1985)
FEDERAL RESERVE NOTES
SERIES OF 1985, SIGNATURES OF ORTEGA-BAKER, GREEN SEAL
★Notes not issued for all banks

BANK	A.B.P.	V.FINE	UNC.	★UNC.	BANK	A.B.P.	V.FINE	UNC.	★UNC.
☐ Boston	—	—	25.00	60.00	☐Chicago	—	—	25.00	—
☐ New York	—	—	25.00	60.00	☐St. Louis	—	—	25.00	60.00
☐ Philadelphia	—	—	25.00	—	☐Minneapolis	—	—	25.00	—
☐ Cleveland	—	—	25.00	60.00	☐Kansas City	—	—	25.00	—
☐ Richmond	—	—	25.00	—	☐Dallas	—	—	25.00	60.00
☐ Atlanta	—	—	25.00	60.00	☐San Francisco	—	—	25.00	60.00

TEN DOLLAR NOTES (1988)
FEDERAL RESERVE NOTES
SERIES OF 1988A, SIGNATURES OF VILLALPANDO-BRADY, GREEN SEAL
★Notes not issued for all banks

BANK	A.B.P.	V.FINE	UNC.	★UNC.	BANK	A.B.P.	V.FINE	UNC.	★UNC.
☐ Boston	—	—	25.00	100.00	☐ Chicago	—	—	25.00	—
☐ New York	—	—	25.00	100.00	☐ St. Louis	—	—	25.00	—
☐ Philadelphia	—	—	25.00	—	☐ Minneapolis	—	—	25.00	—
☐ Cleveland	—	—	25.00	100.00	☐ Kansas City	—	—	25.00	—
☐ Richmond	—	—	25.00	—	☐ Dallas	—	—	25.00	—
☐ Atlanta	—	—	25.00	—	☐ San Francisco	—	—	25.00	100.00

TEN DOLLAR NOTES (1990)
FEDERAL RESERVE NOTES
SERIES OF 1990, SIGNATURES OF VILLALPANDO-BRADY, GREEN SEAL

★Notes not issued for all banks

BANK	A.B.P.	V.FINE	UNC.	★UNC.	BANK	A.B.P.	V.FINE	UNC.	★UNC.
☐ Boston	—	—	15.00	—	☐ Chicago	—	—	12.00	35.00
☐ New York	—	—	15.00	35.00	☐ St. Louis	—	—	12.00	35.00
☐ Philadelphia	—	—	15.00	35.00	☐ Minneapolis	—	—	12.00	—
☐ Cleveland	—	—	15.00	—	☐ Kansas City	—	—	12.00	—
☐ Richmond	—	—	15.00	—	☐ Dallas	—	—	12.00	—
☐ Atlanta	—	—	15.00	—	☐ San Francisco	—	—	12.00	—

TEN DOLLAR NOTES (1993)
FEDERAL RESERVE NOTES
SERIES OF 1993, SIGNATURES OF WITHROW-BENTSEN, GREEN SEAL

★Notes not issued for all banks

BANK	A.B.P.	V.FINE	UNC.	★UNC.	BANK	A.B.P.	V.FINE	UNC.	★UNC.
☐ Boston	—	—	15.00	—	☐ Chicago	—	—	12.00	35.00
☐ New York	—	—	15.00	35.00	☐ St. Louis	—	—	12.00	—
☐ Philadelphia	—	—	15.00	35.00					
☐ Cleveland	—	—	15.00	—	☐ Kansas City	—	—	12.00	—
☐ Atlanta	—	—	15.00	—	☐ San Francisco	—	—	12.00	—

TEN DOLLAR NOTES (1995)
FEDERAL RESERVE NOTES
SERIES OF 1995, SIGNATURES OF WITHROW-RUBIN, GREEN SEAL

★Notes not issued for all banks

BANK	A.B.P.	V.FINE	UNC.	★UNC.	BANK	A.B.P.	V.FINE	UNC.	★UNC.
☐ Boston	—	13.00	15.00	—	☐ Chicago	—	—	12.00	35.00
☐ New York	—	13.00	15.00	—	☐ St. Louis	—	—	12.00	35.00
☐ Philadelphia	—	13.00	15.00	—	☐ Minneapolis	—	—	12.00	—
☐ Cleveland	—	13.00	15.00	35.00	☐ Kansas City	—	—	12.00	—
☐ Richmond		13.00	15.00	35.00	☐ Dallas	—	—	12.00	—
☐ Atlanta	—	—	15.00	50.00	☐ San Francisco	—	—	12.00	35.00

TEN DOLLAR NOTES (1915–1918)
FEDERAL RESERVE BANK NOTES
(Large Size)

Face Design: Portrait of President Jackson to left, bank and city in center, blue seal to the right.

Back Design: Similar to 1914 note.

BANK	SERIES	GOV'T SIGNATURES	BANK SIGNATURES	A.B.P.	GOOD	V.FINE	UNC.
☐New York	1918	Teehee-Burke	Hendricks-Strong				
				450.00	650.00	2000.00	5000.00
☐Atlanta	1915	Teehee-Burke	Bell-Wellborn				
				685.00	950.00	3200.00	6700.00
☐Atlanta	1918	Elliott-Burke	Bell-Wellborn				
				450.00	650.00	2000.00	5000.00
☐Chicago	1915	Teehee-Burke	McLallen-McDougal				
				450.00	650.00	2000.00	5000.00
☐Chicago	1918	Teehee-Burke	McCloud-McDougal				
				450.00	650.00	2000.00	5100.00
☐St. Louis	1918	Teehee-Burke	Attebery-Wells				
				450.00	650.00	2000.00	5100.00
☐Kansas City	1915	Teehee-Burke	Anderson-Miller				
				450.00	650.00	2000.00	5100.00

BANK	SERIES	GOV'T SIGNATURES	BANK SIGNATURES	A.B.P.	GOOD	V.FINE	UNC.
☐ Kansas City	1915	Teehee-Burke	Cross-Miller	260.00	655.00	1975.00	5000.00
☐ Kansas City	1915	Teehee-Burke	Helm-Miller	400.00	4450.00	3175.00	6100.00
☐ Dallas	1915	Teehee-Burke	Hoopes-Van Zandt	260.00	2060.00	1975.00	5100.00
☐ Dallas	1915	Teehee-Burke	Gilbert-Van Zandt	400.00	8660.00	3200.00	6600.00
☐ Dallas	1918	Teehee-Burke	Talley-Van Zandt	260.00	750.00	2975.00	5700.00

TEN DOLLAR NOTES (1929)
FEDERAL RESERVE BANK NOTES
(Small Size)

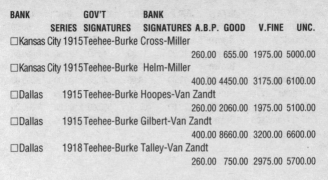

Face Design: Portrait of Alexander Hamilton.

Back Design: Same as all Small Size $10 notes.
SIGNATURES OF JONES-WOODS, BROWN SEAL

BANK	SEAL	A.B.P.	GOOD	V.FINE	UNC.	★UNC.
☐ Boston	Brown	12.00	18.00	42.00	255.00	8000.00
☐ New York	Brown	12.00	18.00	42.00	180.00	2500.00
☐ Philadelphia	Brown	12.00	18.00	42.00	255.00	3500.00
☐ Cleveland	Brown	12.00	18.00	42.00	255.00	3500.00

BANK	SEAL	A.B.P.	GOOD	V.FINE	UNC.	★UNC.
☐Richmond	Brown	12.00	18.00	42.00	455.00	3500.00
☐Atlanta	Brown	12.00	18.00	42.00	380.00	3800.00
☐Chicago	Brown	12.00	18.00	42.00	405.00	3500.00
☐St. Louis	Brown	12.00	18.00	42.00	330.00	2800.00
☐Minneapolis	Brown	12.00	18.00	42.00	330.00	3000.00
☐Kansas City	Brown	12.00	18.00	42.00	330.00	3000.00
☐Dallas	Brown	200.00	400.00	850.00	2500.00	6000.00
☐San Francisco	Brown	12.00	18.00	42.00	1500.00	4000.00

TWENTY DOLLAR NOTES

TWENTY DOLLAR NOTES (1861) DEMAND NOTES
(Large Size)

Face Design: Liberty with sword and shield.

Back Design: Intricate design of numerals, "20." Demand
Notes have no Treasury Seal.

SERIES	PAYABLE AT	A.B.P.	GOOD	V.GOOD
☐1861	Boston (I)	RARE	RARE	RARE
☐1861	New York (I)	6700.00	2000.00	22500.00
☐1861	Philadelphia (I)	6700.00	2000.00	22500.00
☐1861	Cincinnati (I)	RARE	RARE	RARE
☐1861	St. Louis (I)	(Unknown in any collection)		
☐1861	Boston (II)	RARE	RARE	RARE
☐1861	New York (II)	6700.00	2000.00	22500.00
☐1861	Philadelphia (II)	6700.00	2000.00	22500.00
☐1861	Cincinnati (II)	RARE	RARE	RARE
☐1861	St. Louis (II)	(Unknown in any collection)		

Counterfeits exist. Use caution in buying.

TWENTY DOLLAR NOTES (1862–1863)
UNITED STATES NOTES
(ALSO KNOWN AS LEGAL TENDER NOTES)
(Large Size)

Face Design: Liberty with sword and shield.

Back Design: Second obligation. This note was also issued with first obligation on the back.

SERIES	SIGNATURES	SEAL	A.B.P.	GOOD	V.FINE	UNC.
☐ 1862	Chittenden-Spinner*	Red	700.00	950.00	3500.00	12000.00
☐ 1862	Chittenden-Spinner**	Red	700.00	950.00	3500.00	12000.00
☐ 1863	Chittenden-Spinner**	Red	700.00	950.00	3500.00	12000.00

* First Obligation: Similar to 1875–1907 $5 note.
** Second Obligation: Shown above.

TWENTY DOLLAR NOTES (1869)
UNITED STATES NOTES
(ALSO KNOWN AS LEGAL TENDER NOTES)
(Large Size)

SERIES	SIGNATURES	SEAL	A.B.P.	GOOD	V.FINE	UNC.
☐1869	Allison-Spinner	Red	390.00	565.00	2625.00	9200.00
Series Back Design: Revised						
☐1875	Allison-New	Red	275.00	415.00	1350.00	5000.00
☐1878	Allison-Gilfillan	Red	260.00	350.00	1025.00	3500.00
☐1878	Watermark Paper		310.00	550.00	1900.00	5000.00
☐1880	Scofield-Gilfillan	Lg. Brown	620.00	925.00	3275.00	14000.00
☐1880	Bruce-Gilfillan	Lg. Brown	220.00	425.00	2675.00	5000.00
☐1880	Bruce-Wyman	Lg. Brown	185.00	415.00	2200.00	4400.00
☐1880	Bruce-Wyman	Lg. Red	600.00	2060.00	2275.00	13700.00
☐1880	Rosecrans-Jordan	Lg. Red	185.00	315.00	1000.00	4200.00
☐1880	Rosecrans-Hyatt	Red Plain	175.00	283.00	1025.00	3800.00
☐1880	Rosecrans-Hyatt	Red Spikes	145.00	182.00	875.00	2700.00
☐1880	Rosecrans-Huston	Lg. Red	145.00	182.00	900.00	2800.00
☐1880	Rosecrans-Huston	Lg. Brown	145.00	182.00	925.00	2900.00
☐1880	Rosecrans-Nebeker	Lg. Brown	145.00	182.00	2400.00	13700.00
☐1800	Rosecrans-Nebeker	Sm. Red	145.00	173.00	600.00	2700.00
☐1880	Tillman-Morgan	Sm. Red	145.00	173.00	600.00	2200.00
☐1880	Bruce-Roberts	Sm. Red	145.00	173.00	600.00	2200.00
☐1880	Lyons-Roberts	Sm. Red	145.00	173.00	700.00	2350.00
☐1880	Vernon-Treat	Sm. Red	145.00	173.00	755.00	2450.00
☐1880	Vernon-McClung	Sm. Red	145.00	173.00	700.00	2350.00
☐1880	Teehee-Burke	Sm. Red	145.00	167.00	675.00	2225.00
☐1880	Elliott-White	Sm. Red	145.00	155.00	600.00	1650.00

TWENTY DOLLAR NOTES (1863–1875)
NATIONAL BANK NOTES
FIRST CHARTER PERIOD (Large Size)

Face Design: Battle of Lexington left, name of bank in center. Columbia with flag right.

Back Design: Green border, black center picture of baptism of Pocahontas.

SERIES	SIGNATURES	SEAL	A.B.P.	GOOD	V.FINE	UNC.
☐Original	Chittenden-Spinner	Red	385.00	535.00	2400.00	9100.00
☐Original	Colby-Spinner	Red	385.00	535.00	2400.00	9100.00
☐Original	Jeffries-Spinner	Red	385.00	785.00	2850.00	11300.00
☐Original	Allison-Spinner	Red	385.00	535.00	2400.00	9000.00
☐1875	Allison-New	Red	385.00	535.00	2400.00	9000.00
☐1875	Allison-Wyman	Red	385.00	535.00	2400.00	9000.00
☐1875	Allison-Gilfillan	Red	385.00	535.00	2400.00	9000.00
☐1875	Scofield-Gilfillan	Red	385.00	535.00	2400.00	9000.00
☐1875	Bruce-Gilfillan	Red	385.00	535.00	2400.00	9000.00
☐1875	Bruce-Wyman	Red	385.00	535.00	2400.00	9000.00
☐1875	Rosecrans-Huston	Red	385.00	535.00	2400.00	9000.00
☐1875	Rosecrans-Nebeker	Red	385.00	635.00	2600.00	9950.00
☐1875	Tillman-Morgan	Red	385.00	635.00	2600.00	9950.00

TWENTY DOLLAR NOTES (1882)
NATIONAL BANK NOTES
SECOND CHARTER PERIOD (Large Size)

First Issue (Brown seal and brown backs.)
Face Design: Similar to First Charter Period note.
Back Design: Similar to 1882 $5 note. Border is brown, green Charter Number in center.

SERIES	SIGNATURES	SEAL	A.B.P.	GOOD	V.FINE	UNC.
☐1882	Bruce-Gilfillan	Brown	150.00	225.00	1000.00	2300.00
☐1882	Bruce-Wyman	Brown	150.00	225.00	1000.00	2300.00
☐1882	Bruce-Jordan	Brown	150.00	225.00	1000.00	2300.00
☐1882	Rosecrans-Jordan	Brown	150.00	225.00	1000.00	2300.00
☐1882	Rosecrans-Hyatt	Brown	150.00	225.00	1000.00	2300.00
☐1882	Rosecrans-Huston	Brown	150.00	225.00	1000.00	2300.00
☐1882	Rosecrans-Nebeker	Brown	150.00	225.00	1000.00	2300.00
☐1882	Rosecrans-Morgan	Brown	1520.00	410.00	1350.00	3400.00
☐1882	Tillman-Morgan	Brown	150.00	225.00	1000.00	2300.00
☐1882	Tillman-Roberts	Brown	150.00	225.00	1000.00	2300.00
☐1882	Bruce-Roberts	Brown	150.00	225.00	1000.00	2300.00
☐1882	Lyons-Roberts	Brown	150.00	225.00	1000.00	2300.00
☐1882	Lyons-Treat	Brown	150.00	225.00	1000.00	2300.00
☐1882	Vernon-Treat	Brown	150.00	225.00	1000.00	2300.00

SECOND CHARTER PERIOD, Second Issue

Face Design: Similar to First Charter Period note.
Back Design: Similar to 1882 $5.00 Second Issue note.

SERIES	SIGNATURES	SEAL	A.B.P.	GOOD	V.FINE	UNC.
☐1882	Rosecrans-Huston	Blue	125.00	200.00	775.00	2000.00
☐1882	Rosecrans-Nebeker	Blue	125.00	200.00	775.00	2000.00
☐1882	Rosecrans-Morgan	Blue	190.00	415.00	1275.00	2675.00
☐1882	Tillman-Morgan	Blue	125.00	200.00	775.00	2000.00
☐1882	Tillman-Roberts	Blue	125.00	200.00	775.00	2000.00
☐1882	Bruce-Roberts	Blue	125.00	200.00	775.00	2000.00
☐1882	Lyons-Roberts	Blue	125.00	200.00	775.00	2000.00
☐1882	Vernon-Treat	Blue	125.00	200.00	775.00	2000.00
☐1882	Napier-McClung	Blue	125.00	200.00	775.00	2000.00

SECOND CHARTER PERIOD, Third Issue. Large Size

Face Design: Similar to First Charter Period note with blue seal.
Back Design: Similar to 1882 Third Issue note, green back, value in block letters.

SERIES	SIGNATURES	SEAL	A.B.P.	GOOD	V.FINE	UNC.
☐1882	Tillman-Morgan	Blue	150.00	215.00	900.00	2975.00
☐1882	Lyons-Roberts	Blue	123.00	340.00	1100.00	3500.00
☐1882	Lyons-Treat	Blue	160.00	240.00	900.00	3500.00
☐1882	Vernon-Treat	Blue	160.00	240.00	900.00	2675.00
☐1882	Napier-McClung	Blue	160.00	240.00	900.00	2675.00
☐1882	Teehee-Burke	Blue	160.00	240.00	1025.00	3500.00

TWENTY DOLLAR NOTES (1902)
NATIONAL BANK NOTES
THIRD CHARTER PERIOD, First Issue (Large Size)

Face Design: Portrait of McCulloch left, name of bank center, Treasury Seal right.

SERIES	SIGNATURES	SEAL	A.B.P.	GOOD	V.FINE	UNC.
☐1902	Lyons-Roberts	Red	180.00	250.00	760.00	2600.00
☐1902	Lyons-Treat	Red	180.00	250.00	760.00	2600.00
☐1902	Vernon-Treat	Red	180.00	250.00	760.00	2600.00

Second Issue (Date "1902–1908" added on back, Treasury Seal and serial numbers blue)

☐1902	Lyons-Roberts	Blue	55.00	80.00	210.00	700.00
☐1902	Lyons-Treat	Blue	55.00	80.00	210.00	700.00
☐1902	Vernon-Treat	Blue	55.00	80.00	210.00	700.00
☐1902	Vernon-McClung	Blue	55.00	80.00	210.00	700.00
☐1902	Napier-McClung	Blue	55.00	80.00	210.00	700.00
☐1902	Napier-Thompson	Blue	55.00	80.00	210.00	895.00
☐1902	Napier-Burke	Blue	55.00	80.00	210.00	700.00
☐1902	Parker-Burke	Blue	55.00	80.00	210.00	700.00

Third Issue (Date "1902–1908" removed from back, seal and serial numbers blue)

☐1902	Lyons-Roberts	Blue	55.00	75.00	175.00	660.00
☐1902	Lyons-Treat	Blue	55.00	75.00	175.00	660.00
☐1902	Vernon-Treat	Blue	55.00	75.00	175.00	660.00
☐1902	Vernon-McClung	Blue	55.00	75.00	175.00	660.00

SERIES	SIGNATURES	SEAL	A.B.P.	GOOD	V.FINE	UNC.
☐1902	Napier-McClung	Blue	55.00	75.00	195.00	660.00
☐1902	Napier-Thompson	Blue	55.00	75.00	195.00	660.00
☐1902	Napier-Burke	Blue	55.00	7500.00	175.00	660.00
☐1902	Parker-Burke	Blue	55.00	7500.00	175.00	660.00
☐1902	Teehee-Burke	Blue	55.00	7500.00	175.00	660.00
☐1902	Elliott-Burke	Blue	55.00	7500.00	175.00	660.00
☐1902	Elliott-White	Blue	55.00	7500.00	175.00	660.00
☐1902	Speelman-White	Blue	55.00	7500.00	175.00	660.00
☐1902	Woods-White	Blue	55.00	7500.00	175.00	660.00
☐1902	Woods-Tate	Blue	55.00	85.00	275.00	805.00
☐1902	Jones-Woods	Blue	63.00	645.00	1230.00	5425.00

TWENTY DOLLAR NOTES (1929)
NATIONAL BANK NOTES

(Small Size)

Face Design, Type I: Portrait of President Jackson in center, name of bank to left, brown seal right. Charter number in black.

Face Design, Type II.

Back Design: The White House, similar to all $20 Small Notes.

SERIES	SIGNATURES	SEAL	A.B.P.	GOOD	V.FINE	UNC.
☐1929, Type I	Jones-Woods	Brown	40.00	60.00	100.00	400.00
☐1929, Type II	Jones-Woods	Brown	40.00	65.00	100.00	400.00

TWENTY DOLLAR NOTES (1880)
SILVER CERTIFICATES

(Large Size)

Face Design: Portrait of Stephen Decatur right. TWENTY SILVER DOLLARS in center.

Back Design: SILVER in large block letters.

SERIES	SIGNATURES	SEAL	A.B.P.	GOOD	V.FINE	UNC.
☐1880	Scofield-Gilfillan	Brown	900.00	1300.00	6000.00	40000.00
☐1880	Bruce-Gilfillan	Brown	900.00	1300.00	6000.00	40000.00
☐1880	Bruce-Wyman	Brown	900.00	1300.00	6000.00	40000.00
☐1880	Bruce-Wyman	Sm. Red	1100.00	1800.00	6500.00	50000.00

This note was also issued in the Series of 1878. They are very rare.

TWENTY DOLLAR NOTES (1886)
SILVER CERTIFICATES

(Large Size)

Face Design: Portrait of Daniel Manning center, Agriculture left, Industry right.

Back Design: Double-diamond design center.

SERIES	SIGNATURES	SEAL	A.B.P.	GOOD	V.FINE	UNC.
☐1886	Rosecrans-Hyatt	Lg. Red	1000.00	1375.00	6550.00	32000.00
☐1886	Rosecrans-Huston	Lg. Brown	1000.00	1375.00	6550.00	29500.00
☐1886	Rosecrans-Nebeker	Lg. Brown	1000.00	1375.00	6550.00	29500.00
☐1886	Rosecrans-Nebeker	Sm. Red	1000.00	1375.00	7000.00	100000.00

TWENTY DOLLAR NOTES (1891)
SILVER CERTIFICATES
(NOT ISSUED IN SMALL SIZE NOTES)
(Large Size)

Face Design: Same as 1886 note.

Back Design: Revised.

SERIES	SIGNATURES	SEAL	A.B.P.	GOOD	V.FINE	UNC.
☐1891	Rosecrans-Nebeker	Red	175.00	225.00	1750.00	5500.00
☐1891	Tillman-Morgan	Red	175.00	225.00	1750.00	5500.00
☐1891	Bruce-Roberts	Red	175.00	225.00	1750.00	5500.00
☐1891	Lyons-Roberts	Red	175.00	225.00	1750.00	5500.00
☐1891	Parker-Burke	Blue	175.00	225.00	1750.00	5500.00
☐1891	Teehee-Burke	Blue	175.00	225.00	1750.00	5500.00

TWENTY DOLLAR NOTES (1882) GOLD CERTIFICATES
(Large Size)

Face Design: Portrait of President Garfield right, TWENTY DOLLARS IN GOLD COIN center.

Back Design: Large "20" left, eagle and arrows center, bright orange color.

SERIES	SIGNATURES	SEAL	A.B.P.	GOOD	V.FINE	UNC.
☐ 1882*	Bruce-Gilfillan	Brown	3550.00	5300.00	18700.00	35000.00
☐ 1882	Bruce-Gilfillan	Brown	2850.00	4300.00	12200.00	35000.00
☐ 1882	Bruce-Wyman	Brown	1550.00	2100.00	12200.00	46500.00
☐ 1882	Rosecrans-Huston	Brown	1850.00	2750.00	12700.00	37500.00
☐ 1882	Lyons-Roberts	Red	160.00	275.00	1300.00	5500.00

*This note has a countersigned signature.

TWENTY DOLLAR NOTES (1905) GOLD CERTIFICATES
(Large Size)

Face Design: Portrait of President Washington center, "XX" left, Treasury Seal right.

Back Design: Eagle and shield center, printed in bright orange color.

SERIES	SIGNATURES	SEAL	A.B.P.	GOOD	V.FINE	UNC.
☐1905	Lyons-Roberts	Red	350.00	450.00	2600.00	9500.00
☐1905	Lyons-Treat	Red	350.00	450.00	2600.00	9500.00
☐1906	Vernon-Treat	Gold	95.00	150.00	400.00	1300.00
☐1906	Vernon-McClung	Gold	95.00	150.00	400.00	1300.00
☐1906	Napier-McClung	Gold	95.00	150.00	400.00	1300.00
☐1906	Napier-Thompson	Gold	110.00	175.00	660.00	2050.00
☐1906	Parker-Burke	Gold	95.00	150.00	400.00	1300.00
☐1906	Tehee-Burke	Gold	95.00	150.00	400.00	1300.00
☐1922	Speelman-White	Gold	95.00	150.00	400.00	1250.00

TWENTY DOLLAR NOTES (1928) GOLD CERTIFICATES
(Small Size)

Face Design: Portrait of President Jackson center, gold seal left, gold serial numbers.

Back Design: The White House, printed green, similar to all Small Size $20 Notes.

SERIES	SIGNATURES	SEAL	A.B.P.	V.FINE	UNC.
☐1928	Woods-Mellon	Gold	45.00	125.00	850.00

TWENTY DOLLAR NOTES (1890) TREASURY NOTES
(Large Size)

Face Design: Portrait of John Marshall, Supreme Court Chief Justice, left, "20" center.

Back Design

SERIES	SIGNATURES	SEAL	A.B.P.	GOOD	V.FINE	UNC.
☐1890	Rosecrans-Huston	Brown	950.00	1250.00	6500.00	18000.00
☐1890	Rosecrans-Nebeker	Brown	950.00	1250.00	6500.00	18000.00
☐1890	Rosecrans-Nebeker	Red	950.00	1250.00	6500.00	18000.00

(Large Size)

Back Design

Face Design: Same as previous note.

SERIES	SIGNATURES	SEAL	A.B.P.	GOOD	V.FINE	UNC.
☐1891	Tillman-Morgan	Red	900.00	1130.00	5400.00	15,500.00
☐1891	Bruce-Roberts	Red	900.00	1130.00	5300.00	15,500.00

TWENTY DOLLAR NOTES (1914)
FEDERAL RESERVE NOTES

(Large Size)
Face Design: Portrait of President Cleveland center, Federal Reserve Seal left, Treasury Seal right.

Back Design: Scenes of transportation. Locomotive left, steamship right.
(Small Size)

SERIES OF 1914, SIGNATURES OF BURKE-McADOO, RED TREASURY SEAL

BANK	A.B.P.	V.FINE	UNC.	BANK	A.B.P.	V.FINE	UNC.
☐ Boston	60.00	600.00	1700.00	☐ Chicago	150.00	750.00	2800.00
☐ New York	60.00	600.00	1700.00	☐ St. Louis	150.00	750.00	2800.00
☐ Philadelphia	60.00	600.00	1700.00	☐ Minneapolis	150.00	750.00	3000.00
☐ Cleveland	60.00	600.00	1700.00	☐ Kansas City	150.00	750.00	2950.00
☐ Richmond	60.00	750.00	2000.00	☐ Dallas	150.00	750.00	2700.00
☐ Atlanta	60.00	950.00	2200.00	☐ San Francisco	150.00	865.00	3000.00

SERIES OF 1914, BLUE TREASURY SEAL AND BLUE SERIAL NUMBERS

(Small Size)

This note was issued with signatures of Burke-McAdoo, Burke-Glass, Burke-Huston, and White-Mellon.

TWENTY DOLLAR NOTES (1914)
FEDERAL RESERVE NOTES
1914, BLUE TREASURY SEAL AND BLUE NUMBERS

DATE	CITY	SIGNATURES	SEAL	A.B.P.	GOOD	V.FINE	UNC.
1914	Boston	Burke-McAdoo	Blue	40.00	55.00	195.00	650.00
1914	Boston	Burke-Glass	Blue	40.00	60.00	725.00	1500.00
1914	Boston	Burke-Huston	Blue	40.00	50.00	165.00	950.00
1914	Boston	White-Mellon	Blue	40.00	50.00	165.00	550.00
1914	New York	Burke-McAdoo	Blue	40.00	50.00	165.00	550.00
1914	New York	Burke-Glass	Blue	40.00	50.00	165.00	550.00
1914	New York	Burke-Huston	Blue	40.00	50.00	165.00	550.00
1914	New York	White-Mellon	Blue	40.00	50.00	165.00	550.00
1914	Phila.	Burke-McAdoo	Blue	40.00	52.00	185.00	600.00
1914	Phila.	Burke-Glass	Blue	40.00	55.00	725.00	1525.00
1914	Phila.	Burke-Huston	Blue	40.00	50.00	165.00	550.00
1914	Phila.	White-Mellon	Blue	40.00	50.00	165.00	550.00
1914	Cleveland	Burke-McAdoo	Blue	40.00	50.00	200.00	650.00

DATE	CITY	SIGNATURES	SEAL	A.B.P.	GOOD	V.FINE	UNC.
1914	Cleveland	Burke-Glass	Blue	40.00	55.00	715.00	1525.00
1914	Cleveland	Burke-Huston	Blue	40.00	50.00	440.00	1400.00
1914	Cleveland	White-Mellon	Blue	40.00	50.00	160.00	550.00
1914	Richmond	Burke-McAdoo	Blue	40.00	60.00	700.00	1570.00
1914	Richmond	Burke-Glass	Blue	40.00	60.00	795.00	1550.00
1914	Richmond	Burke-Huston	Blue	40.00	57.00	265.00	970.00
1914	Richmond	White-Mellon	Blue	40.00	55.00	185.00	520.00
1914	Atlanta	Burke-McAdoo	Blue	40.00	50.00	235.00	850.00
1914	Atlanta	Burke-Glass	Blue	95.00	175.00	1095.00	1650.00
1914	Atlanta	Burke-Huston	Blue	40.00	50.00	185.00	700.00
1914	Atlanta	White-Mellon	Blue	40.00	60.00	715.00	1450.00
1914	Chicago	Burke-McAdoo	Blue	40.00	50.00	140.00	550.00
1914	Chicago	Burke-Glass	Blue	40.00	50.00	140.00	550.00
1914	Chicago	Burke-Huston	Blue	40.00	50.00	140.00	550.00
1914	Chicago	White-Mellon	Blue	40.00	50.00	140.00	550.00
1914	St. Louis	Burke-McAdoo	Blue	40.00	50.00	140.00	550.00
1914	St. Louis	Burke-Glass	Blue	40.00	60.00	715.00	1225.00
1914	St. Louis	Burke-Huston	Blue	40.00	50.00	145.00	550.00
1914	St. Louis	White-Mellon	Blue	40.00	55.00	265.00	550.00
1914	Minneapolis	Burke-McAdoo	Blue	40.00	50.00	160.00	550.00
1914	Minneapolis	Burke-Glass	Blue	49.00	75.00	865.00	1270.00
1914	Minneapolis	Burke-Huston	Blue	40.00	50.00	240.00	550.00
1914	Minneapolis	White-Mellon	Blue	40.00	50.00	145.00	550.00
1914	Kansas City	Burke-McAdoo	Blue	40.00	50.00	265.00	550.00
1914	Kansas City	Burke-Glass	Blue	94.00	175.00	1085.00	1710.00
1914	Kansas City	Burke-Huston	Blue	40.00	50.00	150.00	550.00
1914	Kansas City	White-Mellon	Blue	44.00	60.00	715.00	1525.00
1914	Dallas	Burke-McAdoo	Blue	40.00	50.00	740.00	1500.00
1914	Dallas	Burke-Glass	Blue	40.00	60.00	715.00	1600.00
1914	Dallas	Burke-Huston	Blue	40.00	50.00	545.00	650.00
1914	Dallas	White-Mellon	Blue	40.00	50.00	165.00	550.00
1914	San Fran.	Burke-McAdoo	Blue	40.00	50.00	445.00	550.00
1914	San Fran.	Burke-Glass	Blue	40.00	50.00	465.00	550.00
1914	San Fran.	Burke-Huston	Blue	40.00	50.00	265.00	550.00
1914	San Fran.	White-Mellon	Blue	40.00	50.00	145.00	550.00

TWENTY DOLLAR NOTES (1928)
FEDERAL RESERVE NOTES
(Small Size)

Face Design: Portrait of President Jackson center, black Federal Reserve Seal with numeral for district in center. City of issuing bank in Seal circle. Green Treasury Seal right.

Back Design: Picture of the White House, similar to all Small Size $20 Notes.
(Small Size)

SERIES OF 1928, SIGNATURES OF TATE-MELLON, GREEN SEAL

BANK	A.B.P.	V.FINE	UNC.	★UNC.	BANK	A.B.P.	V.FINE	UNC.	★UNC.
☐ Boston	32.00	55.00	280.00	2200.00	☐ Chicago	32.00	46.00	230.00	1800.00
☐ New York	32.00	45.00	255.00	1500.00	☐ St. Louis	32.00	55.00	255.00	2200.00
☐ Philadelphia	32.00	55.00	355.00	2000.00	☐ Minneapolis	32.00	55.00	405.00	2200.00
☐ Cleveland	32.00	75.00	330.00	1800.00	☐ Kansas City	32.00	65.00	255.00	1800.00
☐ Richmond	32.00	75.00	355.00	3000.00	☐ Dallas	32.00	65.00	405.00	7500.00
☐ Atlanta	32.00	65.00	405.00	3000.00	☐ San Francisco	32.00	65.00	355.00	2000.00

(Small Size)

SERIES OF 1928A, SIGNATURES OF WOODS-MELLON, GREEN SEAL

CITY	A.B.P.	V.FINE	UNC.	★UNC.	CITY	A.B.P.	V.FINE	UNC.	★UNC.
☐ Boston	33.00	65.00	400.00	4250.00	☐ Chicago	33.00	65.00	250.00	4250.00
☐ New York	33.00	65.00	300.00	4250.00	☐ St. Louis	33.00	75.00	450.00	4250.00
☐ Philadelphia	33.00	70.00	300.00	4250.00	☐ Minneapolis			NOT ISSUED	
☐ Cleveland	33.00	75.00	300.00	4250.00	☐ Kansas City	45.00	85.00	800.00	4250.00
☐ Richmond	25.00	55.00	300.00	4250.00	☐ Dallas	25.00	65.00	300.00	4250.00
☐ Atlanta	33.00	65.00	300.00	4250.00	☐ San Francisco			NOT ISSUED	

TWENTY DOLLAR NOTES (1928)
FEDERAL RESERVE NOTES

(Small Size)

SERIES OF 1928B,
SIGNATURES OF WOODS-MELLON, GREEN SEAL
The face and back design are similar to previous note. Numeral in Federal Reserve Seal is now changed to a letter.

BANK	A.B.P.	V.FINE	UNC.	★UNC.	BANK	A.B.P.	V.FINE	UNC.	★UNC.
☐ Boston	24.00	42.00	225.00	1000.00	☐ Chicago	22.00	37.00	225.00	1000.00
☐ New York	24.00	42.00	225.00	1000.00	☐ St. Louis	22.00	52.00	225.00	1000.00
☐ Philadelphia	24.00	42.00	225.00	1000.00	☐ Minneapolis	22.00	52.00	225.00	1500.00
☐ Cleveland	24.00	32.00	225.00	1000.00	☐ Kansas City	22.00	37.00	225.00	1000.00
☐ Richmond	24.00	37.00	225.00	1000.00	☐ Dallas	22.00	67.00	225.00	1000.00
☐ Atlanta	24.00	22.00	225.00	1000.00	☐ San Francisco	22.00	37.00	225.00	1000.00

SERIES OF 1928C, SIGNATURES OF WOODS-MILLS, GREEN SEAL
Only two banks issued this note.

BANK	A.B.P.	V.FINE	UNC.	★UNC.	BANK	A.B.P.	V.FINE	UNC.	★UNC.
☐ Chicago	100.00	700.00	2000.00	NONE	☐ San Francisco	100.00	1000.00	4500.00	NONE

TWENTY DOLLAR NOTES (1934)
FEDERAL RESERVE NOTES

(Small Size)
SIGNATURES OF JULIAN-MORGENTHAU, GREEN SEAL
Face and back design are similar to previous note. "Redeemable in Gold" removed from obligation over Federal Reserve Seal.

BANK	A.B.P.	V.FINE	UNC.	★UNC.	BANK	A.B.P.	V.FINE	UNC.	★UNC.
☐ Boston	22.00	25.00	100.00	600.00	☐ St. Louis	22.00	25.00	80.00	600.00
☐ New York	22.00	25.00	100.00	600.00	☐ Minneapolis	22.00	25.00	115.00	600.00
☐ Philadelphia	22.00	25.00	100.00	600.00	☐ Kansas City	22.00	25.00	100.00	600.00
☐ Cleveland	22.00	25.00	100.00	600.00	☐ Dallas	22.00	25.00	105.00	600.00
☐ Richmond	22.00	25.00	105.00	600.00	☐ San Francisco	22.00	25.00	85.00	600.00
☐ Atlanta	22.00	25.00	105.00	600.00	☐ San Francisco*				
☐ Chicago	22.00	25.00	100.00	600.00	(HAWAII)		37.00	150.00	2500.0012000.00

* The San Francisco Federal Reserve Note with brown seal and brown serial numbers, and overprinted HAWAII on face and back, was a special issue for the armed forces in the Pacific area during World War II.

TWENTY DOLLAR NOTES (1934A)
FEDERAL RESERVE NOTES

(Small Size)

SERIES OF 1934A, SIGNATURES OF JULIAN-MORGENTHAU

BANK	A.B.P.	V.FINE	UNC.	★UNC.	BANK	A.B.P.	V.FINE	UNC.	★UNC.
☐ Boston	22.00	28.00	70.00	500.00	☐ St. Louis	22.00	33.00	70.00	500.00
☐ New York	22.00	28.00	80.00	500.00	☐ Minneapolis	31.00	48.00	115.00	500.00
☐ Philadelphia	22.00	28.00	80.00	500.00	☐ Kansas City	22.00	35.00	80.00	500.00
☐ Cleveland	22.00	28.00	75.00	500.00	☐ Dallas	22.00	35.00	80.00	500.00
☐ Richmond	22.00	28.00	95.00	500.00	☐ San Francisco	22.00	30.00	80.00	500.00
☐ Atlanta	22.00	28.00	75.00	500.00	☐ San Francisco*				
☐ Chicago	22.00	28.00	90.00	500.00	(HAWAII)	28.00	75.00	1250.00	10000.00

* The San Francisco Federal Reserve Note with brown seal and brown serial numbers, and overprinted HAWAII on face and back, was a special issue for the armed forces in the Pacific area during World War II.

(Small Size)

SERIES OF 1934B,
SIGNATURES OF JULIAN-VINSON, GREEN SEAL

BANK	A.B.P.	V.FINE	UNC.	★UNC.	BANK	A.B.P.	V.FINE	UNC.	★UNC.
☐ Boston	21.00	28.00	115.00	950.00	☐ Chicago	21.00	28.00	115.00	950.00
☐ New York	21.00	28.00	115.00	950.00	☐ St. Louis	21.00	28.00	115.00	950.00
☐ Philadelphia	21.00	28.00	115.00	950.00	☐ Minneapolis	21.00	28.00	115.00	950.00
☐ Cleveland	21.00	28.00	115.00	950.00	☐ Kansas City	21.00	28.00	115.00	950.00
☐ Richmond	21.00	28.00	115.00	950.00	☐ Dallas	21.00	28.00	115.00	950.00
☐ Atlanta	21.00	28.00	115.00	950.00	☐ San Francisco	21.00	28.00	115.00	950.00

SERIES OF 1934C,
SIGNATURES OF JULIAN-SNYDER, GREEN SEAL

Back Design: This has been modified with this series, with or without balcony added to the White House.

BANK	A.B.P.	V.FINE	UNC.	★UNC.	BANK	A.B.P.	V.FINE	UNC.	★UNC.
☐ Boston	22.00	27.00	110.00	600.00	☐ Chicago	22.00	28.00	110.00	600.00
☐ New York	22.00	27.00	110.00	600.00	☐ St. Louis	22.00	28.00	110.00	600.00
☐ Philadelphia	22.00	27.00	110.00	600.00	☐ Minneapolis	22.00	28.00	110.00	600.00
☐ Cleveland	22.00	27.00	110.00	600.00	☐ Kansas City	22.00	28.00	110.00	600.00
☐ Richmond	22.00	27.00	110.00	600.00	☐ Dallas	22.00	28.00	110.00	600.00
☐ Atlanta	22.00	27.00	110.00	600.00	☐ San Francisco	22.00	28.00	110.00	600.00

SERIES OF 1934D,
SIGNATURES OF CLARK-SNYDER, GREEN SEAL

BANK	A.B.P.	V.FINE	UNC.	★UNC.	BANK	A.B.P.	V.FINE	UNC.	★UNC.
☐ Boston	22.00	27.00	75.00	800.00	☐ Chicago	22.00	28.00	75.00	800.00
☐ New York	22.00	27.00	75.00	800.00	☐ St. Louis	22.00	28.00	75.00	800.00
☐ Philadelphia	22.00	27.00	75.00	800.00	☐ Minneapolis	22.00	28.00	75.00	800.00
☐ Cleveland	22.00	27.00	75.00	800.00	☐ Kansas City	22.00	28.00	75.00	800.00
☐ Richmond	22.00	27.00	75.00	800.00	☐ Dallas	22.00	28.00	75.00	800.00
☐ Atlanta	22.00	27.00	75.00	800.00	☐ San Francisco	22.00	28.00	75.00	800.00

TWENTY DOLLAR NOTES (1950)
FEDERAL RESERVE NOTES

(Small Size)

SERIES OF 1950,
SIGNATURES OF CLARK-SNYDER, GREEN SEAL

The black Federal Seal and green Treasury Seal are slightly smaller.

BANK	A.B.P.	V.FINE	UNC.	★UNC.	BANK	A.B.P.	V.FINE	UNC.	★UNC.
☐ Boston	22.00	28.00	115.00	500.00	☐ Chicago	22.00	28.00	115.00	500.00
☐ New York	22.00	28.00	115.00	500.00	☐ St. Louis	22.00	28.00	115.00	500.00
☐ Philadelphia	22.00	28.00	115.00	500.00	☐ Minneapolis	22.00	28.00	115.00	500.00
☐ Cleveland	22.00	28.00	115.00	500.00	☐ Kansas City	22.00	28.00	115.00	500.00

BANK	A.B.P.	V.FINE	UNC.	★UNC.	BANK	A.B.P.	V.FINE	UNC.	★UNC.
☐ Richmond	22.00	27.00	120.00	500.00	☐ Dallas		26.00	28.00	115.00	500.00
☐ Atlanta	22.00	27.00	120.00	500.00	☐ San Francisco	26.00	28.00	115.00	500.00

SERIES OF 1950A, SIGNATURES OF PRIEST-HUMPHERY, GREEN SEAL

BANK	A.B.P.	V.FINE	UNC.	★UNC.	BANK	A.B.P.	V.FINE	UNC.	★UNC.
☐ Boston	21.00	24.00	95.00	350.00	☐ Chicago	21.00	24.00	95.00	350.00
☐ New York	21.00	24.00	95.00	350.00	☐ St. Louis	21.00	24.00	95.00	350.00
☐ Philadelphia	21.00	24.00	95.00	350.00	☐ Minneapolis	21.00	26.00	95.00	350.00
☐ Cleveland	21.00	24.00	95.00	350.00	☐ Kansas City	21.00	23.00	95.00	350.00
☐ Richmond	21.00	24.00	95.00	350.00	☐ Dallas	21.00	23.00	95.00	350.00
☐ Atlanta	21.00	24.00	95.00	350.00	☐ San Francisco	21.00	23.00	95.00	350.00

SERIES OF 1950B, SIGNATURES OF PRIEST-ANDERSON, GREEN SEAL

BANK	A.B.P.	V.FINE	UNC.	★UNC.	BANK	A.B.P.	V.FINE	UNC.	★UNC.
☐ Boston	21.00	24.00	65.00	300.00	☐ Chicago	21.00	24.00	65.00	300.00
☐ New York	21.00	24.00	65.00	300.00	☐ St. Louis	21.00	24.00	65.00	300.00
☐ Philadelphia	21.00	24.00	65.00	300.00	☐ Minneapolis	21.00	24.00	65.00	300.00
☐ Cleveland	21.00	24.00	65.00	300.00	☐ Kansas City	21.00	24.00	65.00	300.00
☐ Richmond	21.00	24.00	65.00	300.00	☐ Dallas	21.00	24.00	65.00	300.00
☐ Atlanta	21.00	24.00	65.00	300.00	☐ San Francisco	21.00	24.00	65.00	300.00

SERIES OF 1950C, SIGNATURES OF SMITH-DILLON, GREEN SEAL

BANK	A.B.P.	V.FINE	UNC.	★UNC.	BANK	A.B.P.	V.FINE	UNC.	★UNC.
☐ Boston	21.00	23.00	75.00	400.00	☐ Chicago	21.00	23.00	75.00	400.00
☐ New York	21.00	23.00	75.00	400.00	☐ St. Louis	21.00	23.00	75.00	400.00
☐ Philadelphia	21.00	23.00	75.00	400.00	☐ Minneapolis	21.00	23.00	75.00	400.00
☐ Cleveland	21.00	23.00	75.00	400.00	☐ Kansas City	21.00	23.00	75.00	400.00
☐ Richmond	21.00	23.00	75.00	400.00	☐ Dallas	21.00	23.00	75.00	400.00
☐ Atlanta	21.00	23.00	75.00	400.00	☐ San Francisco	21.00	23.00	75.00	400.00

SERIES OF 1950D, SIGNATURES OF GRANAHAN-DILLON, GREEN SEAL

BANK	A.B.P.	V.FINE	UNC.	★UNC.	BANK	A.B.P.	V.FINE	UNC.	★UNC.
☐ Boston	21.00	23.00	75.00	375.00	☐ Chicago	21.00	23.00	75.00	375.00
☐ New York	21.00	23.00	75.00	375.00	☐ St. Louis	21.00	23.00	75.00	375.00
☐ Philadelphia	21.00	23.00	75.00	375.00	☐ Minneapolis	21.00	23.00	75.00	375.00
☐ Cleveland	21.00	23.00	75.00	375.00	☐ Kansas City	21.00	23.00	75.00	375.00
☐ Richmond	21.00	23.00	75.00	375.00	☐ Dallas	21.00	23.00	75.00	375.00
☐ Atlanta	21.00	23.00	75.00	375.00	☐ San Francisco	21.00	22.00	75.00	375.00

SERIES OF 1950E, SIGNATURES OF GRANAHAN-FOWLER, GREEN SEAL

BANK	A.B.P.	V.FINE	UNC.	★UNC.	BANK	A.B.P.	V.FINE	UNC.	★UNC.
☐ Boston	21.00	24.00	90.00	750.00	☐ Chicago	21.00	24.00	90.00	750.00
					☐ San Francisco	21.00	24.00	90.00	750.00

TWENTY DOLLAR NOTES (1963)
FEDERAL RESERVE NOTES
SERIES OF 1963, SIGNATURES OF GRANAHAN-FOWLER, GREEN SEAL

BANK	A.B.P.	V.FINE	UNC.	★UNC.	BANK	A.B.P.	V.FINE	UNC.	★UNC.
☐ Boston	21.00	24.00	70.00	150.00	☐ Chicago	21.00	24.00	70.00	150.00
☐ New York	21.00	24.00	70.00	150.00	☐ St. Louis	21.00	24.00	70.00	150.00
☐ Cleveland	21.00	24.00	70.00	150.00	☐ Kansas City	21.00	24.00	70.00	150.00
☐ Richmond	21.00	24.00	70.00	150.00	☐ Dallas	21.00	24.00	70.00	150.00
☐ Atlanta	21.00	24.00	70.00	150.00	☐ San Francisco	21.00	24.00	70.00	150.00

SERIES OF 1963A, SIGNATURES OF GRANAHAN-FOWLER, GREEN SEAL

BANK	A.B.P.	V.FINE	UNC.	★UNC.	BANK	A.B.P.	V.FINE	UNC.	★UNC.
☐ Boston	21.00	23.00	70.00	125.00	☐ Chicago	21.00	23.00	70.00	125.00
☐ New York	21.00	23.00	70.00	125.00	☐ St. Louis	21.00	23.00	70.00	125.00
☐ Philadelphia	21.00	23.00	70.00	125.00	☐ Minneapolis	21.00	23.00	70.00	125.00
☐ Cleveland	21.00	23.00	70.00	125.00	☐ Kansas City	21.00	23.00	70.00	125.00
☐ Richmond	21.00	23.00	70.00	125.00	☐ Dallas	21.00	23.00	70.00	125.00
☐ Atlanta	21.00	23.00	70.00	125.00	☐ San Francisco	21.00	23.00	70.00	125.00

TWENTY DOLLAR NOTES (1969)
FEDERAL RESERVE NOTES
SERIES OF 1969, SIGNATURES OF ELSTON-KENNEDY, GREEN SEAL

BANK	A.B.P.	V.FINE	UNC.	★UNC.	BANK	A.B.P.	V.FINE	UNC.	★UNC.
☐ Boston	—	22.00	50.00	100.00	☐ Chicago	—	22.00	50.00	100.00
☐ New York	—	22.00	50.00	100.00	☐ St. Louis	—	22.00	50.00	100.00
☐ Philadelphia	—	22.00	50.00	100.00	☐ Minneapolis	—	22.00	50.00	100.00
☐ Cleveland	—	22.00	50.00	100.00	☐ Kansas City	—	22.00	50.00	100.00
☐ Richmond	—	22.00	50.00	100.00	☐ Dallas	—	22.00	50.00	100.00
☐ Atlanta	—	22.00	50.00	100.00	☐ San Francisco	—	22.00	50.00	100.00

SERIES OF 1969A, SIGNATURES OF KABIS-CONNALLY, GREEN SEAL

BANK	A.B.P.	V.FINE	UNC.	★UNC.	BANK	A.B.P.	V.FINE	UNC.	★UNC.
☐ Boston	—	22.00	55.00	110.00	☐ Chicago	—	22.00	55.00	110.00
☐ New York	—	22.00	55.00	110.00	☐ St. Louis	—	22.00	55.00	110.00
☐ Philadelphia	—	22.00	55.00	110.00	☐ Minneapolis	—	22.00	55.00	110.00
☐ Cleveland	—	22.00	55.00	110.00	☐ Kansas City	—	22.00	55.00	110.00
☐ Richmond	—	22.00	55.00	110.00	☐ Dallas	—	22.00	55.00	110.00
☐ Atlanta	—	22.00	55.00	110.00	☐ San Francisco	—	22.00	55.00	110.00

SERIES OF 1969B, SIGNATURES OF BANUELOS-CONNALLY, GREEN SEAL

BANK	A.B.P.	V.FINE	UNC.	★UNC.	BANK	A.B.P.	V.FINE	UNC.	★UNC.
☐ New York	—	22.00	140.00	500.00	☐ Chicago	—	22.00	165.00	500.00
☐ Cleveland	—	22.00	165.00	—	☐ St. Louis	—	22.00	165.00	—
☐ Richmond	—	22.00	165.00	—	☐ Minneapolis	—	22.00	240.00	—
☐ Atlanta	—	22.00	165.00	500.00	☐ Kansas City	—	22.00	240.00	500.00
					☐ Dallas	—	22.00	190.00	—
					☐ San Francisco	—	22.00	165.00	500.00

SERIES of 1969C, SIGNATURES OF BANUELOS-SHULTZ, GREEN SEAL

BANK	A.B.P.	V.FINE	UNC.	★UNC.	BANK	A.B.P.	V.FINE	UNC.	★UNC.
☐ Boston	—	22.00	70.00	150.00	☐ Chicago	—	22.00	70.00	150.00
☐ New York	—	22.00	70.00	150.00	☐ St. Louis	—	22.00	70.00	150.00
☐ Philadelphia	—	22.00	70.00	150.00	☐ Minneapolis	—	22.00	70.00	150.00
☐ Cleveland	—	22.00	70.00	150.00	☐ Kansas City	—	22.00	70.00	150.00
☐ Richmond	—	22.00	70.00	150.00	☐ Dallas	—	22.00	70.00	150.00
☐ Atlanta	—	22.00	70.00	150.00	☐ San Francisco	—	22.00	70.00	150.00

TWENTY DOLLAR NOTES (1974)
FEDERAL RESERVE NOTES
SERIES OF 1974, SIGNATURES OF NEFF-SIMON, GREEN SEAL

BANK	A.B.P.	V.FINE	UNC.	★UNC.	BANK	A.B.P.	V.FINE	UNC.	★UNC.
☐ Boston	—	22.00	55.00	125.00	☐ Chicago	—	22.00	60.00	125.00
☐ New York	—	22.00	55.00	125.00	☐ St. Louis	—	22.00	55.00	125.00
☐ Philadelphia	—	22.00	55.00	125.00	☐ Minneapolis	—	25.00	55.00	125.00
☐ Cleveland	—	22.00	55.00	125.00	☐ Kansas City	—	25.00	55.00	125.00
☐ Richmond	—	22.00	55.00	125.00	☐ Dallas	—	25.00	55.00	125.00
☐ Atlanta	—	22.00	55.00	125.00	☐ San Francisco	—	22.00	55.00	125.00

TWENTY DOLLAR NOTES (1977)
FEDERAL RESERVE NOTES
SERIES OF 1977, SIGNATURES OF MORTON-BLUMENTHAL, GREEN SEAL

BANK	A.B.P.	V.FINE	UNC.	★UNC.	BANK	A.B.P.	V.FINE	UNC.	★UNC.
☐ Boston	—	22.00	50.00	90.00	☐ Chicago	—	22.00	50.00	90.00
☐ New York	—	22.00	50.00	90.00	☐ St. Louis	—	22.00	50.00	90.00
☐ Philadelphia	—	22.00	50.00	90.00	☐ Minneapolis	—	25.00	50.00	90.00
☐ Cleveland	—	22.00	50.00	90.00	☐ Kansas City	—	25.00	50.00	90.00
☐ Richmond	—	25.00	50.00	90.00	☐ Dallas	—	25.00	50.00	90.00
☐ Atlanta	—	25.00	50.00	90.00	☐ San Francisco	—	22.00	50.00	90.00

TWENTY DOLLAR NOTES (1981)
FEDERAL RESERVE NOTES
SERIES OF 1981, SIGNATURES OF BUCHANAN-REGAN, GREEN SEAL

BANK	A.B.P.	V.FINE	UNC.	★UNC.	BANK	A.B.P.	V.FINE	UNC.	★UNC.
☐ Boston	—	21.00	75.00	140.00	☐ Chicago	—	21.00	75.00	140.00
☐ New York	—	21.00	75.00	140.00	☐ St. Louis	—	21.00	75.00	140.00
☐ Philadelphia	—	21.00	75.00	140.00	☐ Minneapolis	—	22.00	75.00	140.00
☐ Cleveland	—	21.00	75.00	140.00	☐ Kansas City	—	22.00	75.00	140.00
☐ Richmond	—	21.00	75.00	140.00	☐ Dallas	—	22.00	75.00	140.00
☐ Atlanta	—	21.00	75.00	140.00	☐ San Francisco	—	21.00	75.00	140.00

SERIES OF 1981A, SIGNATURES OF ORTEGA-REGAN, GREEN SEAL
★Notes not issued for all banks

BANK	A.B.P.	V.FINE	UNC.	★UNC.	BANK	A.B.P.	V.FINE	UNC.	★UNC.
☐ Boston	—	21.00	65.00	—	☐ Chicago	—	21.00	65.00	—
☐ New York	—	21.00	65.00	—	☐ St. Louis	—	21.00	65.00	—
☐ Philadelphia	—	21.00	65.00	—	☐ Minneapolis	—	22.00	65.00	—
☐ Cleveland	—	21.00	65.00	190.00	☐ Kansas City	—	22.00	65.00	—
☐ Richmond	—	21.00	65.00	—	☐ Dallas	—	22.00	65.00	—
☐ Atlanta	—	21.00	65.00	190.00	☐ San Francisco	—	21.00	65.00	200.00

TWENTY DOLLAR NOTES (1985)
FEDERAL RESERVE NOTES
SERIES OF 1985, SIGNATURES OF ORTEGA-BAKER, GREEN SEAL
★Notes not issued for all banks

BANK	A.B.P.	V.FINE	UNC.	★UNC.	BANK	A.B.P.	V.FINE	UNC.	★UNC.
☐ Boston	—	21.00	50.00	65.00	☐ Chicago	—	21.00	50.00	65.00
☐ New York	—	21.00	50.00	65.00	☐ St. Louis	—	21.00	50.00	—
☐ Philadelphia	—	21.00	50.00	65.00	☐ Minneapolis	—	21.00	50.00	—
☐ Cleveland	—	21.00	50.00	65.00	☐ Kansas City	—	21.00	50.00	65.00
☐ Richmond	—	21.00	50.00	65.00	☐ Dallas	—	21.00	50.00	65.00
☐ Atlanta	—	21.00	50.00	—	☐ San Francisco	—	21.00	50.00	65.00

TWENTY DOLLAR NOTES (1988)
FEDERAL RESERVE NOTES
SERIES OF 1988A, SIGNATURES OF VILLALPANDO-BRADY, GREEN SEAL

★Notes not issued for all banks

BANK	A.B.P.	V.FINE	UNC.	★UNC.	BANK	A.B.P.	V.FINE	UNC.	★UNC.
☐ Boston	—	21.00	40.00	—	☐ Chicago	—	21.00	40.00	100.00
☐ New York	—	21.00	40.00	100.00	☐ St. Louis	—	21.00	40.00	—
☐ Philadelphia	—	21.00	40.00	100.00	☐ Minneapolis	—	21.00	40.00	—
☐ Cleveland	—	21.00	40.00	—	☐ Kansas City	—	21.00	40.00	—
☐ Richmond	—	21.00	40.00	—	☐ Dallas	—	21.00	40.00	100.00
☐ Atlanta	—	21.00	40.00	100.00	☐ San Francisco	—	21.00	40.00	—

TWENTY DOLLAR NOTES (1990)
FEDERAL RESERVE NOTES
SERIES OF 1990, SIGNATURES OF VILLALPANDO-BRADY, GREEN SEAL

★Notes not issued for all banks

BANK	A.B.P.	V.FINE	UNC.	★UNC.	BANK	A.B.P.	V.FINE	UNC.	★UNC.
☐ Boston	—	21.00	45.00	75.00	☐ Chicago	—	21.00	30.00	75.00
☐ New York	—	21.00	45.00	75.00	☐ St. Louis	—	21.00	30.00	75.00
☐ Philadelphia	—	21.00	45.00	—	☐ Minneapolis	—	21.00	30.00	75.00
☐ Cleveland	—	21.00	45.00	75.00	☐ Kansas City	—	21.00	30.00	—
☐ Richmond	—	21.00	45.00	75.00	☐ Dallas	—	21.00	30.00	—
☐ Atlanta	—	21.00	45.00	75.00	☐ San Francisco	—	21.00	30.00	—

TWENTY DOLLAR NOTES (1993)
FEDERAL RESERVE NOTES
SERIES OF 1993, SIGNATURES OF WITHROW-BENTSEN, GREEN SEAL

★Notes are not issued for all banks

BANK	A.B.P.	V.FINE	UNC.	★UNC.	BANK	A.B.P.	V.FINE	UNC.	★UNC.
☐ Boston	—	21.00	40.00	60.00	☐ Chicago	—	21.00	35.00	—
☐ New York	—	21.00	40.00	60.00	☐ St. Louis	—	21.00	35.00	—
☐ Philadelphia	—	21.00	40.00	—	☐ Kansas City	—	21.00	35.00	—
☐ Cleveland	—	21.00	40.00	60.00	☐ Dallas	—	21.00	35.00	—
☐ Richmond	—	21.00	40.00	60.00	☐ San Francisco	—	21.00	35.00	60.00
☐ Atlanta	—	21.00	40.00	60.00					

TWENTY DOLLAR NOTES (1995)
FEDERAL RESERVE NOTES
SERIES OF 1995, SIGNATURES OF WITHROW-RUBIN, GREEN SEAL
★Notes not issued for all banks

BANK	A.B.P.	V.FINE	UNC.	★UNC.	BANK	A.B.P.	V.FINE	UNC.	★UNC.
☐ Boston	—	22.00	39.00	42.00	☐ Chicago	—	22.00	39.00	47.00
☐ New York	—	22.00	39.00	42.00	☐ St. Louis	—	22.00	39.00	47.00
☐ Philadelphia	—	22.00	39.00	42.00	☐ Minneapolis	—	22.00	41.00	47.00
☐ Cleveland	—	22.00	41.00	42.00	☐ Kansas City	—	22.00	41.00	47.00
☐ Richmond	—	22.00	39.00	42.00	☐ Dallas	—	22.00	39.00	47.00
☐ Atlanta	—	22.00	39.00	42.00	☐ San Francisco	—	22.00	39.00	47.00

TWENTY DOLLAR NOTES (1915–1918)
FEDERAL RESERVE BANK NOTES
(ALL HAVE BLUE SEALS)

(Large Size)

Face Design:
Portrait of
President
Cleveland left,
name of bank
and city center,
blue seal right.

Back Design:
Locomotive
and steamship,
similar to
1914 note.

BANK	SERIES	GOV'T SIGNATURES	BANK SIGNATURES	A.B.P.	GOOD	V.FINE	UNC.
☐Atlanta	1915	Teehee-Burke	Bell-Wellborn	610.00	925.00	2950.00	11850.00
	1915	Teehee-Burke	Pike-McCord	810.00	1125.00	2950.00	11850.00
☐Atlanta	1918	Elliott-Burke	Bell-Wellborn	450.00	625.00	2850.00	8500.00
☐Chicago	1915	Teehee-Burke	McLallen-McDougal	450.00	625.00	2550.00	8500.00
☐St. Louis	1918	Teehee-Burke	Attebery-Wells	450.00	625.00	2550.00	8500.00

BANK	SERIES	GOV'T SIGNATURES	BANK SIGNATURES	A.B.P.	GOOD	V.FINE	UNC.
☐ Kansas City	1915	Teehee-Burke	Anderson-Miller				
				400.00	585.00	2600.00	7000.00
☐ Kansas City	1915	Teehee-Burke	Cross-Miller				
				450.00	585.00	2575.00	7000.00
☐ Dallas	1915	Teehee-Burke	Hoopes-Van Zandt				
				450.00	585.00	2700.00	7000.00
☐ Dallas	1915	Teehee-Burke	Gilbert-Van Zandt				
				470.00	835.00	4625.00	10100.00
☐ Dallas	1915	Teehee-Burke	Talley-Van Zandt				
				470.00	835.00	4500.00	10300.00

TWENTY DOLLAR NOTES (1929)
FEDERAL RESERVE BANK NOTES
(Small Size)

Face Design:
Portrait of
President
Jackson center,
name of bank
and city left,
blue seal right.

Back Design: The White House.

BANK	A.B.P.	V.FINE	UNC.	★UNC.	BANK	A.B.P.	V.FINE	UNC.	★UNC.
☐ Boston	25.00	100.00	340.00	4000.00	☐ Chicago	23.00	100.00	220.00	3500.00
☐ New York	25.00	100.00	300.00	3200.00	☐ St. Louis	23.00	100.00	295.00	3500.00
☐ Philadelphia	25.00	100.00	305.00	3500.00	☐ Minneapolis	23.00	100.00	270.00	3800.00
☐ Cleveland	25.00	100.00	305.00	4000.00	☐ Kansas City	23.00	100.00	1000.00	3800.00
☐ Richmond	25.00	100.00	450.00	3500.00	☐ Dallas	23.00	215.00	1500.00	5000.00
☐ Atlanta	25.00	100.00	630.00	4000.00	☐ San Francisco	29.00	80.00	1000.00	5000.00

FIFTY DOLLAR NOTES

ORDER OF ISSUE

FIFTY DOLLAR NOTES (1862–1863)
UNITED STATES NOTES
(ALSO KNOWN AS LEGAL TENDER NOTES)
(Large Size)

Face Design: Portrait of Hamilton to left.

Back Design

SERIES	SIGNATURES	SEAL	A.B.P.	GOOD	V.FINE	UNC.
☐1862	Chittenden-Spinner*	Red	3150.00	4100.00	13000.00	140,000.00
☐1862	Chittenden-Spinner**	Red	3150.00	4100.00	13000.00	140,000.00
☐1863	Chittenden-Spinner**	Red	3150.00	4100.00	13000.00	140,000.00

*First Obligation: Similar to 1862 $5 note.
**Second Obligation: Shown above.

FIFTY DOLLAR NOTES (1869) UNITED STATES NOTES
(ALSO KNOWN AS LEGAL TENDER NOTES)
(Large Size)

Face Design: Portrait of Henry Clay to right.

Back Design

SERIES	SIGNATURES	SEAL	A.B.P.	GOOD	V.FINE	UNC.
☐1869	Allison-Spinner	Red	4500.00	5600.00	27500.00	72000.00

Only twenty-four pieces of this note remain unredeemed.

FIFTY DOLLAR NOTES (1874–1880)
UNITED STATES NOTES
(Large Size)

Face Design: Franklin to left.

Back Design

SERIES	SIGNATURES	SEAL	A.B.P.	GOOD	V.FINE	UNC.
☐1874	Allison-Spinner	Sm. Red	1500.00	1900.00	6500.00	31000.00
☐1875	Allison-Wyman	Sm. Red	12000.00	17500.00	76500.00	RARE
☐1878	Allison-Gilfillan	Sm. Red	1500.00	1950.00	7500.00	39500.00
☐1880	Bruce-Gilfillan	Lg. Brown	1100.00	1650.00	6000.00	28000.00
☐1880	Bruce-Wyman	Lg. Brown	2000.00	2600.00	6000.00	15500.00
☐1880	Rosecrans-Jordan	Lg. Red	2000.00	2600.00	11000.00	29500.00
☐1880	Rosecrans-Hyatt	Red Plain	VERY RARE 65,000.00			
☐1880	Rosecrans-Hyatt	Red Spike	1600.00	2200.00	7400.00	48000.00
☐1880	Rosecrans-Huston	Lg. Red	20000.00	300.00	13000.00	38000.00
☐1880	Rosecrans-Huston	Lg. Brown	1250.00	1750.00	6000.00	15000.00
☐1880	Tillman-Morgan	Sm. Red	1650.00	2200.00	6200.00	18000.00
☐1880	Bruce-Roberts	Sm. Red	5050.00	8000.00	28000.00	73000.00
☐1880	Lyons-Roberts	Sm. Red	1150.00	1500.00	4500.00	15000.00

FIFTY DOLLAR NOTES (1875) NATIONAL BANK NOTES
FIRST CHARTER PERIOD (Large Size)

Face Design: Washington crossing Delaware left, Washington at Valley Forge, right.

Back Design: Embarkation of the Pilgrims.

SERIES	SIGNATURES	SEAL	A.B.P.	GOOD	V.FINE	UNC.
☐ Original	Chittenden-Spinner	Red w/r	2000.00	2500.00	7500.00	27500.00
☐ Original	Colby-Spinner	Red w/r	2000.00	2500.00	7500.00	27500.00
☐ Original	Allison-Spinner	Red w/r	2000.00	2500.00	7500.00	27500.00
☐ 1875	Allison-New	Red w/s	2000.00	2500.00	7500.00	27500.00
☐ 1875	Allison-Wyman	Red w/s	2000.00	2500.00	7500.00	27500.00
☐ 1875	Allison-Gilfillan	Red w/s	2000.00	2500.00	7500.00	27500.00
☐ 1875	Scofield-Gilfillan	Red w/s	2000.00	2500.00	7500.00	27500.00
☐ 1875	Bruce-Gilfillan	Red w/s	2000.00	2500.00	7500.00	27500.00
☐ 1875	Bruce-Wyman	Red w/s	2000.00	2500.00	7500.00	27500.00
☐ 1875	Rosecrans-Huston	Red w/s	2000.00	2500.00	7500.00	27500.00
☐ 1875	Rosecrans-Nebeker	Red w/s	2000.00	2500.00	7500.00	27500.00
☐ 1875	Tillman-Morgan	Red w/s	2000.00	2500.00	7500.00	27500.00

FIFTY DOLLAR NOTES (1882) NATIONAL BANK NOTES
SECOND CHARTER PERIOD (Large Size)

First Issue (Brown seal and brown back)
Back Design
Face Design: Similar to First Charter Period note.

SERIES	SIGNATURES	SEAL	A.B.P.	GOOD	V.FINE	UNC.
☐1882	Bruce-Gilfillan	Brown	675.00	800.00	4500.00	12500.00
☐1882	Bruce-Wyman	Brown	675.00	800.00	4500.00	12500.00
☐1882	Bruce-Jordan	Brown	675.00	800.00	4500.00	12500.00
☐1882	Rosecrans-Jordan	Brown	675.00	800.00	4500.00	12500.00
☐1882	Rosecrans-Hyatt	Brown	675.00	800.00	4500.00	12500.00
☐1882	Rosecrans-Huston	Brown	675.00	800.00	4500.00	12500.00
☐1882	Rosecrans-Nebeker	Brown	675.00	800.00	4500.00	12500.00
☐1882	Rosecrans-Morgan	Brown	700.00	1100.00	5050.00	13500.00
☐1882	Tillman-Morgan	Brown	600.00	850.00	4500.00	12500.00
☐1882	Tillman-Roberts	Brown	600.00	850.00	4500.00	12500.00
☐1882	Bruce-Roberts	Brown	600.00	850.00	4500.00	12500.00
☐1882	Lyons-Roberts	Brown	600.00	850.00	4500.00	12500.00
☐1882	Vernon-Treat	Brown	725.00	1175.00	5050.00	13500.00

FIFTY DOLLAR NOTES (1882) NATIONAL BANK NOTES
SECOND CHARTER PERIOD (Large Size)

Second Issue (Blue seal, green back with date "1882–1908".)
Face Design: Washington crossing Delaware left, Washington at Valley Forge right.

Back Design

SERIES	SIGNATURES	SEAL	A.B.P.	GOOD	V.FINE	UNC.
☐1882	Rosecrans-Huston	Blue	450.00	600.00	1700.00	8000.00
☐1882	Rosecrans-Nebeker	Blue	450.00	600.00	1700.00	8000.00
☐1882	Tillman-Morgan	Blue	450.00	600.00	1700.00	8000.00
☐1882	Tillman-Roberts	Blue	450.00	600.00	1700.00	8000.00
☐1882	Bruce-Roberts	Blue	450.00	600.00	1700.00	8000.00
☐1882	Lyons-Roberts	Blue	450.00	600.00	1700.00	8000.00
☐1882	Vernon-Treat	Blue	450.00	600.00	1700.00	8000.00
☐1882	Napier-McClung	Blue	450.00	600.00	1700.00	8000.00

Third Issue (As above, "FIFTY DOLLARS" replaces 1882–1908—excessively rare!)

☐1882	Lyons-Roberts	21,000.00	26,000.00	46,000.00	96,000.00

FIFTY DOLLAR NOTES (1902) NATIONAL BANK NOTES
THIRD CHARTER PERIOD (Large Size)

First Issues (Red seal and numbers)
Face Design: Portrait of Sherman left. Name of bank center. Treasury Seal and numbers.

SERIES	SIGNATURES	SEAL	A.B.P.	GOOD	V.FINE	UNC.
☐1902	Lyons-Roberts	Red	425.00	600.00	2900.00	10000.00
☐1902	Lyons-Treat	Red	425.00	600.00	2900.00	10000.00
☐1902	Vernon-Treat	Red	425.00	600.00	2900.00	10000.00

Second Issue (Treasury Seal)
Numbers remain blue, date "1902–1908" added on back.

☐1902	Lyons-Roberts	Blue	365.00	2200.00	2100.00	5000.00
☐1902	Lyons-Treat	Blue	365.00	2200.00	2100.00	5000.00
☐1902	Vernon-Treat	Blue	365.00	2200.00	2100.00	5000.00
☐1902	Vernon-McClung	Blue	365.00	2200.00	2100.00	5000.00
☐1902	Napier-McClung	Blue	365.00	2200.00	2100.00	5000.00
☐1902	Napier-Thompson	Blue	365.00	2200.00	2100.00	5000.00
☐1902	Napier-Burke	Blue	365.00	2200.00	2100.00	5000.00
☐1902	Parker-Burke	Blue	365.00	2200.00	2100.00	5000.00
☐1902	Teehee-Burke	Blue	365.00	2200.00	2100.00	5000.00

Third Issue (Treasury Seal)
Numbers remain blue, date "1902–1908" removed from back.

☐1902	Lyons-Roberts	Blue	200.00	275.00	2000.00	4800.00
☐1902	Lyons-Treat	Blue	200.00	275.00	2000.00	4800.00
☐1902	Vernon-Treat	Blue	200.00	275.00	2000.00	4800.00
☐1902	Vernon-McClung	Blue	200.00	275.00	2000.00	4800.00
☐1902	Napier-McClung	Blue	200.00	275.00	2000.00	4800.00
☐1902	Napier-Thompson	Blue	200.00	275.00	2000.00	4800.00
☐1902	Napier-Burke	Blue	200.00	275.00	2000.00	4800.00
☐1902	Parker-Burke	Blue	200.00	275.00	2000.00	4800.00
☐1902	Teehee-Burke	Blue	200.00	275.00	2000.00	4800.00
☐1902	Elliott-Burke	Blue	200.00	275.00	2000.00	4800.00
☐1902	Elliott-White	Blue	200.00	275.00	2000.00	4800.00

SERIES	SIGNATURES	SEAL	A.B.P.	GOOD	V.FINE	UNC.
☐1902	Speelman-White	Blue	190.00	275.00	2000.00	4800.00
☐1902	Woods-White	Blue	190.00	275.00	2000.00	4800.00

FIFTY DOLLAR NOTES (1929) NATIONAL BANK NOTES
(Small Size)

Face Design: Portrait of President Grant center. Bank left, brown seal right. Brown serial numbers, black Charter Numbers.

Back Design: The Capitol.

SERIES	SIGNATURES	SEAL	A.B.P.	V.FINE	UNC.
☐1929, Type I*	Jones-Wood	Brown	875.00	250.00	750.00
☐1929, Type II*	Jones-Wood	Brown	100.00	450.00	1250.00

*See Page 92. Type I—Charter Number in black. Type II—Similar. Charter Number added in brown.

FIFTY DOLLAR NOTES (1878–1880)
SILVER CERTIFICATES
(Large Size)

Face Design: Portrait of Edward Everett.

Back Design

SERIES	SIGNATURES	SEAL	A.B.P.	GOOD	V.FINE	UNC.
☐ 1878	Varied	Red	15000.00	—	—	VERY RARE
☐ 1880	Scofield-Gilfillan	Brown	16000.00	22500.00	53000.00	150000.00
☐ 1880	Bruce-Gilfillan	Brown	9500.00	13500.00	35000.00	UNKNOWN
☐ 1880	Bruce-Wyman	Brown	9500.00	14000.00	41000.00	95000.00
☐ 1880	Rosecrans-Huston	Brown	3500.00	5000.00	18000.00	150000.00
☐ 1880	Rosecrans-Nebeker	Red	3000.00	4000.00	16000.00	85000.00

FIFTY DOLLAR NOTES (1891) SILVER CERTIFICATES
(Large Size)

Face Design: Portrait of Edward Everett.

Back Design

SERIES	SIGNATURES	SEAL	A.B.P.	GOOD	V.FINE	UNC.
☐1891	Rosecrans-Nebeker	Red	800.00	3550.00	10000.00	19500.00
☐1891	Tillman-Morgan	Red	800.00	1050.00	4100.00	15500.00
☐1891	Bruce-Roberts	Red	800.00	1050.00	4000.00	16000.00
☐1891	Lyons-Roberts	Red	800.00	1050.00	4400.00	21000.00
☐1891	Vernon-Treat	Red	800.00	1050.00	4100.00	27000.00
☐1891	Parker-Burke	Blue	800.00	1050.00	3300.00	17500.00

FIFTY DOLLAR NOTES (1882) GOLD CERTIFICATES
(Large Size)

Face Design: Portrait of Silas Wright to left.

Back Design: Bright yellow color.

SERIES	SIGNATURES	SEAL	A.B.P.	GOOD	V.FINE	UNC.
☐1882	Bruce-Gilfillan	Brown	2600.00	3900.00	30000.00	75,000.00
☐1882	Bruce-Wyman	Brown	2600.00	3900.00	30000.00	82,500.00
☐1882	Rosecrans-Hyatt	Red	1350.00	1900.00	14000.00	65,000.00
☐1882	Rosecrans-Huston	Brown	6050.00	8050.00	21000.00	250,000.00
☐1882	Lyons-Roberts	Red	2500.00	4400.00	30000.00	85,000.00
☐1882	Lyons-Treat	Red	490.00	900.00	3250.00	21,000.00
☐1882	Vernon-Treat	Red	445.00	700.00	3250.00	21,000.00
☐1882	Vernon-McClung	Red	475.00	900.00	3250.00	21,000.00
☐1882	Napier-McClung	Red	375.00	600.00	2250.00	16,500.00

FIFTY DOLLAR NOTES (1913) GOLD CERTIFICATES
(Large Size)

Face Design: Portrait of President Grant.

Back Design: Bright yellow color.

SERIES	SIGNATURES	SEAL	A.B.P.	GOOD	V.FINE	UNC.
☐1913	Parker-Burke	Gold	180.00	275.00	1700.00	4500.00
☐1913	Teehee-Burke	Gold	180.00	250.00	1000.00	3500.00
☐1922	Speelman-White	Gold	205.00	275.00	800.00	4400.00

FIFTY DOLLAR NOTES (1928) GOLD CERTIFICATES
(Small Size)

Back Design: Same as 1929 note.

SERIES	SIGNATURES	SEAL	A.B.P.	GOOD	V.FINE	UNC.
☐1928	Woods-Mellon	Gold	90.00	125.00	400.00	4000.00

FIFTY DOLLAR NOTES (1891) TREASURY OR COIN NOTES
(Large Size)

Face Design: Portrait of William H. Seward. Only twenty-five pieces remain unredeemed.
Back Design: Green.

SERIES	SIGNATURES	SEAL	A.B.P.	GOOD	V.FINE	UNC.
☐1891	Rosecrans-Nebeker	Red	6500.00	8500.00	38,500.00	180,000.00

FIFTY DOLLAR NOTES (1914)
FEDERAL RESERVE NOTES

(Large Size)

SERIES OF 1914,
SIGNATURES OF BURKE-McADOO, RED SEAL AND
RED SERIAL NUMBERS

BANK	A.B.P.	V.FINE	UNC.	CITY	A.B.P.	V.FINE	UNC.
☐Boston	475.00	1800.00	5950.00	☐ Chicago	500.00	1750.00	6500.00
☐New York	475.00	1650.00	5950.00	☐ St. Louis	500.00	1675.00	6400.00
☐Philadelphia	475.00	1650.00	5950.00	☐ Minneapolis	500.00	1700.00	6500.00
☐Cleveland	475.00	1650.00	6100.00	☐ Kansas City	500.00	1730.00	6500.00
☐Richmond	475.00	1650.00	6050.00	☐ Dallas	500.00	1700.00	6500.00
☐Atlanta	475.00	1650.00	6100.00	☐ San Francisco	475.00	1700.00	6500.00

FIFTY DOLLAR NOTES (1914)
FEDERAL RESERVE NOTES
1914, BLUE TREASURY SEAL AND BLUE NUMBERS

DATE	BANK	SIGNATURES	SEAL	A.B.P.	GOOD	V.FINE	UNC.
1914	Boston	Burke-McAdoo	Blue	85.00	110.00	670.00	2400.00
1914	Boston	Burke-Glass	Blue	85.00	110.00	575.00	2350.00
1914	Boston	Burke-Huston	Blue	180.00	335.00	2150.00	4100.00
1914	Boston	White-Mellon	Blue	85.00	95.00	400.00	2750.00
1914	New York	Burke-McAdoo	Blue	85.00	110.00	800.00	3750.00
1914	New York	Burke-Glass	Blue	85.00	100.00	825.00	3500.00
1914	New York	Burke-Huston	Blue	85.00	95.00	400.00	2750.00
1914	New York	White-Mellon	Blue	85.00	95.00	400.00	2750.00

DATE	BANK	SIGNATURES	SEAL	A.B.P.	GOOD	V.FINE	UNC.
1914	Philadelphia	Burke-McAdoo	Blue	85.00	110.00	875.00	4000.00
1914	Philadelphia	Burke-Glass	Blue	85.00	135.00	1225.00	3800.00
1914	Philadelphia	Burke-Huston	Blue	85.00	95.00	400.00	2950.00
1914	Philadelphia	White-Mellon	Blue	85.00	95.00	400.00	2750.00
1914	Cleveland	Burke-McAdoo	Blue	85.00	95.00	400.00	2950.00
1914	Cleveland	Burke-Glass	Blue	85.00	135.00	700.00	3400.00
1914	Cleveland	Burke-Huston	Blue	85.00	115.00	875.00	3700.00
1914	Cleveland	White-Mellon	Blue	85.00	100.00	400.00	2750.00
1914	Richmond	Burke-McAdoo	Blue	85.00	135.00	1125.00	3750.00
1914	Richmond	Burke-Glass	Blue	85.00	175.00	925.00	3900.00
1914	Richmond	Burke-Huston	Blue	85.00	110.00	425.00	2750.00
1914	Richmond	White-Mellon	Blue	85.00	135.00	1075.00	2950.00
1914	Atlanta	Burke-McAdoo	Blue	85.00	135.00	875.00	4000.00
1914	Atlanta	Burke-Glass	Blue	130.00	235.00	1500.00	4500.00
1914	Atlanta	Burke-Huston	Blue	85.00	95.00	400.00	2750.00
1914	Atlanta	White-Mellon	Blue	85.00	135.00	625.00	3300.00
1914	Chicago	Burke-McAdoo	Blue	85.00	100.00	400.00	2750.00
1914	Chicago	Burke-Glass	Blue	85.00	100.00	400.00	2950.00
1914	Chicago	Burke-Huston	Blue	85.00	110.00	475.00	2950.00
1914	Chicago	White-Mellon	Blue	85.00	110.00	475.00	2750.00
1914	St. Louis	Burke-McAdoo	Blue	85.00	135.00	1600.00	3250.00
1914	St. Louis	Burke-Glass	Blue	85.00	110.00	1000.00	3750.00
1914	St. Louis	Burke-Huston	Blue	85.00	95.00	400.00	2750.00
1914	St. Louis	White-Mellon	Blue	155.00	335.00	2130.00	4100.00
1914	Minneapolis	Burke-McAdoo	Blue	85.00	135.00	900.00	3500.00
1914	Minneapolis	Burke-Glass	Blue	155.00	335.00	1400.00	4100.00
1914	Minneapolis	Burke-Huston	Blue	130.00	285.00	1975.00	4400.00
1914	Minneapolis	White-Mellon	Blue	155.00	335.00	6000.00	3000.00
1914	Kansas City	Burke-McAdoo	Blue	85.00	115.00	1000.00	3400.00
1914	Kansas City	White-Mellon	Blue		ONLY 1 KNOWN—RARE		
1914	Dallas	Burke-McAdoo	Blue	85.00	135.00	1100.00	4000.00
1914	Dallas	Burke-Glass	Blue	155.00	335.00	1025.00	5000.00
1914	Dallas	Burke-Huston	Blue	155.00	335.00	1025.00	5000.00
1914	Dallas	White Mellon	Blue	155.00	335.00	1025.00	3500.00
1914	San Francisco	Burke-McAdoo	Blue	85.00	100.00	425.00	3250.00
1914	San Francisco	Burke-Glass	Blue	155.00	335.00	3025.00	3250.00
1914	San Francisco	Burke-Huston	Blue	85.00	100.00	425.00	2750.00
1914	San Francisco	White-Mellon	Blue	85.00	130.00	575.00	2750.00

FIFTY DOLLAR NOTES (1928)
FEDERAL RESERVE NOTES

(Small Size)

Face Design: Portrait of President Grant center. Black Federal Reserve Seal with number to left. Green Treasury Seal to right.
Back Design: Same as 1929 note.

FIFTY DOLLAR NOTES (1928)
FEDERAL RESERVE NOTES
SERIES OF 1928, SIGNATURES OF WOODS-MELLON, GREEN SEAL

BANK	A.B.P.	V.FINE	UNC.	★UNC.	BANK	A.B.P.	V.FINE	UNC.	★UNC.
☐ Boston	75.00	130.00	1000.00	—	☐ Chicago	70.00	125.00	800.00	—
☐ New York	75.00	130.00	700.00	—	☐ St. Louis	70.00	125.00	900.00	—
☐ Philadelphia	75.00	130.00	900.00	—	☐ Minneapolis	70.00	125.00	1250.00	—
☐ Cleveland	70.00	130.00	700.00	—	☐ Kansas City	75.00	130.00	1000.00	—
☐ Richmond	70.00	130.00	900.00	—	☐ Dallas	75.00	130.00	1000.00	—
☐ Atlanta	70.00	130.00	900.00	—	☐ San Francisco	75.00	130.00	800.00	—

SERIES OF 1928A, SIGNATURES OF WOODS-MELLON, GREEN SEAL

BANK	A.B.P.	V.FINE	UNC.	★UNC.	BANK	A.B.P.	V.FINE	UNC.	★UNC.
☐ Boston	65.00	985.00	550.00	—	☐ Chicago	65.00	110.00	500.00	—
☐ New York	65.00	985.00	550.00	—	☐ St. Louis	65.00	110.00	550.00	—
☐ Philadelphia	65.00	985.00	550.00	—	☐ Minneapolis	65.00	120.00	750.00	—
☐ Cleveland	65.00	985.00	550.00	—	☐ Kansas City	65.00	120.00	1200.00	—
☐ Richmond	65.00	985.00	550.00	—	☐ Dallas	65.00	120.00	1000.00	—
☐ Atlanta	65.00	985.00	550.00	—	☐ San Francisco	65.00	110.00	800.00	—

FIFTY DOLLAR NOTES (1934)
FEDERAL RESERVE NOTES
SERIES OF 1934, SIGNATURES OF JULIAN-MORGENTHAU, GREEN SEAL

BANK	A.B.P.	V.FINE	UNC.	★UNC.	BANK	A.B.P.	V.FINE	UNC.	★UNC.
☐ Boston	60.00	90.00	275.00	750.00	☐ Chicago	60.00	90.00	275.00	750.00
☐ New York	60.00	90.00	275.00	750.00	☐ St. Louis	60.00	90.00	275.00	750.00
☐ Philadelphia	60.00	90.00	275.00	750.00	☐ Minneapolis	60.00	90.00	275.00	750.00
☐ Cleveland	60.00	90.00	275.00	750.00	☐ Kansas City	60.00	90.00	275.00	750.00
☐ Richmond	60.00	90.00	275.00	750.00	☐ Dallas	60.00	90.00	275.00	750.00
☐ Atlanta	60.00	90.00	275.00	750.00	☐ San Francisco	60.00	90.00	275.00	750.00

SERIES OF 1934A, SIGNATURES OF JULIAN-MORGENTHAU, GREEN SEAL

BANK	A.B.P.	V.FINE	UNC.	★UNC.	BANK	A.B.P.	V.FINE	UNC.	★UNC.
☐ Boston	58.00	110.00	400.00	1500.00	☐ Chicago	58.00	110.00	400.00	1500.00
☐ New York	58.00	110.00	400.00	1500.00	☐ St. Louis	58.00	110.00	400.00	1500.00
☐ Philadelphia	58.00	110.00	400.00	1500.00	☐ Minneapolis	58.00	120.00	400.00	1500.00
☐ Cleveland	58.00	110.00	400.00	1500.00	☐ Kansas City	58.00	120.00	400.00	1500.00
☐ Richmond	58.00	110.00	400.00	1500.00	☐ Dallas	58.00	120.00	400.00	1500.00
☐ Atlanta	58.00	110.00	400.00	1500.00	☐ San Francisco	58.00	110.00	400.00	1500.00

SERIES OF 1934B, SIGNATURES OF JULIAN-VINSON, GREEN SEAL

BANK	A.B.P.	V.FINE	UNC.	★UNC.	BANK	A.P.B.	V.FINE	UNC.	★UNC.
					☐ Chicago	55.00	105.00	450.00	—
					☐ St. Louis	55.00	105.00	450.00	—
☐ Philadelphia	58.00	105.00	450.00	3500.00	☐ Minneapolis	65.00	125.00	450.00	
☐ Cleveland	58.00	105.00	450.00	3500.00	☐ Kansas City	65.00	125.00	450.00	3500.00
☐ Richmond	58.00	105.00	450.00	3500.00	☐ Dallas	65.00	125.00	450.00	
☐ Atlanta	58.00	105.00	450.00	—	☐ San Francisco	55.00	105.00	450.00	

SERIES OF 1934C, SIGNATURES OF JULIAN-SNYDER, GREEN SEAL

BANK	A.B.P.	V.FINE	UNC.	★UNC.	BANK	A.B.P.	V.FINE	UNC.	★UNC.
☐ Boston	58.00	110.00	300.00	—	☐ Chicago	58.00	110.00	300.00	2000.00
☐ New York	58.00	110.00	300.00	2000.00	☐ St. Louis	58.00	110.00	300.00	
☐ Philadelphia	58.00	110.00	300.00	2000.00	☐ Minneapolis	58.00	110.00	300.00	2000.00
☐ Cleveland	58.00	105.00	300.00	2000.00	☐ Kansas City	58.00	105.00	300.00	
☐ Richmond	58.00	105.00	300.00	2000.00	☐ Dallas	58.00	105.00	300.00	2000.00
☐ Atlanta	58.00	105.00	300.00	—					

SERIES OF 1934D, SIGNATURES OF CLARK-SNYDER, GREEN SEAL

BANK	A.B.P.	V.FINE	UNC.	★UNC.	BANK	A.B.P.	V.FINE	UNC.	★UNC.
☐ Boston	68.00	125.00	550.00	5000.00	☐ Chicago	55.00	95.00	550.00	4000
☐ New York	53.00	95.00	550.00	5000.00					
☐ Philadelphia	53.00	95.00	550.00	4000.00	☐ Minneapolis	55.00	95.00	550.00	—
☐ Richmond	68.00	125.00	550.00	—	☐ Dallas	65 .00	125.00	550.00	—
☐ Atlanta	68.00	125.00	550.00	5000.00					

FIFTY DOLLAR NOTES (1950)
FEDERAL RESERVE NOTES
SERIES OF 1950, SIGNATURES OF CLARK-SNYDER, GREEN SEAL

BANK	A.B.P.	V.FINE	UNC.	★UNC.	BANK	A.P.B.	V.FINE	UNC.	★UNC.
☐ Boston	58.00	110.00	375.00	1000.00	☐ Chicago	55.00	110.00	375.00	1000.00
☐ New York	58.00	110.00	375.00	1000.00	☐ St. Louis	55.00	110.00	375.00	1000.00
☐ Philadelphia	58.00	110.00	375.00	1000.00	☐ Minneapolis	55.00	110.00	375.00	1000.00
☐ Cleveland	53.00	105.00	375.00	1000.00	☐ Kansas City	55.00	110.00	375.00	1000.00
☐ Richmond	53.00	105.00	375.00	1000.00	☐ Dallas	55.00	110.00	375.00	1000.00
☐ Atlanta	53.00	105.00	375.00	1000.00	☐ San Francisco	55.00	110.00	375.00	1000.00

SERIES OF 1950A, SIGNATURES OF PRIEST-HUMPHERY, GREEN SEAL

BANK	A.B.P.	V.FINE	UNC.	★UNC.	BANK	A.B.P.	V.FINE	UNC.	★UNC.
☐ Boston	55.00	90.00	300.00	850.00	☐ Chicago	55.00	80.00	300.00	850.00
☐ New York	55.00	90.00	300.00	850.00	☐ St. Louis	55.00	80.00	300.00	850.00
☐ Philadelphia	55.00	90.00	300.00	850.00	☐ Minneapolis	55.00	80.00	300.00	850.00
☐ Cleveland	55.00	90.00	300.00	850.00	☐ Kansas City	55.00	80.00	300.00	850.00
☐ Richmond	55.00	90.00	300.00	850.00	☐ Dallas	55.00	80.00	300.00	850.00
☐ Atlanta	55.00	90.00	300.00	850.00	☐ San Francisco	55.00	80.00	300.00	850.00

SERIES OF 1950B, SIGNATURES OF PRIEST-ANDERSON, GREEN SEAL

BANK	A.B.P.	V.FINE	UNC.	★UNC.	BANK	A.B.P.	V.FINE	UNC.	★UNC.
☐ Boston	52.00	85.00	250.00	700.00	☐ Chicago	52.00	85.00	250.00	700.00
☐ New York	52.00	85.00	250.00	700.00	☐ St. Louis	52.00	85.00	250.00	700.00
☐ Philadelphia	52.00	85.00	250.00	700.00	☐ Minneapolis	52.00	85.00	250.00	700.00
☐ Cleveland	52.00	85.00	250.00	700.00	☐ Kansas City	52.00	85.00	250.00	700.00
☐ Richmond	52.00	85.00	250.00	700.00	☐ Dallas	52.00	85.00	250.00	700.00
☐ Atlanta	52.00	85.00	250.00	700.00	☐ San Francisco	52.00	85.00	250.00	700.00

SERIES OF 1950C, SIGNATURES OF SMITH-DILLON, GREEN SEAL

BANK	A.B.P.	V.FINE	UNC.	★UNC.	BANK	A.B.P.	V.FINE	UNC.	★UNC.
☐ Boston	52.00	85.00	225.00	650.00	☐ Chicago	52.00	85.00	225.00	650.00
☐ New York	52.00	85.00	225.00	650.00	☐ St. Louis	52.00	85.00	225.00	650.00
☐ Philadelphia	52.00	85.00	225.00	650.00	☐ Minneapolis	52.00	85.00	225.00	650.00
☐ Cleveland	52.00	85.00	225.00	650.00	☐ Kansas City	52.00	85.00	225.00	650.00
☐ Richmond	52.00	85.00	225.00	650.00	☐ Dallas	52.00	85.00	225.00	650.00
☐ Atlanta	52.00	85.00	225.00	650.00	☐ San Francisco	52.00	85.00	225.00	650.00

SERIES OF 1950D, SIGNATURES OF GRANAHAN-DILLON, GREEN SEAL

BANK	A.B.P.	V.FINE	UNC.	★UNC.	BANK	A.B.P.	V.FINE	UNC.	★UNC.
☐ Boston	65.00	120.00	225.00	600.00	☐ Chicago	58.00	115.00	225.00	600.00
☐ New York	65.00	120.00	225.00	600.00	☐ St. Louis	58.00	115.00	225.00	600.00
☐ Philadelphia	65.00	120.00	225.00	600.00	☐ Minneapolis	58.00	115.00	225.00	600.00
☐ Cleveland	58.00	110.00	225.00	600.00	☐ Kansas City	58.00	115.00	225.00	600.00
☐ Richmond	58.00	110.00	225.00	600.00	☐ Dallas	65.00	115.00	225.00	600.00
☐ Atlanta	58.00	110.00	225.00	600.00	☐ San Francisco	65.00	115.00	225.00	600.00

SERIES OF 1950E, SIGNATURES OF GRANAHAN-FOWLER, GREEN SEAL

BANK	A.B.P.	V.FINE	UNC.	★UNC.	BANK	A.B.P.	V.FINE	UNC.	★UNC.
					☐ Chicago	75.00	140.00	1200.00	5000.00
☐ New York	75.00	125.00	900.00	2000.00					
					☐ San Francisco	80.00	140.00	900.00	3000.00

FIFTY DOLLAR NOTES (1963)
FEDERAL RESERVE NOTES
SERIES OF 1963,
(THERE WERE NOT ANY NOTES PRINTED FOR THIS SERIES.)

SERIES OF 1963A, SIGNATURES OF GRANAHAN-FOWLER, GREEN SEAL

BANK	A.B.P.	V.FINE	UNC.	BANK	A.B.P.	V.FINE	UNC.
☐ Boston	51.00	60.00	225.00	☐ Chicago	51.00	60.00	225.00
☐ New York	51.00	60.00	225.00	☐ St. Louis	51.00	85.00	225.00
☐ Philadelphia	51.00	60.00	225.00	☐ Minneapolis	51.00	85.00	225.00
☐ Cleveland	51.00	60.00	225.00	☐ Kansas City	51.00	85.00	225.00
☐ Richmond	51.00	60.00	225.00	☐ Dallas	51.00	60.00	225.00
☐ Atlanta	51.00	60.00	225.00	☐ San Francisco	51.00	60.00	225.00

FIFTY DOLLAR NOTES (1969)
FEDERAL RESERVE NOTES
(WORDING IN GREEN TREASURY SEAL IS CHANGED FROM LATIN TO ENGLISH)

SERIES OF 1969, SIGNATURES OF ELSTON-KENNEDY, GREEN SEAL

BANK	A.B.P.	V.FINE	UNC.	BANK	A.B.P.	V.FINE	UNC.
☐ Boston	51.00	70.00	150.00	☐ Chicago	51.00	70.00	150.00
☐ New York	51.00	70.00	150.00	☐ St. Louis	51.00	85.00	150.00
☐ Philadelphia	51.00	70.00	150.00	☐ Minneapolis	51.00	85.00	150.00
☐ Cleveland	51.00	70.00	150.00	☐ Kansas City	51.00	85.00	150.00
☐ Richmond	51.00	70.00	150.00	☐ Dallas	51.00	70.00	150.00
☐ Atlanta	51.00	85.00	150.00	☐ San Francisco	51.00	70.00	150.00

SERIES OF 1969A, SIGNATURES OF KABIS-CONNALLY, GREEN SEAL

BANK	A.B.P.	V.FINE	UNC.	BANK	A.B.P.	V.FINE	UNC.
☐ Boston	51.00	55.00	145.00	☐ Chicago	51.00	55.00	145.00
☐ New York	51.00	55.00	145.00	☐ St. Louis	51.00	60.00	145.00
☐ Philadelphia	51.00	55.00	145.00	☐ Minneapolis	51.00	60.00	145.00
☐ Cleveland	51.00	55.00	145.00	☐ Kansas City	51.00	60.00	145.00
☐ Richmond	51.00	55.00	145.00	☐ Dallas	51.00	60.00	145.00
☐ Atlanta	51.00	55.00	145.00	☐ San Francisco	51.00	55.00	145.00

SERIES OF 1969B, SIGNATURES OF BANUELOS-CONNALLY, GREEN SEAL

BANK	A.B.P.	V.FINE	UNC.	BANK	A.B.P.	V.FINE	UNC.
☐ Boston	51.00	60.00	725.00	☐ Chicago	51.00	60.00	725.00
☐ New York	51.00	60.00	275.00				
☐ Richmond	51.00	60.00	725.00	☐ Dallas	51.00	60.00	725.00
☐ Atlanta	51.00	70.00	725.00				

SERIES OF 1969C, SIGNATURES OF BANUELOS-SHULTZ, GREEN SEAL

BANK	A.B.P.	V.FINE	UNC.	BANK	A.B.P.	V.FINE	UNC.
☐ Boston	51.00	65.00	115.00	☐ Chicago	51.00	55.00	100.00
☐ New York	51.00	65.00	115.00	☐ St. Louis	51.00	55.00	100.00
☐ Philadelphia	51.00	65.00	115.00	☐ Minneapolis	51.00	55.00	115.00
☐ Cleveland	51.00	55.00	100.00	☐ Kansas City	51.00	55.00	100.00
☐ Richmond	51.00	55.00	100.00	☐ Dallas	51.00	55.00	100.00
☐ Atlanta	51.00	55.00	100.00	☐ San Francisco	51.00	55.00	100.00

FIFTY DOLLAR NOTES (1974)
FEDERAL RESERVE NOTES
SERIES OF 1974, SIGNATURES OF NEFF-SIMON, GREEN SEAL

BANK	A.B.P.	V.FINE	UNC.	BANK	A.B.P.	V.FINE	UNC.
☐ Boston	51.00	60.00	100.00	☐ Chicago	51.00	60.00	100.00
☐ New York	51.00	60.00	100.00	☐ St. Louis	51.00	60.00	100.00
☐ Philadelphia	51.00	60.00	100.00	☐ Minneapolis	51.00	65.00	100.00
☐ Cleveland	51.00	60.00	100.00	☐ Kansas City	51.00	65.00	100.00
☐ Richmond	51.00	60.00	100.00	☐ Dallas	51.00	60.00	100.00
☐ Atlanta	51.00	60.00	100.00	☐ San Francisco	51.00	60.00	100.00

FIFTY DOLLAR NOTES (1977)
FEDERAL RESERVE NOTES
SERIES OF 1977, SIGNATURES OF MORTON-BLUMENTHAL, GREEN SEAL

BANK	A.B.P.	V.FINE	UNC.	BANK	A.B.P.	V.FINE	UNC.
☐ Boston	—	50.00	85.00	☐ Chicago	—	55.00	85.00
☐ New York	—	50.00	85.00	☐ St. Louis	—	55.00	85.00
☐ Philadelphia	—	50.00	85.00	☐ Minneapolis	—	55.00	85.00
☐ Cleveland	—	50.00	85.00	☐ Kansas City	—	55.00	85.00
☐ Richmond	—	50.00	85.00	☐ Dallas	—	55.00	85.00
☐ Atlanta	—	50.00	85.00	☐ San Francisco	—	55.00	85.00

FIFTY DOLLAR NOTES (1981)
FEDERAL RESERVE NOTES
SERIES OF 1981, SIGNATURES OF BUCHANAN-REGAN, GREEN SEAL

BANK	A.B.P.	V.FINE	UNC.	BANK	A.B.P.	V.FINE	UNC.
☐ Boston	—	44.00	100.00	☐ Chicago	—	52.00	100.00
☐ New York	—	44.00	100.00	☐ St. Louis	—	52.00	100.00
☐ Philadelphia	—	44.00	100.00	☐ Minneapolis	—	54.00	100.00
☐ Cleveland	—	44.00	100.00	☐ Kansas City	—	54.00	100.00
☐ Richmond	—	44.00	100.00	☐ Dallas	—	54.00	100.00
☐ Atlanta	—	44.00	100.00	☐ San Francisco	—	52.00	100.00

SERIES OF 1981A, SIGNATURES OF ORTEGA-REGAN, GREEN SEAL

BANK	A.B.P.	V.FINE	UNC.	BANK	A.B.P.	V.FINE	UNC.
☐ Boston	—	54.00	125.00	☐ Chicago	—	54.00	125.00
☐ New York	—	54.00	125.00	☐ St. Louis	—	54.00	125.00
☐ Philadelphia	—	54.00	125.00	☐ Minneapolis	—	56.00	125.00
☐ Cleveland	—	54.00	125.00	☐ Kansas City	—	56.00	125.00
☐ Richmond	—	54.00	125.00	☐ Dallas	—	56.00	125.00
☐ Atlanta	—	54.00	125.00	☐ San Francisco	—	54.00	125.00

FIFTY DOLLAR NOTES (1985)
FEDERAL RESERVE NOTES
SERIES OF 1985, SIGNATURES OF ORTEGA-BAKER, GREEN SEAL

BANK	A.B.P.	V.FINE	UNC.	BANK	A.B.P.	V.FINE	UNC.
☐ Boston	—	55.00	60.00	☐ Chicago	—	55.00	60.00
☐ New York	—	55.00	60.00	☐ St. Louis	—	55.00	60.00
☐ Philadelphia	—	55.00	60.00	☐ Minneapolis	—	55.00	60.00
☐ Cleveland	—	55.00	60.00	☐ Kansas City	—	55.00	60.00
☐ Richmond	—	55.00	60.00	☐ Dallas	—	55.00	60.00
☐ Atlanta	—	55.00	60.00	☐ San Francisco	—	55.00	60.00

FIFTY DOLLAR NOTES (1988)
FEDERAL RESERVE NOTES
SERIES OF 1988, SIGNATURES OF ORTEGA-BRADY, GREEN SEAL

BANK	A.B.P.	V.FINE	UNC.	BANK	A.B.P.	V.FINE	UNC.
☐ Boston	—	53.00	75.00	☐ Chicago	—	53.00	75.00
☐ New York	—	53.00	75.00	☐ St. Louis	—	53.00	75.00
☐ Philadelphia	—	53.00	75.00	☐ Minneapolis	—	53.00	75.00
☐ Cleveland	—	53.00	75.00	☐ Kansas City	—	53.00	75.00
☐ Richmond	—	53.00	75.00	☐ Dallas	—	53.00	75.00
☐ Atlanta	—	53.00	75.00	☐ San Francisco	—	53.00	75.00

FIFTY DOLLAR NOTES (1990)
FEDERAL RESERVE NOTES
SERIES OF 1990, SIGNATURES OF VILLALPANDO-BRADY, GREEN SEAL

BANK	A.B.P.	V.FINE	UNC.	BANK	A.B.P.	V.FINE	UNC.
☐ Boston	—	52.00	55.00	☐ Chicago	—	52.00	55.00
☐ New York	—	52.00	55.00	☐ St. Louis	—	52.00	55.00
☐ Philadelphia	—	52.00	55.00	☐ Minneapolis	—	52.00	55.00
☐ Cleveland	—	52.00	55.00	☐ Kansas City	—	52.00	55.00
☐ Richmond	—	52.00	55.00	☐ Dallas	—	52.00	55.00
☐ Atlanta	—	52.00	55.00	☐ San Francisco	—	52.00	55.00

FIFTY DOLLAR NOTES (1993)
FEDERAL RESERVE NOTES
SERIES OF 1993, SIGNATURES OF WITHROW-BENTSEN, GREEN
SEAL

BANK	A.B.P.	V.FINE	UNC.	BANK	A.B.P.	V.FINE	UNC.
☐ Boston	—	52.00	70.00	☐ Chicago	—	52.00	70.00
☐ New York	—	52.00	70.00	☐ St. Louis	—	52.00	70.00
☐ Philadelphia	—	52.00	70.00	☐ Minneapolis	—	52.00	70.00
☐ Cleveland	—	52.00	70.00	☐ Kansas City	—	52.00	70.00
☐ Richmond	—	52.00	70.00	☐ Dallas	—	52.00	70.00
☐ Atlanta	—	52.00	70.00	☐ San Francisco	—	52.00	70.00

FIFTY DOLLAR NOTES (1996)
FEDERAL RESERVE NOTES
SERIES OF 1995, SIGNATURES OF WITHROW-BENTSEN, GREEN
SEAL

BANK	A.B.P.	V.FINE	UNC.	BANK	A.B.P.	V.FINE	UNC.
☐ Boston	—	52.00	60.00	☐ Chicago	—	52.00	60.00
☐ New York	—	52.00	60.00	☐ St. Louis	—	52.00	60.00
☐ Philadelphia	—	52.00	60.00	☐ Minneapolis	—	52.00	60.00
☐ Cleveland	—	52.00	60.00	☐ Kansas City	—	52.00	60.00
☐ Richmond	—	52.00	60.00	☐ Dallas	—	52.00	60.00
☐ Atlanta	—	52.00	60.00	☐ San Francisco	—	52.00	60.00

FIFTY DOLLAR NOTES (1918)

FEDERAL RESERVE BANK NOTES

(Large Size)

Face Design: Portrait of President Grant to left, Federal Reserve Bank in center, blue seal right.

Back Design: Female figure of Panama between merchant ship and battleship. Plates were made for all twelve Federal Reserve Districts. Only St. Louis bank issued. Less than thirty notes are known today.

BANK	SERIES	GOV'T SIGNATURES	BANK SIGNATURES	A.B.P.	VF	UNC.
☐ St. Louis	1918	Teehee-Burke	Attebery-Wells	1000.00	5600.00	22500.00

FIFTY DOLLAR NOTES (1929)
FEDERAL RESERVE BANK NOTES

(Small Size)

Face Design:
Portrait of Grant center, name of bank left, brown serial numbers, black letter for Federal Reserve District.

Back Design:
Same as 1929 $50 note.

BANK	SERIES	SIGNATURES	SEAL	A.B.P.	V.FINE	UNC.	★UNC.
☐ New York	1929	Jones-Woods	Brown	70.00	125.00	400.00	3000.00
☐ Cleveland	1929	Jones-Woods	Brown	74.00	135.00	400.00	3500.00
☐ Chicago	1929	Jones-Woods	Brown	70.00	125.00	500.00	5000.00
☐ Minneapolis	1929	Jones-Woods	Brown	70.00	125.00	700.00	4000.00
☐ Kansas City	1929	Jones-Woods	Brown	70.00	105.00	400.00	1000.00
☐ Dallas	1929	Jones-Woods	Brown	74.00	155.00	2450.00	5000.00
☐ San Francisco	1929	Jones-Woods	Brown	129.00	230.00	950.00	5000.00

ONE HUNDRED
DOLLAR NOTES

ONE HUNDRED DOLLAR NOTES (1862–1863)
UNITED STATES NOTES
(ALSO KNOWN AS LEGAL TENDER NOTES)
(Large Size)

Face Design: Eagle with spread wings left, three discs with "100," red seal numbers.

Back Design: Green, two variations of the wording in obligation.

SERIES	SIGNATURES	SEAL	A.B.P.	GOOD	V.FINE	UNC.
☐1862	Chittenden-Spinner*	Red	4200.00	5600.00	20000.00	82000.00
☐1862	Chittenden-Spinner**	Red	4200.00	5600.00	20000.00	82000.00
☐1863	Chittenden-Spinner**	Red	4200.00	5600.00	20000.00	82000.00

*First Obligation: Similar to 1875–1907 $5 note.
**Second Obligation: Shown above.

ONE HUNDRED DOLLAR NOTES (1869–1880)
UNITED STATES NOTES

(Large Size)

Face Design: Portrait of President Lincoln.

Back Design: First Issue

Back Design: Second Issue.

SERIES	SIGNATURES	SEAL	A.B.P.	GOOD	V.FINE	UNC.
☐1869	Allison-Spinner	Red	3800.00	5500.00	24,500.00	62,000.00

The following notes have a modified back design.
(Small Size)
Second Issue

SERIES	SIGNATURES	SEAL	A.B.P.	GOOD	V.FINE	UNC.
☐1875	Allison-New	Sm. Red	2500.00	3800.00	18000.00	51000.00
☐1875	Allison-Wyman	Sm. Red	3900.00	5900.00	23000.00	78500.00
☐1878	Allison-Gilfillan	Sm. Red	2200.00	3100.00	20500.00	48000.00
☐1880	Bruce-Gilfillan	Lg. Brown	1700.00	2400.00	17000.00	90500.00
☐1880	Bruce-Wyman	Lg. Brown	1700.00	2500.00	17000.00	90500.00
☐1880	Rosecrans-Jordan	Lg. Red	1700.00	2300.00	27000.00	43500.00
☐1880	Rosecrans-Hyatt	Red Plain	2200.00	3300.00	26500.00	100000.00
☐1880	Rosecrans-Hyatt	Red Spike	1700.00	2300.00	17000.00	43500.00
☐1880	Rosecrans-Huston	Lg. Red	1700.00	2300.00	14500.00	66000.00
☐1880	Rosecrans-Huston	Lg. Brown	1700.00	2700.00	14500.00	39500.00
☐1880	Tillman-Morgan	Sm. Red	1600.00	1700.00	12000.00	26500.00
☐1880	Bruce-Roberts	Sm. Red	1600.00	1700.00	11000.00	25500.00
☐1880	Lyons-Roberts	Sm. Red	1600.00	1700.00	11000.00	25500.00

ONE HUNDRED DOLLAR NOTES (1966) U.S. NOTES
(ALSO KNOWN AS LEGAL TENDER NOTES)
(Small Size)

Face Design: Portrait of Franklin, red seal, red serial numbers.

Back Design: Independence Hall.

SERIES	SIGNATURES	SEAL	A.B.P.	V.FINE	UNC.	*UNC
☐1966*	Granahan-Fowler	Red	135.00	175.00	550.00	2000.00
☐1966A	Elston-Kennedy	Red	135.00	240.00	1300.00	—

*This is the first note to be issued with the new Treasury Seal with wording in English instead of Latin.

ONE HUNDRED DOLLAR NOTES (1875)
NATIONAL BANK NOTES

FIRST CHARTER PERIOD (Large Size)

Face Design: Perry leaving the Saint Lawrence, left.

Back Design: Border green, center black, signing of the Declaration of Independence.

SERIES	SIGNATURES	SEAL	A.B.P.	GOOD	V.FINE	UNC.
☐Original	Chittenden-Spinner	Red	2100.00	2750.00	9000.00	40000.00
☐Original	Colby-Spinner	Red	2100.00	2750.00	9000.00	40000.00
☐Original	Allison-Spinner	Red	2100.00	2750.00	9000.00	40000.00
☐1875	Allison-New	Red	1900.00	2750.00	9000.00	41500.00
☐1875	Allison-Wyman	Red	1900.00	2750.00	9000.00	41500.00
☐1875	Allison-Gilfillan	Red	1900.00	2750.00	9000.00	41500.00
☐1875	Scofield-Gilfillan	Red	1900.00	2750.00	9000.00	41500.00
☐1875	Bruce-Gilfillan	Red	1900.00	2750.00	9000.00	41500.00
☐1875	Bruce-Wyman	Red	1900.00	2750.00	9000.00	41500.00
☐1875	Rosecrans-Huston	Red	1900.00	2750.00	9000.00	41500.00
☐1875	Tillman-Morgan	Red	1900.00	2750.00	9000.00	41500.00

ONE HUNDRED DOLLAR NOTES (1882)
NATIONAL BANK NOTES
SECOND CHARTER PERIOD (Large Size)
First Issue (Brown seal and brown backs.)

SERIES	SIGNATURES	SEAL	A.B.P.	GOOD	V.FINE	UNC.
☐1882	Bruce-Gilfillan	Brown	700.00	950.00	3000.00	14500.00
☐1882	Bruce-Wyman	Brown	700.00	950.00	3000.00	14500.00
☐1882	Bruce-Jordan	Brown	700.00	950.00	3000.00	14500.00
☐1882	Rosecrans-Jordan	Brown	700.00	950.00	3000.00	14500.00
☐1882	Rosecrans-Hyatt	Brown	700.00	950.00	3000.00	14500.00
☐1882	Rosecrans-Huston	Brown	700.00	950.00	3000.00	14500.00
☐1882	Rosecrans-Nebeker	Brown	700.00	950.00	3000.00	14500.00
☐1882	Rosecrans-Morgan	Brown	700.00	1375.00	3500.00	14500.00
☐1882	Tillman-Morgan	Brown	700.00	950.00	3000.00	14500.00
☐1882	Tillman-Roberts	Brown	700.00	950.00	3000.00	14500.00
☐1882	Bruce-Roberts	Brown	700.00	950.00	3000.00	14500.00
☐1882	Lyons-Roberts	Brown	700.00	950.00	3000.00	14500.00

SECOND CHARTER PERIOD (Large Size)
Second Issue (Blue seal, green back with date "1882–1908")

Back Design: Green with date "1882–1908" center.

SERIES	SIGNATURES	SEAL	A.B.P.	GOOD	V.FINE	UNC.
☐1882	Rosecrans-Huston	Blue	550.00	800.00	5750.00	12000.00
☐1882	Rosecrans-Nebeker	Blue	550.00	800.00	5750.00	12000.00
☐1882	Tillman-Morgan	Blue	550.00	800.00	5750.00	12000.00
☐1882	Tillman-Roberts	Blue	550.00	800.00	5750.00	12000.00
☐1882	Bruce-Roberts	Blue	550.00	800.00	5750.00	12000.00
☐1882	Lyons-Roberts	Blue	550.00	800.00	5750.00	12000.00
☐1882	Vernon-Treat	Blue	550.00	800.00	5750.00	12000.00
☐1882	Napier-McClung	Blue	550.00	800.00	5750.00	12000.00

This note was also issued with (value) ONE HUNDRED DOLLARS
on the back. Very rare. — 45,000.00 60,000.00 95,000.00 —

ONE HUNDRED DOLLAR NOTES (1902)
NATIONAL BANK NOTES
THIRD CHARTER PERIOD (Large Size)

Face Design: Portrait of John J. Knox left.

Back Design: Male figures with shield and flags.
First Issue (Red seal)

SERIES	SIGNATURES	SEAL	A.B.P.	GOOD	V.FINE	UNC.
☐1902	Lyons-Roberts	Red	700.00	950.00	5000.00	17500.00
☐1902	Lyons-Treat	Red	700.00	950.00	5000.00	17500.00
☐1902	Vernon-Treat	Red	700.00	950.00	5000.00	17500.00

Second Issue*

Design is similar to previous note. Seal and serial numbers are now blue; back of note has date "1902–1908" added.

SERIES	SIGNATURES	SEAL	A.B.P.	GOOD	V.FINE	UNC.
		Blue	170.00	235.00	1400.00	4000.00

Third Issue*

Design continues as previous notes. Seal and serial numbers remain blue, date "1902–1908" removed from back.

SERIES	SIGNATURES	SEAL	A.B.P.	GOOD	V.FINE	UNC.
		Blue	160.00	215.00	1300.00	3900.00

* The notes of the **Second and Third Issue** appeared with various signatures: Lyons-Roberts, Lyons-Treat, Vernon-Treat, Vernon-McClung, Napier-McClung, Parker-Burke, Teehee-Burke, Elliott-Burke, Elliott-White, Speelman-White, Woods-White.

ONE HUNDRED DOLLAR NOTES (1929)
NATIONAL BANK NOTES
(Small Size)

Face Design: Portrait of Franklin center. Name of bank and city left. Brown seal right.

SERIES SIGNATURES	SEAL	A.B.P.	V.FINE	UNC.
☐ 1929 Type I Jones-Woods	Brown	125.00	175.00	625.00
☐ 1929 Type II Jones-Woods	Brown	150.00	275.00	1525.00

ONE HUNDRED DOLLAR NOTES (1878)
SILVER CERTIFICATES

SERIES SIGNATURES	SEAL	A.B.P.	GOOD	V.FINE	UNC.
☐ 1878 Scofield-Gilfillan-White	Red				UNIQUE
☐ 1878 Scofield-Gilfillan-Hopper	Red		NO SPECIMENS KNOWN		
☐ 1878 Scofield-Gilfillan-Hillhouse	Red		NO SPECIMENS KNOWN		
☐ 1878 Scofield-Gilfillan-Anthony	Red				UNIQUE
☐ 1878 Scofield-Gilfillan-Wyman (printed signature of Wyman)	Red		NO SPECIMENS KNOWN		
☐ 1878 Scofield-Gilfillan	Red				VERY RARE
☐ 1880 Scofield-Gilfillan	Brown		EXTREMELY RARE		
☐ 1880 Bruce-Gilfillan	Brown	3350.00	4900.00	18500.00	65000.00
☐ 1880 Bruce-Wyman	Brown	2350.00	3700.00	16000.00	55000.00
☐ 1880 Rosecrans-Huston	Brown	2350.00	3700.00	16000.00	205000.00
☐ 1880 Rosecrans-Nebeker	Brown	2350.00	3700.00	16000.00	180000.00

ONE HUNDRED DOLLAR NOTES (1891)
SILVER CERTIFICATES

(Large Size)

Face Design: Portrait of President Monroe.

SERIES	SIGNATURES	SEAL	A.B.P.	GOOD	V.FINE	UNC.
☐1891	Rosecrans-Nebeker	Red	3000.00	4500.00	18000.00	60000.00
☐1891	Tillman-Morgan	Red	3000.00	4500.00	18000.00	60000.00

This note was also issued in the Series of 1878 and 1880. They are very rare.

ONE HUNDRED DOLLAR NOTES (1882–1922)
GOLD CERTIFICATES

(Large Size)

Face Design: Portrait of Thomas H. Benton.

SERIES	SIGNATURES	SEAL	A.B.P.	GOOD	V.FINE	UNC.
☐1882	Bruce-Gilfillan	Brown	1840.00	2985.00	21000.00	260000.00
☐1882	Bruce-Wyman	Brown	3800.00	7100.00	51100.00	285000.00
☐1882	Rosecrans-Hyatt	Lg. Red	3800.00	6100.00	48000.00	260000.00
☐1882	Rosecrans-Huston	Lg. Brown	3500.00	5100.00	33000.00	260000.00
☐1882	Lyons-Roberts	Sm. Red	250.00	320.00	1900.00	6600.00
☐1882	Lyons-Treat	Sm. Red	250.00	530.00	2700.00	28600.00
☐1882	Vernon-Treat	Sm. Red	250.00	420.00	2100.00	8600.00
☐1882	Vernon-McClung	Sm. Red	250.00	420.00	2175.00	8600.00
☐1882	Napier-McClung	Sm. Red	250.00	335.00	2100.00	8600.00
☐1882	Napier-Thompson	Sm. Red	250.00	440.00	1800.00	10850.00
☐1882	Napier-Burke	Sm. Red	250.00	310.00	1050.00	8600.00
☐1882	Parker-Burke	Sm. Red	250.00	310.00	1050.00	8600.00
☐1882	Teehee-Burke	Sm. Red	250.00	310.00	1050.00	8600.00
☐1922	Speelman-White	Sm. Red	250.00	310.00	950.00	8600.00

ONE HUNDRED DOLLAR NOTES (1928)
GOLD CERTIFICATES
(Small Size)

Face Design: Portrait of Franklin center. Yellow seal to left. Yellow numbers.

SERIES	SIGNATURES	SEAL	A.B.P.	GOOD	V.FINE	UNC.
☐1928	Woods-Mellon	Gold	145.00	220.00	535.00	3500.00

ONE HUNDRED DOLLAR NOTES (1890–1891)
TREASURY OR COIN NOTES

(Large Size)

Face Design: Portrait of Commodore Farragut to right.

Back Design: Large "100," called "Watermelon Note."

Back Design: ONE HUNDRED in scalloped medallion.

SERIES	SIGNATURES	SEAL	A.B.P.	GOOD	V.FINE	UNC.
☐1890	Rosecrans-Huston	Brown	7500.00	10500.00	75000.00	180000.00+
☐1890	Rosecrans-Nebeker	Red	7500.00	10500.00	75000.00	180000.00+

ONE HUNDRED DOLLAR NOTES (1914)
FEDERAL RESERVE NOTES
(Large Size)

Face Design: Portrait of Franklin in center.
Back Design: Group of five allegorical figures.

SERIES OF 1914,
SIGNATURES OF BURKE-McADOO, RED SEAL
AND RED SERIAL NUMBERS

BANK	A.B.P.	GOOD	V.FINE	UNC.	BANK	A.B.P.	GOOD	V.FINE	UNC.
☐ Boston	800.00	1000.00	5000.00	17000.00	☐Chicago	800.00	1100.00	5000.00	17000.00
☐ New York	800.00	1000.00	5000.00	17000.00	☐St. Louis	800.00	1100.00	5000.00	17000.00
☐ Philadelphia	800.00	1000.00	5000.00	17000.00	☐Minneapolis	800.00	1100.00	5000.00	17000.00
☐ Cleveland	800.00	1000.00	5000.00	17000.00	☐Kansas City	800.00	1100.00	5000.00	17000.00
☐ Richmond	800.00	1000.00	5000.00	17000.00	☐Dallas	800.00	1100.00	5000.00	17000.00
☐ Atlanta	800.00	1000.00	5000.00	17000.00	☐San Francisco	800.00	1100.00	5000.00	17000.00

SERIES OF 1914, DESIGN CONTINUES AS PREVIOUS NOTE, BLUE
SEAL AND BLUE SERIAL NUMBERS

This note was issued with various signatures for each bank (Burke-McAdoo, Burke-Glass, Burke-Huston, White-Mellon).

BANK	A.B.P.	V.FINE	UNC.	BANK	A.B.P.	V.FINE	UNC.
☐Boston	375.00	775.00	2000.00	☐ Chicago	375.00	775.00	2000.00
☐New York	375.00	775.00	2000.00	☐ St. Louis	375.00	775.00	2000.00
☐Philadelphia	375.00	775.00	2000.00	☐ Minneapolis	375.00	775.00	2000.00
☐Cleveland	375.00	775.00	2000.00	☐ Kansas City	375.00	775.00	2000.00
☐Richmond	375.00	775.00	2000.00	☐ Dallas	375.00	775.00	2000.00
☐Atlanta	375.00	775.00	2000.00	☐ San Francisco	375.00	775.00	2000.00

ONE HUNDRED DOLLAR NOTES (1928)
FEDERAL RESERVE NOTES
(Small Size)

Face Design: Portrait of Franklin, black Federal Reserve Seal left with number, green Treasury Seal right.

SERIES OF 1928,
SIGNATURES OF WOODS-MELLON, GREEN SEAL

BANK	A.B.P.	V.FINE	UNC.	BANK	A.B.P.	V.FINE	UNC.
☐Boston	120.00	230.00	850.00	☐ Chicago	120.00	220.00	650.00
☐New York	120.00	190.00	850.00	☐ St. Louis	120.00	195.00	650.00
☐Philadelphia	120.00	190.00	850.00	☐ Minneapolis	120.00	195.00	650.00
☐Cleveland	120.00	230.00	850.00	☐ Kansas City	120.00	195.00	650.00
☐Richmond	120.00	230.00	850.00	☐ Dallas	170.00	220.00	650.00
☐Atlanta	120.00	230.00	850.00	☐ San Francisco	120.00	185.00	650.00

SERIES OF 1928A,
SIGNATURES OF WOODS-MELLON, GREEN SEAL

The number is in black and the Federal Reserve Seal is changed to a letter.
(Small Size)

BANK	A.B.P.	V.FINE	UNC.	BANK	A.B.P.	V.FINE	UNC.
☐Boston	120.00	230.00	700.00	☐ Chicago	120.00	180.00	500.00
☐New York	120.00	200.00	700.00	☐ St. Louis	120.00	180.00	500.00
☐Philadelphia	120.00	230.00	700.00	☐ Minneapolis	120.00	200.00	500.00
☐Cleveland	120.00	195.00	700.00	☐ Kansas City	120.00	220.00	500.00
☐Richmond	120.00	245.00	700.00	☐ Dallas	120.00	180.00	500.00
☐Atlanta	170.00	220.00	700.00	☐ San Francisco	120.00	180.00	500.00

ONE HUNDRED DOLLAR NOTES (1934)
FEDERAL RESERVE NOTES
SERIES OF 1934, SIGNATURES OF JULIAN-MORGENTHAU, GREEN SEAL

BANK	A.B.P.	V.FINE	UNC.	BANK	A.B.P.	V.FINE	UNC.
☐ Boston	115.00	125.00	200.00	☐ Chicago	115.00	125.00	200.00
☐ New York	115.00	125.00	200.00	☐ St. Louis	115.00	125.00	200.00

☐ Philadelphia	110.00	120.00	250.00	☐ Minneapolis	110.00	120.00	300.00
☐ Cleveland	110.00	120.00	250.00	☐ Kansas City	110.00	120.00	300.00
☐ Richmond	110.00	120.00	250.00	☐ Dallas	110.00	120.00	300.00
☐ Atlanta	110.00	120.00	250.00	☐ San Francisco	110.00	120.00	300.00

SERIES OF 1934A, SIGNATURES OF JULIAN-MORGENTHAU, GREEN SEAL

BANK	A.B.P.	V.FINE	UNC.	BANK	A.B.P.	V.FINE	UNC.
☐ Boston	110.00	120.00	250.00	☐ Chicago	110.00	120.00	250.00
☐ New York	110.00	120.00	250.00	☐ St. Louis	110.00	120.00	250.00
☐ Philadelphia	110.00	120.00	250.00	☐ Minneapolis	110.00	120.00	250.00
☐ Cleveland	110.00	120.00	250.00	☐ Kansas City	110.00	120.00	250.00
☐ Richmond	110.00	120.00	250.00	☐ Dallas	110.00	120.00	250.00
☐ Atlanta	110.00	120.00	250.00	☐ San Francisco	110.00	120.00	250.00

SERIES OF 1934B, SIGNATURES OF JULIAN-VINSON, GREEN SEAL

BANK	A.B.P.	V.FINE	UNC.	BANK	A.B.P.	V.FINE	UNC.
☐ Boston	120.00	150.00	350.00	☐ Chicago	125.00	165.00	350.00
☐ New York	120.00	150.00	350.00	☐ St. Louis	125.00	165.00	350.00
☐ Philadelphia	125.00	165.00	350.00	☐ Minneapolis	125.00	165.00	350.00
☐ Cleveland	125.00	165.00	350.00	☐ Kansas City	120.00	150.00	350.00
☐ Richmond	125.00	165.00	350.00	☐ Dallas	120.00	150.00	350.00
☐ Atlanta	125.00	165.00	350.00	☐ San Francisco	120.00	150.00	350.00

SERIES OF 1934C, SIGNATURES OF JULIAN-SNYDER, GREEN SEAL

BANK	A.B.P.	V.FINE	UNC.	BANK	A.B.P.	V.FINE	UNC.
☐ Boston	120.00	150.00	350.00	☐ Chicago	120.00	185.00	350.00
☐ New York	120.00	150.00	350.00	☐ St. Louis	120.00	185.00	350.00
☐ Philadelphia	120.00	150.00	350.00	☐ Minneapolis	120.00	185.00	350.00
☐ Cleveland	120.00	165.00	350.00	☐ Kansas City	120.00	185.00	350.00
☐ Richmond	120.00	165.00	350.00	☐ Dallas	120.00	185.00	350.00
☐ Atlanta	120.00	165.00	350.00	☐ San Francisco	120.00	185.00	350.00

SERIES OF 1934D, SIGNATURES OF JULIAN-SNYDER, GREEN SEAL

BANK	A.B.P.	V.FINE	UNC.	BANK	A.B.P.	V.FINE	UNC.
☐ New York	110.00	5000.00	8000.00	☐ St. Louis	110.00	215.00	900.00
☐ Philadelphia	110.00	280.00	1000.00	☐ Dallas	110.00	265.00	1000.00
☐ Atlanta	110.00	280.00	1000.00				
☐ Chicago	110.00	280.00	1000.00				

ONE HUNDRED DOLLAR NOTES (1950)
FEDERAL RESERVE NOTES
SERIES OF 1950, SIGNATURES OF CLARK-SNYDER, GREEN SEAL

BANK	A.B.P.	V.FINE	UNC.	UNC.★	BANK	A.B.P.	V.FINE	UNC.	UNC.★
☐ Boston	110.00	120.00	300.00	1500.00	☐ Chicago	110.00	120.00	100.00	1500.00
☐ New York	110.00	120.00	300.00	1500.00	☐ St. Louis	110.00	120.00	100.00	1500.00
☐ Philadelphia	105.00	105.00	300.00	1500.00	☐ Minneapolis	105.00	105.00	100.00	1500.00
☐ Cleveland	110.00	120.00	300.00	1500.00	☐ Kansas City	110.00	120.00	100.00	1500.00
☐ Richmond	110.00	120.00	300.00	1500.00	☐ Dallas	110.00	120.00	110.00	1500.00
☐ Atlanta	110.00	120.00	300.00	1500.00	☐ San Francisco	105.00	105.00	110.00	1500.00

SERIES OF 1950A, SIGNATURES OF PRIEST-HUMPHERY, GREEN SEAL

BANK	A.B.P.	V.FINE	UNC.	UNC.★	BANK	A.B.P.	V.FINE	UNC.	UNC.★
☐ Boston	105.00	125.00	175.00	750.00	☐ Chicago	105.00	125.00	175.00	750.00
☐ New York	105.00	125.00	175.00	750.00	☐ St. Louis	105.00	115.00	175.00	750.00
☐ Philadelphia	105.00	110.00	175.00	750.00	☐ Minneapolis	105.00	125.00	175.00	750.00
☐ Cleveland	105.00	110.00	175.00	750.00	☐ Kansas City	105.00	125.00	175.00	750.00
☐ Richmond	105.00	110.00	175.00	750.00	☐ Dallas	105.00	110.00	175.00	750.00
☐ Atlanta	105.00	120.00	175.00	750.00	☐ San Francisco	105.00	110.00	175.00	750.00

SERIES OF 1950B, SIGNATURES OF PRIEST-ANDERSON, GREEN SEAL

BANK	A.B.P.	V.FINE	UNC.	UNC.★	BANK	A.B.P.	V.FINE	UNC.	UNC.★
☐ Boston	110.00	120.00	150.00	720.00	☐ Chicago	100.00	110.00	150.00	720.00
☐ New York	110.00	120.00	150.00	720.00	☐ St. Louis	100.00	120.00	150.00	720.00
☐ Philadelphia	100.00	100.00	150.00	720.00	☐ Minneapolis	100.00	120.00	150.00	720.00
☐ Cleveland	110.00	120.00	150.00	720.00	☐ Kansas City	100.00	120.00	150.00	720.00
☐ Richmond	110.00	120.00	150.00	720.00	☐ Dallas	100.00	120.00	150.00	720.00
☐ Atlanta	100.00	100.00	150.00	720.00	☐ San Francisco	100.00	120.00	150.00	720.00

SERIES OF 1950C, SIGNATURES OF SMITH-DILLON, GREEN SEAL

BANK	A.B.P.	V.FINE	UNC.	UNC.★	BANK	A.B.P.	V.FINE	UNC.	UNC.★
☐ Boston	105.00	120.00	175.00	650.00	☐ Chicago	105.00	110.00	175.00	650.00
☐ New York	105.00	120.00	175.00	650.00	☐ St. Louis	105.00	120.00	175.00	650.00
☐ Philadelphia	105.00	120.00	175.00	650.00	☐ Minneapolis	105.00	120.00	175.00	650.00
☐ Cleveland	105.00	110.00	175.00	650.00	☐ Kansas City	105.00	120.00	175.00	650.00
☐ Richmond	105.00	110.00	175.00	650.00	☐ Dallas	105.00	120.00	175.00	650.00
☐ Atlanta	105.00	120.00	175.00	650.00	☐ San Francisco	105.00	120.00	175.00	650.00

SERIES OF 1950D, SIGNATURES OF GRANAHAN-DILLON, GREEN SEAL

BANK	A.B.P.	V.FINE	UNC.	UNC.★	BANK	A.B.P.	V.FINE	UNC.	UNC.★
☐ Boston	105.00	135.00	200.00	960.00	☐ Chicago	105.00	135.00	200.00	915.00
☐ New York	105.00	135.00	200.00	960.00	☐ St. Louis	105.00	135.00	200.00	915.00
☐ Philadelphia	105.00	115.00	175.00	960.00	☐ Minneapolis	105.00	135.00	200.00	915.00
☐ Cleveland	105.00	115.00	175.00	960.00	☐ Kansas City	105.00	120.00	175.00	915.00
☐ Richmond	105.00	115.00	175.00	960.00	☐ Dallas	105.00	120.00	175.00	915.00
☐ Atlanta	105.00	115.00	175.00	960.00	☐ San Francisco	105.00	120.00	175.00	915.00

SERIES OF 1950E, SIGNATURES OF GRANAHAN-FOWLER, GREEN SEAL

BANK	A.B.P.	V.FINE	UNC.	BANK	A.B.P.	V.FINE	UNC.
				☐ Chicago	130.00	200.00	1200.00
☐ New York	130.00	175.00	950.00				
				☐ San Francisco	130.00	225.00	900.00

ONE HUNDRED DOLLAR NOTES (1963)
FEDERAL RESERVE NOTES
SERIES OF 1963, (THERE WERE NOT ANY NOTES PRINTED FOR THIS SERIES.)

SERIES OF 1963A, SIGNATURES OF GRANAHAN-FOWLER, GREEN SEAL

BANK	A.B.P.	V.FINE	UNC.	UNC.★	BANK	A.B.P.	V.FINE	UNC.	UNC.★
☐ Boston	105.00	120.00	200.00	675.00	☐ Chicago	105.00	120.00	200.00	675.00
☐ New York	105.00	120.00	200.00	675.00	☐ St. Louis	105.00	120.00	200.00	675.00
☐ Philadelphia	102.00	110.00	200.00	675.00	☐ Minneapolis	105.00	120.00	200.00	675.00
☐ Cleveland	102.00	110.00	200.00	675.00	☐ Kansas City	105.00	120.00	200.00	675.00
☐ Richmond	102.00	110.00	200.00	675.00	☐ Dallas	105.00	120.00	200.00	675.00
☐ Atlanta	102.00	110.00	200.00	675.00	☐ San Francisco	105.00	120.00	200.00	675.00

ONE HUNDRED DOLLAR NOTES (1969)
FEDERAL RESERVE NOTES
SERIES OF 1969, SIGNATURES OF ELSTON-KENNEDY, GREEN SEAL

BANK	A.B.P.	V.FINE	UNC.	UNC.★	BANK	A.B.P.	V.FINE	UNC.	UNC.★
☐ Boston	102.00	110.00	175.00	400.00	☐ Chicago	102.00	110.00	175.00	400.00
☐ New York	102.00	110.00	175.00	400.00	☐ St. Louis	102.00	110.00	175.00	400.00
☐ Philadelphia	102.00	110.00	175.00	400.00	☐ Minneapolis	102.00	110.00	175.00	400.00
☐ Cleveland	102.00	110.00	175.00	400.00	☐ Kansas City	102.00	110.00	175.00	400.00
☐ Richmond	102.00	110.00	175.00	400.00	☐ Dallas	102.00	110.00	175.00	400.00
☐ Atlanta	102.00	110.00	175.00	400.00	☐ San Francisco	102.00	110.00	175.00	400.00

SERIES OF 1969A, SIGNATURES OF KABIS-CONNALLY, GREEN SEAL

BANK	A.B.P.	V.FINE	UNC.	UNC.★	BANK	A.B.P.	V.FINE	UNC.	UNC.★
☐ Boston	—	110.00	150.00	375.00	☐ Chicago	—	110.00	150.00	375.00
☐ New York	—	110.00	150.00	375.00	☐ St. Louis	—	110.00	150.00	375.00
☐ Philadelphia	—	110.00	150.00	375.00	☐ Minneapolis	—	110.00	150.00	375.00
☐ Cleveland	—	110.00	150.00	375.00	☐ Kansas City	—	110.00	150.00	375.00
☐ Richmond	—	110.00	150.00	375.00	☐ Dallas	—	110.00	150.00	375.00
☐ Atlanta	—	110.00	150.00	375.00	☐ San Francisco	—	110.00	150.00	375.00

SERIES OF 1969B, (THERE WERE NOT ANY NOTES PRINTED FOR THIS SERIES.)

SERIES OF 1969C, SIGNATURES OF BANUELOS-SHULTZ, GREEN SEAL

BANK	A.B.P.	V.FINE	UNC.	UNC.★	BANK	A.B.P.	V.FINE	UNC.	UNC.★
☐ Boston	—	110.00	175.00	400.00	☐ Chicago	—	110.00	150.00	400.00
☐ New York	—	110.00	175.00	400.00	☐ St. Louis	—	110.00	150.00	400.00
☐ Philadelphia	—	110.00	175.00	400.00	☐ Minneapolis	—	110.00	150.00	400.00
☐ Cleveland	—	110.00	175.00	400.00	☐ Kansas City	—	110.00	150.00	400.00
☐ Richmond	—	110.00	175.00	400.00	☐ Dallas	—	110.00	150.00	400.00
☐ Atlanta	—	110.00	175.00	400.00	☐ San Francisco	—	110.00	150.00	400.00

ONE HUNDRED DOLLAR NOTES (1974)
FEDERAL RESERVE NOTES
SERIES OF 1974, SIGNATURES OF NEFF-SIMON, GREEN SEAL

BANK	A.B.P.	V.FINE	UNC.	UNC.★	BANK	A.B.P.	V.FINE	UNC.	UNC.★
☐ Boston	—	110.00	175.00	350.00	☐ Chicago	—	110.00	150.00	350.00
☐ New York	—	110.00	175.00	350.00	☐ St. Louis	—	110.00	150.00	350.00
☐ Philadelphia	—	110.00	175.00	350.00	☐ Minneapolis	—	110.00	150.00	350.00
☐ Cleveland	—	110.00	175.00	350.00	☐ Kansas City	—	110.00	150.00	350.00
☐ Richmond	—	110.00	175.00	350.00	☐ Dallas	—	110.00	150.00	350.00
☐ Atlanta	—	110.00	175.00	350.00	☐ San Francisco	—	110.00	150.00	350.00

ONE HUNDRED DOLLAR NOTES (1977)
FEDERAL RESERVE NOTES
SERIES OF 1977, SIGNATURES OF MORTON-BLUMENTHAL, GREEN SEAL

BANK	A.B.P.	V.FINE	UNC.	UNC.★	BANK	A.B.P.	V.FINE	UNC.	UNC.★
☐ Boston	—	110.00	125.00	325.00	☐ Chicago	—	110.00	125.00	325.00
☐ New York	—	110.00	125.00	325.00	☐ St. Louis	—	110.00	125.00	325.00
☐ Philadelphia	—	110.00	125.00	325.00	☐ Minneapolis	—	110.00	125.00	325.00
☐ Cleveland	—	110.00	125.00	325.00	☐ Kansas City	—	110.00	125.00	325.00
☐ Richmond	—	110.00	125.00	325.00	☐ Dallas	—	110.00	125.00	325.00
☐ Atlanta	—	110.00	125.00	325.00	☐ San Francisco	—	110.00	125.00	325.00

ONE HUNDRED DOLLAR NOTES (1981)
FEDERAL RESERVE NOTES
SERIES OF 1981, SIGNATURES OF BUCHANAN-REGAN, GREEN SEAL

BANK	A.B.P.	V.FINE	UNC.	BANK	A.B.P.	V.FINE	UNC.
☐ Boston	—	110.00	200.00	☐ Chicago	—	110.00	200.00
☐ New York	—	110.00	200.00	☐ St. Louis	—	110.00	200.00
☐ Philadelphia	—	110.00	200.00	☐ Minneapolis	—	110.00	200.00
☐ Cleveland	—	110.00	200.00	☐ Kansas City	—	110.00	200.00
☐ Richmond	—	110.00	200.00	☐ Dallas	—	110.00	200.00
☐ Atlanta	—	110.00	200.00	☐ San Francisco	—	110.00	200.00

SERIES OF 1981A, SIGNATURES OF ORTEGA-REGAN, GREEN SEAL

BANK	A.B.P.	V.FINE	UNC.	BANK	A.B.P.	V.FINE	UNC.
☐ Boston	—	110.00	175.00	☐ Chicago	—	110.00	175.00
☐ New York	—	110.00	175.00	☐ St. Louis	—	110.00	175.00
☐ Philadelphia	—	110.00	175.00	☐ Minneapolis	—	110.00	175.00
☐ Cleveland	—	110.00	175.00	☐ Kansas City	—	110.00	175.00
☐ Richmond	—	110.00	175.00	☐ Dallas	—	110.00	175.00
☐ Atlanta	—	110.00	175.00	☐ San Francisco	—	110.00	175.00

ONE HUNDRED DOLLAR NOTES (1985)
FEDERAL RESERVE NOTES
SERIES OF 1985, SIGNATURES OF ORTEGA-REGAN, GREEN SEAL

BANK	A.B.P.	V.FINE	UNC.	BANK	A.B.P.	V.FINE	UNC.
☐ Boston	—	110.00	140.00	☐ Chicago	—	110.00	140.00
☐ New York	—	110.00	140.00	☐ St. Louis	—	110.00	140.00
☐ Philadelphia	—	110.00	140.00	☐ Minneapolis	—	110.00	140.00
☐ Cleveland	—	110.00	140.00	☐ Kansas City	—	110.00	140.00
☐ Richmond	—	110.00	140.00	☐ Dallas	—	110.00	140.00
☐ Atlanta	—	110.00	140.00	☐ San Francisco	—	110.00	140.00

ONE HUNDRED DOLLAR NOTES (1988)
FEDERAL RESERVE NOTES
SERIES OF 1988, SIGNATURES OF ORTEGA-BRADY, GREEN SEAL

BANK	A.B.P.	V.FINE	UNC.	BANK	A.B.P.	V.FINE	UNC.
☐ Boston	—	110.00	130.00	☐ Chicago	—	110.00	130.00
☐ New York	—	110.00	130.00	☐ St. Louis	—	110.00	130.00
☐ Philadelphia	—	110.00	130.00	☐ Minneapolis	—	110.00	130.00
☐ Cleveland	—	110.00	130.00	☐ Kansas City	—	110.00	130.00
☐ Richmond	—	110.00	130.00	☐ Dallas	—	110.00	130.00
☐ Atlanta	—	110.00	130.00	☐ San Francisco	—	110.00	130.00

ONE HUNDRED DOLLAR NOTES (1990)
FEDERAL RESERVE NOTES
SERIES OF 1990, SIGNATURES OF VILLALPANDO-BRADY, GREEN SEAL

BANK	A.B.P.	V.FINE	UNC.	BANK	A.B.P.	V.FINE	UNC.
☐ Boston	—	—	125.00	☐ Chicago	—	—	125.00
☐ New York	—	—	125.00	☐ St. Louis	—	—	125.00
☐ Philadelphia	—	—	125.00	☐ Minneapolis	—	—	125.00
☐ Cleveland	—	—	125.00	☐ Kansas City	—	—	125.00
☐ Richmond	—	—	125.00	☐ Dallas	—	—	125.00
☐ Atlanta	—	—	125.00	☐ San Francisco	—	—	125.00

ONE HUNDRED DOLLAR NOTES (1993)
FEDERAL RESERVE NOTES
SERIES OF 1993, SIGNATURES OF WITHROW-BENTSEN, GREEN SEAL

BANK	A.B.P.	V.FINE	UNC.	BANK	A.B.P.	V.FINE	UNC.
☐ Boston	—	—	120.00	☐ Chicago	—	—	120.00
☐ New York	—	—	120.00	☐ St. Louis	—	—	120.00
☐ Philadelphia	—	—	120.00	☐ Minneapolis	—	—	120.00
☐ Cleveland	—	—	120.00	☐ Kansas City	—	—	120.00
☐ Richmond	—	—	120.00	☐ Dallas	—	—	120.00
☐ Atlanta	—	—	120.00	☐ San Francisco	—	—	120.00

ONE HUNDRED DOLLAR NOTES (1996)
FEDERAL RESERVE NOTES
SERIES OF 1996, SIGNATURES OF WITHROW-RUBIN, GREEN SEAL

BANK	A.B.P.	V.FINE	UNC.	BANK	A.B.P.	V.FINE	UNC.
☐ Boston	—	—	105.00	☐ Chicago	—	—	105.00
☐ New York	—	—	105.00	☐ St. Louis	—	—	105.00
☐ Philadelphia	—	—	105.00	☐ Minneapolis	—	—	105.00
☐ Cleveland	—	—	105.00	☐ Kansas City	—	—	105.00
☐ Richmond	—	—	105.00	☐ Dallas	—	—	105.00
☐ Atlanta	—	—	105.00	☐ San Francisco	—	—	105.00

ONE HUNDRED DOLLAR NOTES (1929)
FEDERAL RESERVE BANK NOTES
(ISSUED ONLY IN SERIES OF 1929)
(Small Size)

Face Design: Portrait of Franklin, brown seal and numbers.

Back Design

BANK & CITY	SIGNATURES	SEAL	A.B.P.	V.FINE	UNC.
☐New York	Jones-Woods	Brown	110.00	165.00	460.00
☐Cleveland	Jones-Woods	Brown	110.00	165.00	460.00
☐Richmond	Jones-Woods	Brown	110.00	175.00	810.00
☐Chicago	Jones-Woods	Brown	110.00	165.00	460.00
☐Minneapolis	Jones-Woods	Brown	110.00	180.00	560.00
☐Kansas City	Jones-Woods	Brown	110.00	140.00	585.00
☐Dallas	Jones-Woods	Brown	110.00	205.00	2000.00

FIVE HUNDRED, ONE THOUSAND, FIVE THOUSAND, AND TEN THOUSAND DOLLAR NOTES

(Production of notes in denominations above one hundred dollars was discontinued in 1969.)

FEDERAL RESERVE
FIVE HUNDRED DOLLAR NOTES

	A.B.P.	V.FINE	UNC.	BANK
☐ 1928	700.00	900.00	2000.00	ALL BANKS
☐ 1934	625.00	850.00	1500.00	ALL BANKS
☐ 1934A	625.00	850.00	1500.00	ALL BANKS EXCEPT BOSTON/ATLANTA
☐ 1934B	—	RARE	RARE	ATLANTA ONLY
☐ 1934C	—	RARE	RARE	BOSTON ONLY

Gold Certs.

☐ 1928	1000.00	4500.00	20,000.00	

ONE THOUSAND DOLLAR NOTES

	A.B.P.	V.FINE	UNC.
☐ 1928	1200.00	1700.00	3800.00
☐ 1934	1200.00	1500.00	2500.00
☐ 1934A	1200.00	1500.00	2500.00

Gold:

☐ 1928	1300.00	6000.00	30,000.00
☐ 1934	RARE	RARE	RARE

FIVE THOUSAND DOLLAR NOTES

	A.B.P.	V.FINE	UNC.	BANK
☐ 1928	10,000.00	30,000.00	65,000.00	
☐ 1934	8000.00	28,000.00	45,000.00	
☐ 1934A	—	RARE	RARE	ST. LOUIS ONLY
☐ 1934B	—	RARE	RARE	NEW YORK
☐ Gold Certs.			VERY RARE	

TEN THOUSAND DOLLAR NOTES

	A.B.P.	V.FINE	UNC.	BANK
☐ 1928	20,000.00	45,000.00	120,000.00	
☐ 1934	15,000.00	37,500.00	65,000.00	
☐ 1934A	—	RARE	RARE	CHICAGO ONLY
☐ Gold Certs.			VERY RARE	

WESTERN SCRIP & OBSOLETES

First a word regarding these western notes. Paper was generally despised in the west, where gold was the main source of exchange. However, certain realities dictated the use of paper currency. Notes listed here fall into six categories:

1) SUTLER NOTES (S): Forts in the military west needed a traceable form of barter payable between pay days.

2) PRIVATE BANK NOTES (B): Western banks isolated from the eastern monetary sources couldn't wait months for gold delivery when their daily existence was tenable at best.

3) MERCHANT SCRIP (M): Businesses needed a means to pay their workers and issue credits to customers. Companies also used scrip to ensure that wages were spent at their company store.

4) WARRANTS and COMMUNAL SCRIP (W): Both civic groups and city, county, and state governments needed a medium of "future" exchange where nonexistent funds or labor could be collected as it became available.

5) ADVERTISING NOTES (A): These represented promises to the holder and either had a face value or were printed on other notes such as Private Bank or CSA notes. Some were printed as close copies of U.S. Federal currency.

6) PANIC or DEPRESSION SCRIP (D): Widespread runs on banks (1907) or the closing of all banks (1933) necessitated a form of currency that could keep commerce operating while Federal notes were in short supply. It should be noted that the Federal government welcomed these notes and ignored currency laws banning them.

Comments or information regarding existing unlisted or listed issues is encouraged and should be sent to Bill Rindone, P.O. Box 790, Aurora, OR 97002 or emailed to Scrip@mystical.ws. Scans and data may be submitted for the states/territories listed and *also* for California, Iowa, Missouri, and Oklahoma, which are currently being compiled. This listing of Western Scrip is part of an ongoing research project.

Prices listed are for the most common of the denominations shown and for the condition most frequently found. A short glossary of terms can be found after the listings.

ALASKA

1920 $100 Valdez Igloo of Pioneers of Alaska

DENOMINATION	PRICE
1954 Alaska Terr. - $100 Black Diamond Certificate (A)	$35
1847–52 Aleutians, AT-10 Kopeks 1 Rouble, etc. Russian-America Sealskin Money (M)	$5000
19-- Dillingham 5¢, 10¢, 25¢, 50¢ Fisherman's Co-Op Trading Post and Roadhouse (M)	Set $10
1907 ND Fairbanks, AT - 25¢ 50¢ Salchaket Trading Co. Scrip (M)	$8500
19-- ND Fairbanks - 1 share Alaska-Colonial Currency (A)	$25
19-- Juneau - 5¢, 10¢, 25¢, 50¢ Juneau Hotel Scrip (M)	$65
1907 Nome, AT - $1, $2, $5, $10, $20, $50, $100 Nome Clearing House (D)	$7500
1920-33 Skagway, AT - $5 $10 $20 $50 White Pass Dance Hall (A)	$250
1920 Valdez, AT - $10 $20 $50 $100 Valdez Igloo, Pioneers of Alaska (A)	$250

ARIZONA

1902 $4 Fiege & Company, Arizona Territory

DENOMINATION	PRICE
1933 Arizona - 50¢ Arizona Grocery Co. (no city shown) (D)	$700
1924–?? ND Arizona - 1¢ 5¢ 10¢ 25¢ 50¢ Arizona State Hospital Script (M)	$15
1907 Benson - $1 Bank of Benson (D)	$1750
1907 Bisbee, AT - $1 Miner's and Merchants Bank (D)	$1500
1913 Bisbee - $50, $100 Miner's and Merchants Bank CD (B)	$1500
1933 Buckeye - 5¢ 10¢ 25¢ 50¢ Buckeye Merchants (D)	$900
1933 Flagstaff - 50¢ Arizona State Teachers College (D)	$350
1907 Globe, AT - $1 Old Dominion Commercial Company (D)	$600
ND Hampden, AT - 50¢, $1, $2 Territorial Script of F S Collins & Co. (M)	$5000
1904 Harshaw, AT - $3 $7 (var.) Mowry Mines, American Industrial Development Co. (M)	$950
ND 1933c Jerome - 25¢/25¢ Ritz Theatre. Issue for Civilian Conservation Corp. (D)	$150
1902 Johnson City, AT - $1, $2, $3, $4 Fiege & Co. Commisary & Meat Market (M)	$2500
1933 Nogales - $1 Nogales Herald Newspaper (D)	$375
1933 Nogales - $1 Herald Newspaper (D)	$250
1933 Phoenix - $1, $5, $10, $20, $50, $100 Phoenix Clearing House Certificate (D)	$600
1933 Phoenix - $1 Arizona Republic and Phoenix Gazette Newspapers (D)	$700
1933 Phoenix - 50¢, $1 Arizona Grocery Co. (D)	$700
1900–03 Russellville, AT - $1, $2, $3, $4 Fiege & Co. Commisary & Meat Market (M)	$2500
1890c Tucson, AT - 25¢ 50¢ L. Zeckendorf & Co. (M)	$3000
1895c Tucson, AT - 5¢ Lord & Williams, Arizona Territory (M)	$2500
1907 Tucson, AT - $1 Arizona Nat'l Bank (D)	$600
1933 Tucson - $20 Consolidated National Bank (D)	$500
1933 Tucson - $1 Arizona Daily Star Newspaper (D)	$500
1940 Tucson - 10¢, 25¢ 50¢ Old Tucson issued during filming of "ARIZONA" (A)	$30
1880c Tucson, AT - $10 Safford, Hudson & Co. Bankers Scrip (B)	$175
1905c Twin Buttes, AT - $2.50, $5, $10 Twin Buttes Mining and Smelting Scrip (M)	$250

COLORADO

1880c Geo. Fechter & Son Clothiers

DENOMINATION	PRICE
1909 ND Boyero - 1¢ 5¢ HF Davis, General Merchandise (M)	$500
1933 Castle Rock - ($ various) Douglas County Treasurer's Warrant (D)	$175
1880c Colorado Springs - $3 Geo. Fechter Advertising Note (M)	$600
ND Colorado Springs - Pelta's Department Store Premium Scrip (A)	$75
1907 Colorado Springs - $2 $5 $10 $20 Commercial Bank & Trust (Clearing House) (D)	$110

DENOMINATION	PRICE
1907 Colorado Springs - $1, 5, 10 First Nat'l Bank (Clearing House) (D)	$195
1933 Crede - 50¢, $1 Town of Crede (D)	$135
1933 Delta - ($ various) - Natural Development Assoc. (D)	$125
1897 Denver - 1/10, 1/4, 1/2, 1, 2 Labor Exchange #158. Good for hours of labor (W)	$150
1899 Denver - $1. Colorado Supply Co. (M)	$1200
1901–05 Denver 5¢, 10¢, 25¢. Colorado Supply Co. (M)	$350
1905 Denver 5¢ Rocky Mountain Supply Co. (M)	$750
1905 Denver - 5¢ 25¢ Western Stores Co. (M)	$300
1905c Denver - 50¢, $1 Western Trading & Supply (M)	$300
1907 Denver - $5 $10 Colorado Nat'l Bank (D)	$225
1907 Denver - $5 Denver Nat'l Bank as cashiers check (D)	$500
1907 Denver - $5 $10 $20 First Nat'l Bank of Denver (D)	$225
1907 Denver - $5 $10 $20 Nat'l Bank of Commerce (D)	$225
1907 Denver - $5 $10 United States Nat'l Bank (D)	$225
1921 Denver - $1 Askin & Marine Company, Green and Gold (A)	$160
1933 Denver - $5 $10 $20 The International Trust Company (D)	$100
1933 (ND) Durango - 5¢ 10¢ 25¢ Community Council Scrip (D)	$140
1907 Fort Collins - $2 $5 $10 Ft. Collins Clearing House (D)	$125
1907 Fort Collins - $2 $5 Commercial Bank & Trust (D)	$135
1907 Fort Collins - $5 $10 Poudre Valley Nat'l Bank of Ft. Collins (D)	$250
1907 Fort Collins - $5 $10 First Nat'l Bank of Ft. Collins (D)	$225
1933 Fort Collins - 1¢ 2¢ 3¢ 4¢ 5¢ 10¢ Edmonds Dry Goods, Stork Savings (D)	$150
1897 Fruita - 1/10, 1/4, 1/2, 1, 2 Labor Exchange. Good for hours of labor (W)	$475
1870 Gilpin, CT - (var.) City of Gilpin Pre-emption Certificate (W)	$750
1933 Golden - $1 Golden Welfare Association (D)	$150
1915 Goldfield - $2 $50 (var.) City of Goldfield Colorado (W)	$50
1933 Hot Sulphur Springs - $5 First State Bank (D)	$125
1933 Julesburg - $1 Town of Julesburg (D)	$125
1933 Kremmling - $1 Bank of Kremmling (D)	$165
1924 Leadville - $50 Days of '79. Leadville Lodge B.P.O.E. (A)	$125
1907 Loveland - $1 $5 Larimer County Bank (D)	$435
1900c Pueblo - 5¢ Herman & Shloss, General Merchandise (M)	$500
1907 Rocky Ford - $1 $5 $10 $20 State Bank of Rocky Ford (D)	$350
1880c Salida - $3 New York Clothing House Adv. Note (A)	$600
1933 Springfield - Various, Baca County Treasurer's Warrant (D)	$350
1933 Sterling - $1 $5 $10 Commercial Savings Bank (D)	$135
1933 Sterling - $1 Sterling, City of, Scrip Certificate (D)	$135
1933 Sterling - $1 Sterling Lions Club (D)	$250
1933 Sterling - $1 $5 Sterling Security State Bank (D)	$135
1935 Sterling - 10¢ 25¢ Logan County Fair (A)	$10
1912 Trinidad - $1 The Aiello Mercantile Company (M)	$650

DAKOTA TERRITORY

1868 $50 First Empire City Outfitting Store

DENOMINATION	PRICE
1868 Cheyenne, DT - $50 First Empire City Outfitting Store (A)	$2400
1888 Canton, DT - (var.) Town Treasurer Canton D.T. (W)	$75
1871 Ft. Rice, DT - $55 U.S. Infantry Pay Voucher (W)	$350

HAWAII

1933 $1 Honolulu Clearing House Certificate, Hawaii Territory

DENOMINATION	PRICE
1933 Honolulu - $1 Honolulu Clearing House Certificate, Hawaii (D)	$150
1933 Honolulu - $5 Honolulu Clearing House Certificate, Hawaii (D)	$300
1933 Honolulu - $10 Honolulu Clearing House Certificate, Hawaii (D)	$500
ND 1942 Kahuilui, Maui - $3 Naval Air Station NASKA (S)	$100
1911 Kona - $3 Kona & Kau Railway Company Coupon (W)	$75

IDAHO

1885 $5 Coeur D'Alene Water Supply Company Territorial

DENOMINATION	PRICE
1888 Alturas County, IT - Idaho Territorial School Warrant. Green (W)	$225
1867 Boise City, IT - $10 $20 $50 $100 Du Rell & Moore, First Nat'l Bank of Idaho (B)	$2000–$6000
1883 Boise City, IT - Treasurer of Idaho Territory Warrant (W)	$350
1928 Boise - 100 Boldts Restaurants - Battleship USS Idaho at Bremerton (A)	$265
1933 Boise - 5¢ 10¢ Farmer-Labor Exchange (D)	$400
1943 Boise - 1¢ Retail Merchants Bureau. Minute Man in "V". Blue (M)	$5
1932 Caldwell - $1 $5 Dairymen's Co-Operative. Blue/Gold (D)	$40
1933 Caldwell - $5 Dairymen's Co-Operative. Gold (D)	$35
1935 Caldwell - $1 $5 Dairymen's Co-Operative. Plum (D)	$37
1937 Caldwell - $5 Dairymen's Co-Operative. Green (D)	$37
1885 Coeur D'Alene - $5 Coeur D'Alene Water Supply Company (M)	$1500
1907 Coeur D'Alene - $5 $10 $20 $50 American Trust Company (D)	$1200
1935 Elk River - $1 Civilian Conservation Corp. 590th Co. (D)	$400
1890c Franklin - 5¢ Oneida Mercantile Union (M)	$3000
1894 Franklin - 10¢ 25¢ Lowe & Company (M)	$3000
1867 Idaho City - $10 $20 $50 $100 Du Rell & Moore FNB of Idaho (B)	$2000–$6000
1895 Idaho Falls - 1/20 1 Labor Exchange (W)	$1500
1936 Lewiston - 25¢ Idaho Spaulding Centennial. Wood (D)	$125
1933 Malad City - 10¢ 25¢ 50¢ Unbankable Certificate, Malad City, ID (D)	$500
1915 Moscow - (var.) Latah County Warrant (W)	$85
1890c Preston - 5¢ 10¢ 50¢ W.C. Parkinson & Co. (M)	$3000
1868 Rocky Bar - Alturas County Territorial Warrant (W)	$350
1867 Silver City - $10 $20 $50 $100 Du Rell & Moore First Nat'l Bank of Idaho (B)	$3500–$7500
1889 Silver City - (various denoms.) Owyhee County Territorial Warrant (W)	$250
1889 Silver City - (var.) Owyhee County Warrant (W)	$75

KANSAS

1871 $1 City of Leavenworth, Kansas Territory

DENOMINATION	PRICE
1907 Atchison - $1000 Clearing House (D)	$900
1907 Atchison - $5 Exchange Nat'l Bank (D)	$150
ND Broken Bow - $10 Broken Bow Business College (B)	$1000
1857c Chetopa, KT - $2 City of Chetopa (B)	$650
1933 Clay Center - 5¢ 50¢ Chamber of Commerce (D)	$17

DENOMINATION	PRICE
1854 Delaware, KT - $1 $2 Delaware City Bank (B)	$350
1854 Fort Leavenworth, KT - $2 $3 $5 $10 Merchants Bank (B)	$275
1856 Fort Leavenworth, KT - $1 Drovers Bank (B)	$300
1880 Fort Scott - 5¢ Kansas Normal College Bank (B)	$950
1933 Garden City - United States Sugar & Land Co. (D)	$600
1933 Gardner - City of Gardner, KS (D)	$130
ND 1870c Greenwood - A.W. Sanders Groceries Ad Note ($100 CSA) (A)	$100
ND Hiawatha - L.S. McNamar Ad Note (A)	$175
1882 Holton - $1 $5 $10 Commercial Institute Bank (B)	$185
1907c Independence - $1 $5 $10 Citizen's Nat'l Bank (D)	$375
1907c Independence - $1 $5 $10 $20 Commercial Nat'l Bank (D)	$375
1907c Independence - $1 First Nat'l Bank (D)	$375
1863 Junction City - 25¢ Streeter & Strickler (M)	$1750
1933 Kansas City - (var.) Goodwill Barter and Exchange Centers (D)	$115
ND Lawrence - 50¢ Durfee House (M)	$700
ND Lawrence - $2 $3 The Bank of Wm. H.R. Lykins (B)	$1400
18-- Lawrence - $3 The Lawrence Bank (B)	$500
1857 Lawrence, KT - $2 $3 Redwing Bank (B)	$1,250
1856 Leavenworth City, KT - $3 $5 $10 Drovers Bank. Ormsby (B)	$400
1856 Leavenworth City, KT - $1 The City Bank (B)	$375
1856 Leavenworth City, KT - $2 $3 The City Bank (B)	$600
1871 Leavenworth - $1 $2 $3 City of Leavenworth (B)	$375
1862 Leavenworth - Scott, Kerr & Co. (B)	$1200
ND Leavenworth - (var.) Western Business College (B)	$275
1856 Lecompton, KT - $3 The State Bank (B)	$900
1933 Neodesha - 5¢ 10¢ 25¢ 50¢, $1 $5 Chamber of Commerce (D)	$50
1933 Oswego - $5 First Nat'l Bank of Oswego (D)	$135
1933 Parsons - $5 Parson's Commercial Bank (D)	$225
1890s Pittsburg - 10¢ Rogers Coal Co.	$375
1894 Pittsburg - 10¢ The Wear Coal Co.	$375
1901 Pittsburg, etc. - $1 A Hood & Sons Implement Co.	$185
1907 Pittsburg - $1 $2 $5 $10 Associated Banks of Pittsburg (D)	$225
1905 Rook County - (var.) State of Kansas Warrant	$60
1933 Russell - 50¢ City of Russell (D)	$45
1933 Sedan - 25¢ Sedan Depressio Scrip (D)	$135
ND Seneca - 50¢ Lappin & Scrafford	$650
1855 Topeka, KT - $20 The State of Kansas	$750
1907 Topeka - $2 $5 Associated Banks of Topeka (D)	$400
1880s Topeka - 50¢ Karp & Turnbull	$80
1880s Topeka - 10¢ Kore & Hackman	$90
1867 Topeka - $1 $10 $20 Union Military Scrip. Bare-breasted maid	$200
1867 Topeka - $100 Union Military Scrip. Lincoln vignette	$500
1915c - 25¢ 50¢, $1 $5 Albert H. Shuler / Citizens State Bank	$15
1880s Wichita - 1¢, $2 $50 Southwestern Business College	$175
1914 Wichita - Wichita Clearing House Assoc.	$75
1933 Wichita - 5¢ Unemployed Trading Post (D)	$250
1934 Wilmore - 1 Jack, Merchants of Wilmore (D)	$15
18-- Wyandott - $1 $2 Kansas State Savings Bank. Green/black	$250

DENOMINATION	PRICE
18-- Wyandott - $3 Kansas State Savings Bank. Green/black	$400
ND 1857c Wyandott - $2 The City of Wyandott	$450

MONTANA

$20 Peoples Nat'l Bank of Helena

DENOMINATION	PRICE
1865 Beaver Head County, MT - (var.) Territorial Warrant	$125
1898 Belt - $1 Labor Exchange	$1900
1900–07 Butte - 25¢ 50¢, $1 Montana Mining Loan & Investment Co.	$75
1964 Butte - $20 Century of Mining	$15
1933 Conrad - $1 Farmers State Bank of Conrad (D)	$850
1905–14 Great Falls - (var.) City of Great Falls, Cascade County warrant	$15
1933 Forsyth - 25¢ 50¢, $1 Forsyth Mercantile (D)	$250
1880c Fort Shaw, MT - $3 J.H. McKnight & Co., Indian Post Trader, Mont. Territory	$1400
1933 Great Falls - $1 Black Eagle Commandery, Conrad Nat'l Bank on Leather (D)	$1200
1866 Helena, MT - (var.) First Nat'l Bank of Helena	$125
1873 Helena, MT - $50 First Nat'l Bank Helena, Territorial CD	$125
ND Helena - $5 10 $20 $50 Peoples Nat'l Bank of Helena	$1000
1887 Helena, MT - (var.) Territory of Montana Warrant (Liberty/shield)	$35
1893- Helena - (var.) State of Montana Warrant (Liberty/shield)	$17
1901 Helena - (var.) State of Montana Warrant (State Capitol) (W)	$50
1919 Helena - $20 $100 Helena Commercial Club "Pay Dirt" (A)	$165
1869 Jefferson County, MT - (var.) Treasurer of Jefferson County (W)	$95
1915c Lewistown - $25 Elk's Fair. Green/stag/brown (A)	$75
ND Lewistown - $10 $20 $25 Days of '49 BPOE Brown/blue (A)	$35
1909 Miles City - $5 $10 Bank of Elkville. Heart of the Yellowstone (B)	$425
1933 Missoula - 5¢ 10¢ 25¢ 50¢, $1 $5 $10 Missoula County Peoples Exchange (D)	$175
1933 Montana - $1 Montana Trade Certificate (D)	$750
1933 Scobey, Poplar & Glascow - 25¢, $1 St. Pauls Rural Parish (D)	$250

NEBRASKA

1857 $5 Brownville Bank & Land Co., Nebraska Territory

DENOMINATION	PRICE
1933 Aurora - $1 Aurora Scrip Money, Republican-Register Newspaper (D)	$95
1933 Beatrice - $1 $5 American Legion/Chamber of Commerce (D)	$75
1856 Bellevue, NT - $1 $2 $3 $5 $10 Fontenelle Bank (B)	$200
1885c Blair - 50¢ Haller Proprietary Co. "Haller's Remedies" on CSA (A)	$125
1856 Brownville, NT - $1 $2 $3 $5 $10 Nemaha Valley Bank (B)	$175
1859 Dakota City, NT - $1 $2 $5 Bank of Dakota (B)	$1200
1885 Dakota City - (var.) Dakota County Cert. of Account (W)	$65
1857 DeSoto, NT - $1 $2 $3 $5 The Waubeek Bank (B)	$185
1857 DeSoto, NT - $1 Western Land & Exchange Co. (ABNCo) (B)	RARE
1857–63 DeSoto, NT - $1 $2 $3 $5 Bank of DeSoto (B)	$135
1860 DeSoto, NT - $1 $2 $3 $5 Corn Exchange Bank (B)	$200
1933 Douglas County - $10 Douglas County Employee's Committee (D)	$400
1856 Florence, NT - $1 $2 $3 $5 $10 The Bank of Florence (B)	$145
1933 Fremont - 5¢ 25¢, $1 Retail Merchants Association (D)	$150
1933 Grand Island - $1 S N Wolbach Sons (D)	$95
1933 Holdrege - 5¢ Chamber of Commerce (D)	$125
1933 Lexington - $1 City of Lexington (D)	$95
1933 Lincoln - $1 $2 The City of Lincoln	$160
1902 Madison - (var.) Madison County Warrant (W)	$35
1858 Nebraska City, NT - $1 $2 $5 $10 Platte Valley Bank (B)	$2250
1870 Nelson - $5 Nelson's College Currency First International Bank (B)	$75
1933 Nelson - 25¢ Moratoriun Shin Plaster (D)	$50
1933 Norfolk - $1 City of Norfolk (D)	$135
1933 Norfolk - $1 Norfolk Cereal & Flour Mills (D)	$135
1861 Omaha City, NT - (var.) Territorial Warrant	$150
1857 Omaha, NT - $3 $5 $10 Brownville Bank & Land Co. (B)	$300
1857 Omaho, NT - $1 $3 $5 City of Omaha (B)	$145
1880c Omaha - Iler & Company American Life Bitters (A)	$200
1857 Omaha, NT - $1 $2 Nebraska Land & Banking (B)	$2250
1857 Omaha, NT - $1 $2 $5 $10 Omaha Bank & Land Co. (B)	$135
1856 Omaha, NT - $1 $2 $5 $10 Bank of Nebraska (B)	$1200
1856 Omaha, NT - $1 $2 $3 $5 $10 $20 Western Exchange Fire & Marine (B)	$85
1857c Omaha, NT - $1 $5 $10 Western Exchange and Land Co. (B)	$1600
1933 Omaha - 5¢ 25¢ 50¢, $1 $5 Married Men's Council of Omaha (D)	$125
1933 Roseland - 10¢ 25¢ 50¢, $1 Snyder's Shop (D)	$60
1857 Tekama, NT - $1 $2 $5 Bank of Tekama (B)	$135

DENOMINATION	PRICE
1908 Wausa - $5 $10 Commercial Bank (D)	$45
1933 York County - 5¢ York County Scrip (D)	$175

NEVADA

1872c $50 Manhattan Silver Mining Co.

DENOMINATION	PRICE
1872c Austin - $1 $3 $5 $10 $20 $50 $100 Manhattan Silver Mining Co. (M)	$95
1876 Carson City - $500 (var.) Carson City Savings Bank (B)	$125
1913–28 Carson City - $1000 Slippery Gulch Currency (A)	$350
187- Eureka - $5 Butter Cup Silver Mining Co. (M)	$1900
1915 Eureka - $5 Lincoln Hotel Cafe punch card (M)	$150
1861–64 Goldhill, NT - (var.) Wells Fargo & Co., Nevada Territory CD (B)	$125
1906 Palisade - One Trip "Scrip" "Issued by Eureka, Hmltn & Ely Stage Line" (M)	$450
1908 Rawhide - 25¢ 50¢ The Northern (Saloon) (M)	$125
1907 Reno - $1 Reno Clearing House (D)	$2000
1907 Rhyolite - $1 $5 $10 $20 Rhyolite Clearing House (D)	$6500
1870 Virginia - (var.) Storey, County of (plum color) (W)	$145
1877 Virginia - $5 $10 $20 Society of Pacific Coast Pioneers (M)	$300
1886 Virginia - County of Storey Warrant (W)	$35

NEW MEXICO

1900c 5¢ Southwestern Mercantile. Jarilla, NM Territory

DENOMINATION	PRICE
1890 ND El Capitan, NMT - 5¢ El Capitan Store (M)	$2000
ND 1933 Gallup - 5¢ 10¢ 25¢ 50¢, $1 $5 $10 Gallup American Coal Co. (M,D)	$500
ND 1900c Jarilla, NMT - 5¢ Southwestern Mercantile. Jarilla became Orogrande in 1905 (M)	$2200
1895 Las Cruces, NMT - $5 Bounty for Mountain Lion (W)	$175
1898 Lincoln County, NMT - Blue/Stag Territory of New Mexico warrant (W)	$195
1904 Lincoln County, NMT - Territory of New Mexico warrant (W)	$175
1914 Obar - $5 New Mexico Land & Immigration Co. (M)	$125
1860c Pinos Altos, NMT - $3 Buckhorn Furnace Store (M)	$3000
1925 Sante Fe - 1/4c Fidel Bros - Nat'l Cert Corp Green (M)	$150
1925 Sante Fe - 1 Fidel Bros - Nat'l Cert Corp Brown (M)	$145

NORTH DAKOTA

DENOMINATION	PRICE
1893c Fargo - $5 $10 $50 $100 $200 $500 Fargo Business College (Bliss) (B)	$145
1933 State - $1 $5 (Two issues of each) State of North Dakota (D)	$175
ND Plaza - 1/2¢ 1¢ 2¢ 4¢ First Nat'l Bank of Plaza, NW Bankers & Merchants (B)	$25

OREGON

1897 1/10 Toledo Labor Exchange. Pay in hours

DENOMINATION	PRICE
1933 Albany - 25¢ 50¢, $1 $5 Albany Scrip Assoc. City of Albany (D)	$125
1933 Albany - $1 Thrift Currency, merchant scrip (D)	$195

DENOMINATION	PRICE
1933 Albany - 10¢ Sternberg Saddlery/Albany Tanning Co. Scallop Leather (D)	$250
1933 Albany - 25¢, $1 Sternberg Saddlery/Albany Tanning Co. Rectangle Leather (D)	$300
1933 Albany - 50¢ Valley Bottling Co. (D)	$160
1933 Astoria - $1 Astoria Budget Newspaper scrip. Blue (D)	$175
1933 Astoria - 10¢ Guardsman's Scrip; Oregon Nat'l Guard. Pink (D)	$75
1934 Astoria - 10¢ Guardsman's Scrip; Oregon Nat'l Guard (D)	$95
1959 Bend - $1 Bend Buck printed on Deerskin (A)	$12
ND Canyon City - $10 Whiskey Gulch Gang (A)	$35
1933c Cascade Locks - Five Dam Bucks - Merrill's BBQ (D)	$350
1907 Clatskanie - $1 $2 $5 Columbia County Clearing House (D)	$300
1933 Clatskanie - 50¢, $2 $5 Merchant's "Windmill" Scrip (D)	$175
1897 Corvallis - 1/2 Labor Exchange (W)	$750
1933 Enterprise - 50¢, $1 Chamber of Commerce, Series A, Buckskin Currency (D)	$175
1933 Enterprise - 50¢, $1 C of C, Series B, Buckskin Currency (Deer Hide) (D)	$500
1933 Enterprise - 25¢ C of C, Series C (paper) (D)	$95
1933 Enterprise - 50¢, $1 C of C, Series D Black, Buckskin Currency (Deer Hide) (D)	$165
1907 Eugene - $1 $2 $5 $10 Eugene Clearing House (D)	$300
1933 Eugene - 50¢ Townsend Recovery Certificate (D)	$700
1850–66 Ft. Dalles - 1 2 3 5 10 20 Loaves of Bread signed Post Treas. Steel (S)	$450
1933 Grant's Pass - 25¢ 50¢, $1 The Oregon Caveman, Inc. (D)	$175
1933 Heppner - 5¢ 25¢ 50¢, $1 $5 Heppner Sheepskin Scrip on paper (D)	$7
1933 Heppner - 25¢ 50¢, $1 $5 Heppner Sheepskin Scrip on Leather (D)	$125
1959 Hermiston - 100th Anniversary of Oregon, Green on Yellow (M)	$25
1959 Independence - 100th Anniversary of Oregon on Leather (M)	$10
1933 Hillsboro - 25¢ 50¢, $1 $5 $10 Washington County Scrip (D)	$5
1933 Klamath Falls - 25¢ Capt. O.C. Applegate/American Legion Wood/round (D)	$18
1896 La Grande - 1/10 hour Labor Exchange, Branch 122 (W)	$400
1933 LaGrande - 5¢ 20¢ LaGrande Emergency Wage (D)	$125
1940 Lake County - 5¢ Lake County Centennial, silver cardboard (M)	$22
1959 Lake County - $1 Lake County Buck printed on Cowhide (M)	$12
1918 Marshfield - $5 $10 $20 Homeguard WW1 Scrip (D)	$175
1910c Marshfield - $1 Marshfield Fuel & Supply Co. (M)	$95
1933 Medford - 10¢ 50¢, $1 $5 Association Labor Agreement (D)	$75
1933 Multnomah - 25¢ 50¢, $1 $5 Mulnomah County Scrip (D)	$10
1860 Napolean - (var.) Treasurer of Josephine County	$250
1858 New Clackamas, OT - New Clackamas Banking House, Territorial (B)	$2200
1933 Newport - Newport Relief Committee Script (D)	$25
1933 North Bend - 50¢, $1 $2 1/2 $5 $10 City of North Bend (1st series wood) (D)	$40
1933 North Bend - 25¢ 50¢, $1 $5 $10 City of North Bend. (2nd series wood) (D)	$25
1959 North Bend - 25¢ 50¢ City of North Bend, Oregon Centennial (wood) (M)	$12
1925 Oakridge - $20 End of Steel (continental railroad) Green Goes 201 form (M)	$35
1925 Oakridge - $20 End of Steel Celebration, Green, Buffaloes (M)	$35
1855 Oregon City, OT - $10 John B. Preston, Surveyor General. Due Bill	$500
1873 ND Pendleton - 25¢ Boston Store (M)	$900
1933 Pendleton - 25¢ 50¢, $1 City of Pendleton (D)	$85
1933 Pendleton - $5 City of Pendleton (D)	$225
1915 Pendleton - $10 Pendleton Round-up (negotiable)	$95
1933 Pilot Rock - 25¢ 50¢, $1 Pilot Rock Wheat Scrip (D)	$100

DENOMINATION	PRICE
1866 Portland - $1 $2 $5 $10 $20 $50 $100 $500 Portland Business College (M)	$185
1880c Portland - $1 $2 $5 $10 $20 $50 $100 $500 Portland Business College (M)	$90
1882 Portland - $1 Portland Business College (M)	$300
1887 Portland - $5 Eastman Printing, Engraving, Photography (A)	$300
1907 Portland - $1 $2 $5 $10 $20 Portland Clearing House. Lion (D)	$25
1933 Portland - $1 $5 $10 $20 Portland Clearing House. Eagle (D)	$12
1933 Portland - $2 Pacific Savings Bank (D)	$450
ND Portland - 50¢ Unemployed Citizens League Montavilla Local (D)	$350
1933 Portland - $1 Western Industrial Pioneers, Inc. (D)	$175
ND (1870–1910) Portland - Oregon Coal & Navigation Co. Due Bill	$95
1959 Prineville - $1 Crook County Centennial Buck printed on deerskin	$12
1933 Reedsport - 25¢, $1 Reedsport Emergency Scrip (D)	$100
1933 Reedsport - $2.50 Reedsport Emergency Scrip (not issued) (D)	$250
1933 St.Helens - $1 $2 $5 St. Helen's Chamber of Commerce (D)	$95
1933 St.Helens - 50¢, $1 $2 $5 Sentinel-Mist Publishing (D)	$125
1896 Salem - 1/2, 1, 2 Labor Exchange (W)	$500
1880c Salem - $1 $2 Capital Business College (M)	$350
1913 Salem - 5 Kopecks Salem Bing Cherry Festival (M)	$375
1922 Salem - 25 Kopecks Salem Bing Cherry Festival (M)	$375
1933 Salem - 25¢ 50¢ Local Exchange/Premium Currency (D)	$85
1933 Sherman County - 25¢ Sherman County Scrip Association (D)	$600
1933 Silverton - 25¢ 50¢, $1 Silverton American Legion Scrip (D)	$25
1897 Toledo - 1/10 Labor Exchange	$750
1933 Union County - 5¢ 25¢ 50¢, $1 Union County Emergency Wage (D)	$75
1933 Union County - 5¢ 10¢ 25¢ 50¢, $1 $5 Labor Exchange Certificate (D)	$95

SOUTH DAKOTA

1932 $1 The City of Elk Point, SD

DENOMINATION	PRICE
1888 Deadwood, DT - I.H. Chase 1888 Baseball Adv. Note (A)	$7200
1895c State - (var.) State of South Dakota, Lawrence County (W)	$65
1895 Tyndall - $1 County of Bon Homme warrant (W)	$125
1932 Elk Point - $1 The City of Elk Point (D)	$250
1933 Madison - $1 The City of Madison (D)	$250
1933 Marion - $1 The City of Marion (D)	$250

DENOMINATION	PRICE
193- Huron - (var.) Huron College Warrant (D)	$300
1948 Rapid City - $5 KOTA Radio, c/s Bean Bag Market (M)	$35
1948 Rapid City - $10 KOTA Radio, c/s Rapid City Clothing (M)	$35

UTAH

1903 25¢ Boden & Grahl, Meats and Groceries, Brigham City

DENOMINATION	PRICE
1876c Brigham City - 10¢ Brigham City Co-Operative (M)	$1400
1903 Brigham City - 25¢ Boden & Grahl, Meats and Groceries (M)	$750
1890s Fairview - 10¢ 50¢ Fairview Co-Op. Mercantile Co. (M)	$1750
1890s Fairview - 10¢ 25¢ Swen & Lars Neilson. Store (M)	$1100
1868 Fort Bridger, UT - $1 to $10 Utah Territory; W.A. Carter Post Trader (S)	$2200
1890s Logan - 10¢ Cache Valley Mercantile Co. (M)	$1700
1890s Logan - 5¢ 10¢ 50¢ Equitable Co-Op. Association, Limited (M)	$1200
1890s Logan - 5¢ 10¢ 25¢ $1 Fourth Ward Co-Op (M)	$750
1890s Logan - 5¢ Fifth Ward Co-Op (M)	$650
1890s Logan - 10¢ 25¢ $1 $2 Goodwin Brothers (M)	$1500
1890s Logan - 10¢ 25¢ 50¢, $1 Logan Branch Z.C.M.I. (M)	$550
1890s Logan - 10¢ 25¢ Logan Meat Market (M)	$550
1890s Logan - 5¢ Logan Meat Market Co. (M)	$600
1890s Logan - 5¢ 15¢ Second Ward Store (M)	$600
1895–97 Logan - 5¢ Cache Stake Tithing Store House (M)	$550
1901 Logan - 5¢ 25¢ - Logan Store House (M)	$450
1890s Magna - Louis Falvo & Son's (M)	$175
1890s Manti City - 5¢ Sanpete Tithing Store House (M)	$500
1890s Murray - 10¢ Workingmen's Store (M)	$175
1907 Ogden - $1 $2 $5 $10 Ogden Clearing House (D)	$275
ND Park City - 10¢ The Cozy (M)	$65
1890s Payson - 5¢ Payson Co-Operative Store (M)	$1500
18-- Pleasant Grove - 5¢ Pleasant Grove, Utah Store (M)	$1550
1890s Provo - 10¢ 25¢ Co-Operative Institution West Branch (M)	$800
1890s Provo - 25¢, $5 Sup't Provo Co-Operative Institution (M)	$800
1890s Provo - 25¢, $5 W.H. Freshwater "in merchandise at retail" (M)	$1500
1890s Scipio - 5¢ 10¢ 15¢ 25¢ 50¢, $1 $2 $5 Co-Op. Mercantile Institution (M)	$400
1900c Provo - 10¢ Provo Woolen Mills Company (M)	$1500
1908 Richfield - $1 $2 $5 $10 Gold Mountain Consolidated Mining Co. (D)	$350

DENOMINATION	PRICE
1933 Roosevelt City - $1 Roosevelt City Scrip (D)	$100
1901 St. George - 5¢ 10¢ St. George StoreHouse (M)	$400
1849 Salt Lake, UT - 25¢ 50¢, $1 $2 $3 Valley Notes w/ embossed seal. "B Young" sig. (M)	$2300
1856 Salt Lake, UT - $1 $2 $3 The Drover's Bank (B)	$750
1858 Salt Lake, UT - $1 $2 $3 $5 Deseret Currency Association (M)	$1950
1858–61 Salt Lake, UT - $3 Utah Territory Mercantile Currency (reprints exist) (M)	RARE
1858 Salt Lake, UT - $10 $50 California & Salt Lake Mail Line (M)	$3500
1862 Salt Lake, UT - $625 Due Bill, United States to Gov. of Utah Terr. (W)	$125
1863 Salt Lake City, UT - 50¢, $3 Walker Brothers (Bankers) (M)	$2000
1865 Salt Lake City, UT - $50 Holladay & Halsey (Bankers) (M)	$2500
1867 Salt Lake, UT - (var.) First Nat'l Bank of Utah (B)	$1800
1866 Salt Lake, UT - 25¢ 50¢, $1 $2 Great Salt Lake City Corporation (B)	$350
1868 Salt Lake, UT - 5¢, $1 $5 $10 $50 Deseret University Bank (B)	$1800
1870 Salt Lake, UT - 25¢ 50¢, $1 $2 $5 $10 Zion's Co-Operative Mercantile Institution (M)	$750
1870 Salt Lake, UT - $1 $2 $5 Series A Zion's Co-Operative Mercantile Institution (M)	$750
1870's Salt Lake, UT - $1 Salt Lake City, Utah Territory "Good to workmen" (M)	$750
1874 Salt Lake, UT - $1 $2 $3 $5 WB Welles, Salt Lake City Nat'l Bank (B)	$1350
1890s ND Salt Lake - $10 Mill Creek Commercial Bank (B)	$1500
1890s Salt Lake City - 5¢ Deseret Meat Market (M)	$1200
1890–95 Salt Lake, UT - Elk Liquor Co. Advertiser (A)	$225
1887–96 Salt Lake, UT - 5¢ 10¢ 25¢ 50¢ Territorial - General Tithing Store House (M)	$275
1896–1897 Salt Lake - 5¢ 10¢ 25¢ 50¢ State - General Tithing Store House (M)	$125
ND Salt Lake - 5¢ 10¢ 25¢ Bishop's Office Coupon. Brn/blk Bishop's Gen'l Store Hse (M)	$350
1896–97 Salt Lake - 5¢ 10¢ 25¢ 50¢, $1 $10 Bishop's General Store House (M)	$125
1898–1906 Salt Lake - 5¢ 10¢ 25¢ 50¢ Bishop's General Store House (M)	$85
1890s ND Salt lake - 25¢, $5 $10 Beaver Wool Manufacturing & Milling Co. (M)	$700
1890c ND Salt Lake, UT - $1000 LDS Business College (B)	$500
1900c Salt Lake - 10¢ United Order of Tailors (M)	$750
1907 Salt Lake - $1 Deseret Nat'l Bank (Cashiers Checks) (D)	$350
1907 Salt Lake - $1 McCormick Bank (D)	$350
1907 Salt Lake - $1 Utah-Idaho Sugar Co. (D)	$450
1907 Salt Lake - $100 Salt Lake City Clearing House (D)	$375
1933 Salt Lake - $1 Church of Jesus Christ of Latter-Day Saints (D)	$650
1933 Salt Lake - 5¢ 10¢ 25¢ 50¢, $1 Natural Development Association (D)	$175
1933 Salt Lake - $1 Trade Stimulus Certificate (D)	$135
1890s Spanish Fork - 25¢ Spanish Fork Co-Op. (M)	$1000
1890s Spanish Fork - 10¢ Young Men's Co-Op. Institution (M)	$1000

WASHINGTON

1933 25¢ Everett, WA Sockeye Trade Note

DENOMINATION	PRICE
1906 Aberdeen - $5 Palace Restaurant Meal Card (M)	$40
1933 Aberdeen - 25¢ Old Ironsides/Samuel Benn Wood/round (D)	$12
1933 Almira - 5¢ Almira Grand Coulee Dam Scrip (D)	$150
1907 Bellingham - $1 $2 $5 $10 $20 Bellingham Clearing House (D)	$135
1933 Bellingham - $1 $5 $10 $20 Bellingham Clearing House (D)	$175
1933 Bellingham - 5¢ Henry Roeder Round/wood (D)	$12
1893 Bellingham - $1 Fair Department Store (M)	$250
1933 Blaine - 5¢ 10¢ 25¢ 50¢, $1 Blaine Relief Assoc. (Reprints exist) (D)	$17
1933 Bremerton - 25¢ Old Ironsides/American Legion Wood/round (D)	$15
1933 Brewster - $1 Townsend Test Fund - 1st Nat'l Bank (D)	$650
1933 Camas - $10 American Legion - 50th Anniv. of Camas (D)	$600
1933 Centralia - 25¢ 50¢, $1 $5 Centralia Daily Chronicle (D)	$125
1933 Chelan - 10¢ 25¢ 50¢, $1 Townsend Test Fund - Miners & Merchants Bank (D)	$500
1933 Callam County - $1 Angeles Co-Operative Creamery (D)	$160
1907 Chehalis County - $1 Associated Banks of Chehalis County (D)	$600
1932–3 Cowlitz County (Port Angeles) - 5¢ 15¢, $1 Liberty Service Token (D)	$150
1933 Deer Park - $5 Deer Park Lumber Co. (D)	$350
1907 Ellensburg - $1 Associated Banks of Ellensburg (D)	$400
1933 Everett - 25¢ Sockeye (Salmon shaped). Convention Committee (D)	$400
1933 Everett - $1 City of Everett Trade Extension Warrant (D)	$400
1933 Friday Harbor - 25¢ 50¢, $1 Haxkett-Larson American Legion Post (D)	$45
1933 Grand Coulee - 25¢ Grand Coulee Dam Quarter (concrete) (D)	$35
1933 Grays Harbor - $1 $5 $10 $20 Grays Harbor Associated Banks (D)	$135
1933 Hoquiam - $1 Olde Ironsides (Round wood) (D)	$18
1933 Hoquiam - 1¢ 2¢ 3¢ 4¢ 5¢ 10¢ 25¢ 50¢ Stork System Savings @ 1912 (D)	$50
1933 Hoquiam - 1¢ 2¢ 3¢ 4¢ 5¢ 10¢ Stork System Savings @ 1917 (D)	$12
1939 Hoquiam - 25¢ Hoquiam Jubilee Assoc. 3" round wood (A)	$17
1933 Ilwaco - 5¢ 25¢ 50¢, $1 Ilwaco Salmon Currency (D)	$125
1933 Issaquah - 25¢ Farmer's Trade Note (D)	$150
1933 Kalama - Port of Kalama Scrip (D)	$125
1933 Kelso - (var.) County Dairymen's Assocation (D)	$200
1933 Linden - City of Linden (D)	$500
1933 Longview - 25¢ Longview Chamber of Commerce (D)	$15
1933 Montesano - 5¢ 10¢ United Producer's Money (D)	$150
1933 Mt. Rainier - $10 Mt. Ranier Clearing House (D)	$500
1933 Okanogan - $1 Okanogan Commercial Club "WineSap" (D)	$165

DENOMINATION	PRICE
1907 Olympia - $1 Associated Banks of Olympia (D)	$250
1933 Olympia - 25¢, $1 $2 $5 Community Service Bureau (D)	$30
1933 Olympia - 25¢ Olympia Oyster Money, Chamber of Commerce (D)	$350
1933 Omak - $1 $5 $10 Bile-Coleman Lumber Co. (D)	$175
1933 Pasco - 50¢, $1 Pasco Relief Scrip (D)	$225
1933 Peshastin - 25¢ 50¢, $1 Peshastin Ponderosa Scrip (D)	$135
1894 Port Angeles - (var.) City of Port Angeles - City Council (W)	$135
1933 Port Townsend - $1 $5 $10 First Nat'l Bank (D)	$45
1933 Raymond - 25¢ 50¢, $1 $5 Raymond Oyster Money (D)	$85
1933 Rock Island - 25¢ Rock Island Dam Scrip (D)	$125
1907 Seattle - $1000 The Seattle Clearing House Assoc. (D)	$1,380
1907 Seattle - $1 $2 $5 $10 $20 Seattle Clearing House Assoc. (D)	$100
1931 Seattle - 1 vote Citizens of the City of Seattle (A)	$45
1932 Seattle - 10¢ Theatre Scrip for Unemployed (D)	$135
1933 Seattle - $1 $5 $10 $20 Seattle Clearing House Assoc. (D)	$150
ND 1915c Sequim - $1 Chas. Fenwick Rifles (A)	$135
1907 Skagit County - $1 $5 Skagit County Clearing House (D)	$400
1933 Skagit County - $1 Skagit Community Scrip (D)	$225
1907 Snohomish - $1 $2 $5 $10 $20 Snohomish County Associated Bank (D)	$300
1933 South Bend - 25¢ 50¢, $1 $5 $10 Willapa Harbor Currency (wood) (D)	$90
1933 South Bend - 25¢ 50¢, $1 $5 $10 Willapa Harbor Currency (paper) (D)	$125
1907 Spokane $1 $2 $5 $10 $20 Clearing House Association (D)	$150
1933 Spokane - 50¢, $1 $5 Baird-Naundorf Lumber Co. (D)	$95
1933 Spokane - $1 Commercial Creamery (D)	$150
1933 Spokane - 25¢ 50¢, $1 Davenport Hotel (D)	$75
1933 Spokane - 25¢ 50¢, $1 $5 Dessert Hotel (D)	$75
1933 Spokane - $2 $5 Federated Exchange Cert. McClintock-Turnkey Co. (D)	$95
1933 Spokane - $1 John W. Graham Co. (D)	$225
1933 Spokane - $1 $5 Long Lake Lumber Co. (D)	$75
1933 Spokane - 50¢, $1 $5 Spokesman-Review Newspaper (D)	$175
1933 Spokane - $1 Tull & Gibbs (D)	$125
1939 Spokane - 5¢ Columbia Cavalcade Golden Jubilee (A)	$20
1880c Tacoma, W.T. - $5 W.H. Fife Advertising Note (A)	$3000
1907 Tacoma - $1 $2 $5 $10 $20 Seattle Clearing House Assoc. (D)	$150
1933 Tacoma - 25¢, $1 $2 $5 $10 Community Service Bureau (D)	$45
1933 Tacoma - 5¢ 10¢ 25¢ 50¢ Natural Development Assoc. Centi/Vallars (D)	$450
1933 Tacoma - 1 U, 5 Units, New Commonwealth (D)	$150
1931–32 Tenino- 25¢, $1 $5 $10 (Paper) Chamber of Commerce (D)	$125
1932–33 Tenino - 25¢ 50¢, $1 (Wood) Chamber of Commerce (D)	$95
1932 Tenino - 25¢ 50¢ (Wood) Chamber of Commerce Double Denomination	RARE
ND 1933 Tenino - 5¢ Jiffy Lunch, small/wood (D)	$125
ND 1933 Tenino - 5¢ D.M. Major, small/wood (D)	$125
ND 1933 Tenino - 5¢ Tenino Chamber of Commerce, small/wood (D)	$85
ND 1933 Tenino - 1¢ 2¢ 3¢ Thurston County Independent, small/wood with postal stamp (D)	$230

ND 1933–35 Tenino A series of 1/5¢ wooden sales tax "chits" approximately 1" square were issued by several firms and are sought after. They include: Campbell & Campbell, Drug Store, Jack Horner, Jiffy Lunch, L.A. McLain,

DENOMINATION	PRICE
Mecca Cafes, Paramount Service Station, Penny's Garage, Tenino Cash Market, Thurston County Independent, E.E. Walker, and White Front Garage. Most are valued in the range of	$35
1939 Tenino - 25¢ Lions Club, Lion Money (A)	$65
1933 Toppenish - $10 The Traders Bank (D)	$750
1933 Toppenish - $1 Toppenish Commercial Club "Toppenish Wampum" (D)	$750
1933 Waitsburg - $1 Waitsburg Civic Relief Committee (D)	$350
1872 Walla Walla, WT - 50¢ A.H. Reynolds Co. (M)	$2200
1933 Wapato - 25¢ Community Service Bureau (D)	$100
1933 Wenatchee - $1 Wenatchee Chamber of Commerce - Apple Jack (D)	$225
1933 Wenatchee - 25¢ 50¢, $1 Wenatchee Daily World Publishing Co. (D)	$20
1933 Woodland - 5¢ 10¢ 25¢ 50¢ City of Woodland - Welfare Scrip (D)	$125

WYOMING

1870 $8 Post Trader, Fort Bridger, Wyoming Territory

DENOMINATION	PRICE
1908 Cambria - $1 Cambria Trading Company. Blue print. Miner on front (M)	$175
1897 Cambria - $5 Kirkpatrick Brothers & Collins. Gray print. Miner	$300
ND Cheyenne, WT - Wyoming Territory - Gray & Pearse Advertising Note	$4000
1931 Cheyenne - $1 Cheyenne Frontier Night Show (blue)	$225
1907 Cheyenne - $1 $5 $10 Cheyenne Clearing House (D)	$400
1933 Cheyenne - $50 City of Cheyenne - The Scrip Commission (D)	$275
1933–34 Cheyenne - $1 Cheyenne Frontier Days (D)	$225
1933 Cheyenne - Natural Development Assoc. Centi/Vallars SENC (D)	RARE
1964 Cheyenne - $1 Cheyenne Autumn Trail Dedication "Cheyenne Wampum" (W)	$25
1877 Evanston, WT - (var.) Territory of Wyoming, County of Uinta warrant (W)	$125
1870 Ft. Bridger. WT - $1 to $8 Sutler note; WA Carter Post Trader, Wyo. Territory (S)	$3500
1933 Laramie - 50¢ City of Laramie Scrip - Scrip Commission (D)	$350
1933 Laramie - 3¢ 25¢ A E Roedel Druggist, Citizen's Nat'l Bank, Stork (1910 Copyright) (D)	$400
1933 Laramie - 50¢ Gem City Grocery, First State Bank, Stork (1910 Copyright) (D)	$400
1933–34 Riverton - 5¢ 10 25¢ 50¢, $1 Riverton Lion's Club. Paper (D)	$300
1933–34 Riverton - 50¢ Riverton Lion's Club. Paper (D)	$200
1933 Riverton - 50¢ Riverton Lions Club. Scrip printed on buckskin (D)	$175

Glossary: Adv.=Advertising; c (following date)=circa; CD=Certificate of Deposit; ND=No Printed Date; (var.)=Various amounts

SPECIAL REPORT:
UNCUT SHEETS

As very few notes exist in the form of full uncut sheets, this is a limited area for the collector. Also, the prices are high, well out of range for most hobbyists.

Uncut sheets available on the market are of Small Size Notes exclusively. In most instances it is not known precisely how they reached public hands. Some were undoubtedly presented as souvenir gifts to Treasury Department officials. In any event, uncut sheets have never been illegal to own, since the notes they comprise are precisely the same as those released into general circulation.

The sheets differ in the number of notes, from a low of six in National Currency sheets to a high of eighteen for some sheets of United States (Legal Tender) Notes and Silver Certificates. Others have twelve notes. These differences are due entirely to the printing method being used at their time of manufacture. Any given note was always printed in sheets of the same size, with the same number of specimens per sheet. If you have an uncut sheet with twelve notes, it means that all notes from the series were printed twelve to a sheet.

The condition standards for uncut sheets are the same as those for single notes. Obviously, an uncut sheet did not circulate as money, but some specimens became worn or damaged as a result of careless storage, accident, or other causes. These impaired sheets do turn up in the market, but there is not much demand for them. Almost every buyer of uncut sheets wants Uncirculated condition. Quite often an uncut sheet will be framed when you buy it. This should be considered a plus, as the frame has probably kept the sheet in immaculate condition. Just to be entirely safe, however, it is wise to examine the reverse side of the sheet for possible staining or other problems.

The following prices were current for uncut sheets in Uncirculated grade at publication time. Gem Uncirculated sheets in absolutely pristine condition command higher prices than those shown.

SILVER CERTIFICATES

DENOMINATION	SERIES	NO. OF NOTES PER SHEET	CURRENT PRICE RANGE IN UNC. CONDITION
$1	1928	12	2000.00–3000.00
$1	1934	12	2400.00–3200.00
$5	1934	12	1500.00–2400.00
$10	1934	12	3900.00–5500.00
$1	1935	12	800.00–1500.00
$5	1953	18	1200.00–1600.00
$10	1953	18	3900.00–5000.00

UNITED STATES NOTES (LEGAL TENDER NOTES)

DENOMINATION	SERIES	NO. OF NOTES PER SHEET	CURRENT PRICE RANGE IN UNC. CONDITION
$1	1928	12	9000.00–12,000.00
$2	1928	12	900.00–12,000.00
$5	1928	12	1450.00–2500.00
$2	1953	18	900.00–1300.00
$5	1953	18	1500.00–2600.00

NATIONAL CURRENCY

DENOMINATION	SERIES	NO. OF NOTES PER SHEET	CURRENT PRICE RANGE IN UNC. CONDITION
$5	1929	6	750.00–2400.00
$10	1929	6	800.00–2800.00
$20	1929	6	825.00–3000.00
$50	1929	6	4000.00–8000.00
$100	1929	6	4500.00–12,000.00
EMERGENCY NOTES:			
Hawaii $1	1935A		4000.00–6500.00
No. Africa $1	1935A		5000.00–9000.00

MULES
(MIXED PLATE NUMBERS)

All U.S. currency has plate numbers on the face and back. These plate numbers are in the lower right corner somewhat close to the fine scroll design. They refer to the number of the engraved plate used to print the sheet of notes. Each plate can be used for about 100,000 impressions. It is then destroyed and a new plate with the next number in sequence is put into use.

During the term of Treasury officials Julian and Morgenthau, the plate numbers were changed from almost a microscopic to a larger size, far easier to read. Due to this improvement the series designation then in use was an advance on United States Notes, Silver Certificates, and Federal Reserve Notes. The signatures remained Julian-Morgenthau. National Currency and Gold Certificates were not affected, as these were discontinued earlier.

During the changeover period in printing, plates were sometimes mixed up, producing a note with a large number on one side and a small number on the other side. Notes of this variety are called "mules," or "mule notes." This is from a term applied to coins struck with the obverse or reverse die of one year and the opposite side from a die of another year.

Many collectors are eager to add one or more of these mule notes to their collection. Some of the most common mule notes are:

$2 UNITED STATES NOTES
1928-C, 1928-D

$1 SILVER CERTIFICATES
1935, 1935-A

$5 UNITED STATES NOTES
1928-B, 1928-C, 1928-D, 1928-E

$5 SILVER CERTIFICATES
1934, 1934-A, 1934-B, 1934-C

$10 SILVER CERTIFICATES
1934, 1934A

Mules were also issued in the Federal Reserve Note Series. However, these are not as popular with collectors as the United States Notes and Silver Certificates because of the higher denominations and the twelve districts involved.

The schedule below shows some of the most common mule notes and their values in new condition. The combination of the prefix and suffix letters of the serial numbers on notes is known as "Blocks." For instance: A—A Block, B—A Block.

			UNC.
$2 UNITED STATES NOTE	1928-D	B—A	575.00
		C—A	100.00
		*—A	135.00
$5 UNITED STATES NOTE	1928-B	E—A	160.00
		*—A	600.00
	1928-C	E—A	134.00
		*—A	160.00
$1 SILVER CERTIFICATE	1935	N—A	
		Thru	210.00
		P—A	
	1935-A	M—A	
		Thru	110.00
		V—A	
		C—B	110.00
$5 SILVER CERTIFICATE	1934-A	D—A	
		Thru	110.00
		G—A	
		*—A	195.00
$10 SILVER CERTIFICATE	1934	A—A	115.00
		*—A	160.00
	1934-A	A—A	260.00

Front	SIZES DIFFERENT	Back

INTRODUCTION TO
UNITED STATES
FRACTIONAL CURRENCY

Events following the outbreak of the Civil War resulted in a shortage of circulating coinage. Trade was hampered as many merchants, especially in large cities, were unable to make change and only customers presenting the exact amount for a purchase could buy—but they were generally as short on coins as the shop proprietors. Various attempts were made to solve this problem by issuing credit slips (which most customers didn't care for), tokens (which they also didn't care for), and using postage stamps as money. Finally, in 1862, the government stepped in, recognizing that the economy was being seriously hurt, and issued a series of small paper notes as equivalents of coinage denominations. They carried designs adapted from the current postage stamps of the day and were known as Postage Currency or Postal Currency. The more popular title is now Fractional Currency. There were five separate issues of Fractional Currency, three of which occurred during the Civil War and two thereafter, the final one as late as 1874. That a need existed for coin substitutes as late as the 1870s demonstrates the drain placed upon coinage during the war and the long period of recovery. A total of six denominations were issued, from 3¢ to 50¢, comprising 23 designs and more than 100 varieties. Because of its small size and lack of visual impact, Fractional Currency was long shunned by collectors. In recent years it has enjoyed an unprecedented surge of popularity, which, if continued, promises to drive prices beyond present levels. All told, more than $360,000,000 worth of Fractional Currency was circulated. It would be extremely plentiful today but for the fact that most notes were redeemed, leaving only about

$2,000,000 outstanding. This is what collectors have to work with, and a good deal of these are badly preserved.

FIRST ISSUE—Postage Currency August 21st, 1862
5-10-25-50

SECOND ISSUE—Fractional Currency October 10th, 1863
5-10-25-50

THIRD ISSUE—Fractional Currency December 5th, 1864
3-5-10-15-25-50

FOURTH ISSUE—Fractional Currency July 14th, 1869
10-15-25-50

FIFTH ISSUE—Fractional Currency February 26th, 1874
10-25-50

THE FRACTIONAL CURRENCY SHIELD

Fractional currency shields were sold by the Treasury Department in 1866. Specimen notes printed only on one side were used. Very Good–condition shields are valued at $3000 to $3500. Choice condition shields in contemporary frames can sell for $4500. Shields with pink, green, or other backgrounds are more valuable.

FRACTIONAL CURRENCY NOTES

The following notes may be collected by issue or by denomination. We list them here by denomination for convenience. Also, since most of these notes were hastily cut from large sheets, the margin size can vary. Specimens are narrow margined while proofs have wide margins. Prices listed are for Nice "well centered" Uncirculated notes.

THREE-CENT NOTES

THIRD ISSUE
Face Design:
Portrait of President Washington.

	SPECIMEN	FACE		REVERSE
	Light Port.	175.00		75.00
	Dark Port.	100.00		75.00
	PROOF			
	Light Port	6000.00		300.00
	Dark Port	350.00		300.00

Back Design:
Large "3" green.

REGULAR ISSUES

	A.B.P.	GOOD	V.FINE	UNC.
☐ With Light Portrait	13.00	20.00	35.00	183.00
☐ With Dark Portrait	14.00	20.00	42.00	310.00

FIVE-CENT NOTES

FIRST ISSUE	SPECIMEN	FACE	100.00	REVERSE	60.00
	PROOF	FACE	400.00	REVERSE	300.00

Face Design:
Portrait of President Jefferson, brown.

Back Design:
"5" black.

REGULAR ISSUES

	A.B.P.	GOOD	V.FINE	UNC.
☐ Perforated edges, monogram ABNCO on back	9.00	13.00	29.00	400.00
☐ Perforated edges, without monogram on back	9.00	12.00	41.00	500.00
☐ Straight edges, monogram ABNCO on back	9.00	11.00	22.00	200.00
☐ Straight edges, without monogram on back	9.00	12.00	25.00	275.00

FIVE-CENT NOTES

SECOND ISSUE	SPECIMEN	FACE	90.00	REVERSE	62.00
	PROOF	FACE	275.00	REVERSE	225.00

Face Design:
Portrait of
President
Washington.

Back Design:
Shield and
brown, "5"s.

REGULAR ISSUES	A.B.P.	GOOD	V.FINE	UNC.
☐Value only in bronze on back	8.00	11.00	20.00	250.00
☐Surcharges 18-63 on back	8.00	11.00	20.00	250.00
☐Surcharges S-18-63 on back	11.00	15.00	20.00	350.00
☐Surcharges R-1-18-63 on back, fiber paper	10.00	15.00	57.00	600.00

FIVE-CENT NOTES

THIRD ISSUE	SPECIMEN	FACE	91.00	REVERSE	62.00
	PROOF	FACE	248.00	REVERSE	180.00

Face Design:
Portrait of
Spencer M.
Clark.

Back Design:
Green or
red.

REGULAR ISSUES	A.B.P.	GOOD	V.FINE	UNC.
☐Without letter "A" on face, red back	8.00	11.00	23.00	400.00
☐With letter "A" on face, red back	8.00	12.00	27.00	450.00
☐Without letter "A" on face, green back	6.00	10.00	19.00	225.00
☐With letter "A" on face, green back	6.00	10.00	19.00	175.00

This note was authorized to have the portraits of the explorers Lewis and Clark on the face. Mr. Spencer M. Clark, who was then head of the Bureau of Currency, flagrantly placed his own portrait on this note. This caused Congress to pass legislation forbidding the likeness of any living person on U.S. currency.

TEN-CENT NOTES

FIRST ISSUE	SPECIMEN	FACE	90.00	REVERSE	65.00
	PROOF	FACE	375.00	REVERSE	325.00

Face Design:
Portrait of
President
Washington.

Back Design:
"10,"
black.

REGULAR ISSUES

	A.B.P.	GOOD	V.FINE	UNC.
☐Perforated edges, monogram ABNCO on back	8.00	9.00	28.00	415.00
☐Perforated edges, without monogram on back	8.00	9.00	29.00	430.00
☐Plain edges, monogram ABNCO on back	6.00	11.00	18.00	200.00
☐Plain edges, without monogram on back	7.00	12.00	39.00	900.00

TEN-CENT NOTES

SECOND ISSUE	SPECIMEN	FACE	95.00	REVERSE	65.00
	PROOF	FACE	325.00	REVERSE	275.00

Face Design:
Portrait of
President
Washington.

Back Design:
"10,"
green.

REGULAR ISSUE

	A.B.P.	GOOD	V.FINE	UNC.
☐Value only surcharge on back	4.00	7.00	20.00	200.00
☐Surcharge 18-63 on back	4.00	7.00	20.00	200.00
☐Surcharge S-18-63 on back	5.00	8.00	21.00	225.00
☐Surcharge I-18-63 on back	9.00	20.00	41.00	400.00
☐Surcharge O-63 on back	140.00	400.00	1000.00	2150.00
☐Surcharge T-1-18-63 on back, fiber paper	12.00	21.00	110.00	800.00

TEN-CENT NOTES

THIRD ISSUE	SPECIMEN	FACE	100.00	REVERSE	110.00
	PROOF	FACE	300.00	REVERSE	250.00

Face Design:
Portrait of
President
Washington.

Back Design:
"10," green
or red.

REGULAR ISSUES

	A.B.P.	GOOD	V.FINE	UNC.
☐Printed signatures Colby-Spinner, green back	6.00	10.00	19.00	132.00
☐As above, figure "1" near left margin on face	6.00	10.00	19.00	143.00
☐Printed signatures Colby-Spinner, red back	7.00	10.00	25.00	350.00
☐As above, figure "1" near left margin, red back				
	7.00	14.00	35.00	375.00
☐Autographed signatures Colby-Spinner, red back				
	11.00	16.00	50.00	500.00
☐Autographed signatures Jeffries-Spinner, red back				
	11.00	16.00	75.00	500.00

TEN-CENT NOTES

FOURTH ISSUE	SPECIMEN	FACE	325.00	REVERSE	RARE
	PROOF	FACE	325.00	REVERSE	RARE

Face Design:
Bust of
Liberty.

Back Design:
Green with
TEN and
"10."

REGULAR ISSUES	A.B.P.	GOOD	V.FINE	UNC.
☐ Large red seal, watermarked paper	7.00	10.00	17.00	125.00
☐ Large red seal, pink fibers in paper	7.00	10.00	18.00	125.00
☐ Large seal, pink fibers in paper, right end blue	7.00	10.00	20.00	125.00
☐ Large brown seal	16.00	30.00	85.00	220.00
☐ Small red seal, pink fibers, right end blue	7.00	10.00	30.00	170.00

TEN-CENT NOTES

FIFTH ISSUE	PROOF	FACE	RARE	REVERSE	$400.00

Face Design:
William
Meredith.

Back Design:
Green.

REGULAR ISSUES

	A.B.P.	GOOD	V.FINE	UNC.
☐ Green seal, long narrow key	6.00	8.00	12.00	125.00
☐ Red seal, long narrow key	6.00	7.00	12.00	75.00
☐ Red seal, short stubby key	6.00	7.00	12.00	75.00

FIFTEEN-CENT NOTES
FACES AND BACKS PRINTED SEPARATELY
THIRD ISSUE ALL ARE SPECIMENS AND UNISSUED.

Face Design:
Sherman and
President
Grant.

Back Design:
Green
or red.

	SPECIMEN UNC.	PROOF UNC.
☐ With printed signatures Colby-Spinner	310.00	600.00
☐ With autographed signatures Colby-Spinner	2100.00	7700.00
☐ With autographed signatures Jeffries-Spinner	280.00	650.00
☐ With autographed signatures Allison-Spinner	290.00	650.00
☐ Green back	180.00	275.00
☐ Red back	175.00	275.00

FIFTEEN-CENT NOTES

| FOURTH ISSUE | PROOF | FACE | RARE | REVERSE 475.00 |

Face Design:
Bust
of Columbia.

Back Design:
Green
with "15"s.

REGULAR ISSUES	A.B.P.	GOOD	V.FINE	UNC.
☐ Large seal, watermarked paper	20.00	31.00	59.00	350.00
☐ Large seal, pink fibers in paper	20.00	32.00	64.00	350.00
☐ Large seal, pink fibers in paper, right end blue				
	20.00	32.00	60.00	350.00
☐ Large brown seal	26.00	46.00	185.00	RARE
☐ Smaller red seal, pink fibers, right end blue	20.00	31.00	62.00	350.00

TWENTY-FIVE-CENT NOTES

FIRST ISSUE	SPECIMEN	FACE	100.00	REVERSE	65.00
	PROOF	FACE	300.00	REVERSE	225.00

Face Design:
Five 5¢
Jefferson
Stamps.

Back Design:
Black,
large "25."

REGULAR ISSUES	A.B.P.	GOOD	V.FINE	UNC.
☐ Perforated edges, monogram ABNCO on back	9.00	12.00	32.00	430.00
☐ Perforated edges, without monogram on back	8.00	13.00	55.00	550.00
☐ Straight edges, monogram ABNCO on back	8.00	10.00	20.00	210.00
☐ Straight edges, without monogram on back	9.00	15.00	68.00	600.00

TWENTY-FIVE-CENT NOTES

SECOND ISSUE	SPECIMEN	FACE	100.00	REVERSE	75.00
	PROOF	FACE	275.00	REVERSE	225.00

Time and climatic condition have changed the purple color on the back of this note into many variations.

Face Design:
Portrait of
President
Washington.

Back Design:
Purple with
"25."

REGULAR ISSUES

	A.B.P.	GOOD	V.FINE	UNC.
☐Value only surcharge on back	8.00	12.00	20.00	250.00
☐Surcharge 18-63 on back	8.00	13.00	20.00	275.00
☐Surcharge A-18-63 on back	8.00	12.00	20.00	275.00
☐Surcharge 1-18-63 on back	19.00	37.00	200.00	645.00
☐Surcharge 2-18-63 on back	8.00	12.00	25.00	325.00
☐Surcharge S-18-63 on back	9.00	16.00	25.00	325.00
☐Surcharge T-1-18-63 on back, fiber paper	11.00	21.00	75.00	375.00
☐Surcharge T-2-18-63 on back, fiber paper	11.00	21.00	75.00	375.00

TWENTY-FIVE-CENT NOTES

THIRD ISSUE	SPECIMEN	FACE	150.00	REVERSE	80.00
	PROOF	FACE	300.00	REVERSE	200.00

All notes have printed signatures of Colby-Spinner.

Face Design:
Portrait of
Fessenden.

Back Design:
Green or
red with "25"

	A.B.P.	GOOD	V.FINE	UNC.
☐Face—bust of Fessenden between solid bronze surcharges, fiber paper, back—green, surcharge M-2-6-5 in corners	125.00	210.00	800.00	3300.00
☐As above, with letter "A" in lower left corner of face	150.00	300.00	900.00	4300.00
☐Face—Fessenden, open scroll bronze surcharges, fiber paper, back—green, surcharges M-2-6-5 in corners	12.00	20.00	85.00	550.00
☐As above with letter "A" in lower left corner of face	10.00	19.00	84.00	555.00
☐Face—Fessenden, open scroll surcharges, plain paper, back—green, value surcharges only	8.00	15.00	31.00	170.00
☐As before, letter "A" in lower left corner of face, back—green, plain paper	10.00	18.00	40.00	175.00
☐Face—Fessenden, red back, value surcharge only	12.00	21.00	44.00	250.00
☐As above, letter "A" in lower left corner of face	12.00	20.00	48.00	300.00

TWENTY-FIVE-CENT NOTES
FOURTH ISSUE SPECIMENS AND PROOFS RARE

Face Design:
Portrait of
President
Washington
and Treasury Seal.

Back Design:
Green.

REGULAR ISSUES	A.B.P.	GOOD	V.FINE	UNC.
☐Large seal, plain watermarked paper	6.00	9.00	21.00	125.00
☐Large seal, pink silk fiber in paper	6.00	9.00	21.00	125.00
☐Large seal, pink fibers in paper, right end blue	6.00	8.50	24.00	135.00
☐Large brown seal, right end blue	35.00	70.00	280.00	1150.00
☐Smaller red seal, right end blue	6.00	10.00	25.00	130.00

TWENTY-FIVE-CENT NOTES
FIFTH ISSUE SPECIMENS AND PROOFS RARE

Face Design:
Portrait of
Walker and
red seal.

Back Design:
Black.

REGULAR ISSUES	A.B.P.	GOOD	V.FINE	UNC.
☐With long narrow key in Treasury Seal.	6.00	9.00	16.00	75.00
☐With short stubby key in Treasury Seal	6.00	9.00	16.00	75.00

FIFTY-CENT NOTES

FIRST ISSUE	SPECIMEN	FACE	135.00	REVERSE	100.00
	PROOF	FACE	600.00	REVERSE	400.00

Face Design:
Five 10¢
Washington
stamps.

Back Design:
Green.

REGULAR ISSUES	A.B.P.	GOOD	V.FINE	UNC.
☐Perforated edges, monogram ABNCO on back	15.00	14.00	80.00	675.00
☐Perforated edges, without monogram on back	13.00	20.00	75.00	700.00
☐Straight edges, monogram ABNCO on back	8.00	10.00	30.00	360.00
☐Straight edges, without monogram	11.00	20.00	80.00	410.00

FIFTY-CENT NOTES

FIRST ISSUE	SPECIMEN	FACE	135.00	REVERSE	110.00
	PROOF	FACE	340.00	REVERSE	270.00

Face Design:
Portrait of
President
Washington.

Back Design:
Red.

REGULAR ISSUES	A.B.P.	GOOD	V.FINE	UNC.
☐Surcharge 18-63 on back	7.00	11.00	38.00	340.00
☐Surcharge A-18-63 on back	7.00	11.00	20.00	335.00
☐Surcharge O-1-18-63, fiber paper	9.00	25.00	81.00	575.00
☐Surcharge R-2-18-63, fiber paper	11.00	17.00	45.00	455.00
☐Surcharge T-1-18-63, fiber paper	7.00	15.00	47.00	460.00

FIFTY-CENT NOTES

THIRD ISSUE	SPECIMENS	FACE	150.00	REVERSE	120.00
	PROOFS	FACE	330.00	REVERSE	280.00

Face Design:
Justice with
sword,
shield,
scales.

Back Design:
Green
or red.

The following notes have printed signatures of Colby-Spinner
and have *green backs*.

REGULAR ISSUES	A.B.P.	GOOD	V.FINE	UNC.
☐Value surcharge and S-2-6-4 on back, fiber paper			12,000.00	25,000.00
☐Value surcharge and A-2-6-5 on back, fiber paper	16.00	30.00	92.00	1350.00
☐As above with "1" and letter "A" on face, A-2-6-5 on back	55.00	85.00	800.00	3600.00
☐As above with "1" only on face, A-2-6-5 on back	14.00	32.00	85.00	725.00
☐As above with letter "A" only on face, A-2-6-5 on back	14.00	36.00	85.00	700.00
☐A-2-6-5 on back, *narrowly spaced*, plain paper	10.00	12.00	74.00	550.00

	A.B.P.	GOOD	V.FINE	UNC.
☐As above, numeral "1" and letter "A" on face				
	10.00	20.00	72.50	510.00
☐As above, numeral "1" only on face	10.00	12.00	65.00	510.00
☐As above, letter "A" only on face	10.00	18.00	75.00	525.00
☐A-2-6-5 on back, *widely spaced,* plain paper	10.00	18.00	75.00	535.00
☐As above, numeral "1" and letter "A" on face				
	20.00	45.00	320.00	1300.00
☐As above, numeral "1" only on face	9.00	12.00	65.00	650.00
☐As above, letter "A" only on face	9.00	12.00	65.00	650.00
☐Without position letters or back surcharges	9.00	12.00	60.00	510.00
☐As above with numeral "1" and letter "A" on face				
	15.00	25.00	150.00	1500.00
☐As above with numeral "1" only on face	7.00	12.00	60.00	510.00
☐As above with letter "A" only on face	7.00	12.50	67.00	500.00

The following notes have printed signatures of Colby-Spinner and *red backs.*

	A.B.P.	GOOD	V.FINE	UNC.
☐Value surcharge and S-2-6-4 on back, fiber				
	150.00	180.00	17,000.00	34,000.00
☐As above, numeral "1" and letter "A"	150.00	350.00	2800.00	51,000.00
☐As above, numeral "1" only on face	125.00	200.00	900.00	32,000.00
☐As above, letter "A" only on face	135.00	225.00	900.00	32,000.00
☐Value surcharge and A-2-6-5 on back, plain				
	10.00	19.00	80.00	740.00
☐As above, numeral "1" and letter "A"	47.00	77.00	500.00	2200.00
☐As above, numeral "1" only on face	10.00	19.00	82.00	610.00
☐As above, letter "A" only on face	10.00	20.00	82.00	610.00
☐No surcharge on back, plain paper	10.00	20.00	84.00	675.00
☐As above, numeral "1" and letter "A" on face				
	25.00	50.00	250.00	2000.00
☐As above, numeral "1" only on face	13.00	24.00	145.00	1000.00
☐As above, letter "A" only on face	13.00	30.00	115.00	750.00

The following notes have autographed signatures of Colby-Spinner and *red backs.*

	A.B.P.	GOOD	V.FINE	UNC.
☐Value surcharge and S-2-6-4 on back, fiber	37.00	90.00	210.00	1500.00
☐Value surcharge and A-2-6-5 on back, fiber	35.00	75.00	195.00	1200.00
☐Value surcharge only on back, plain paper	16.00	30.00	84.00	900.00

FIFTY-CENT NOTES

THIRD ISSUE	SPECIMEN	FACE	135.00	REVERSE	125.00
	PROOF	FACE	400.00	REVERSE	300.00

Face Design: Bust of Spinner with surcharges.
Back Design: Green or red.

The following notes have printed signatures of Colby-Spinner, and *green backs*.

REGULAR ISSUES	A.B.P.	GOOD	V.FINE	UNC.
☐Value surcharge and A-2-6-5 on back	9.00	27.00	110.00	365.00
☐As above, numeral "1" and letter "A" on face	22.00	41.00	225.00	740.00
☐As above, numeral "1" only on face	9.00	19.00	62.00	370.00
☐As above, letter "A" only on face	9.00	18.00	100.00	500.00
☐Value surcharge only on back	9.00	12.00	50.00	410.00
☐As above, numeral "1" and letter "A" on face	12.00	28.00	60.00	410.00
☐As above, numeral "1" only on face	9.00	15.00	55.00	410.00
☐As above, letter "A" only on face	9.00	15.00	50.00	425.00

TYPE II BACK DESIGN

	A.B.P.	GOOD	V.FINE	UNC.
☐No back surcharge	9.00	18.00	56.00	380.00
☐Numeral "1" and letter "A" on face	20.00	37.00	95.00	460.00
☐Numeral "1" only on face	9.00	17.00	57.00	380.00
☐Letter "A" only on face	9.00	22.00	74.00	460.00

The following notes have a portrait of Spinner, printed signatures of Colby-Spinner, *red backs*, and are Type I.

REGULAR ISSUES	A.B.P.	GOOD	V.FINE	UNC.
☐Value surcharge and A-2-6-5 on back	10.00	45.00	60.00	360.00
☐As above with numeral "1" and letter "A"	20.00	45.00	130.00	875.00
☐As above with numeral "1" only on face	10.00	17.00	65.00	450.00
☐As above with letter "A" only on face	10.00	25.00	75.00	525.00

The following notes have autographed signatures, *red backs,* and are Type I.

	A.B.P.	GOOD	V.FINE	UNC.
☐Autographed signatures COLBY-SPINNER, back surcharged value and A-2-6-5	12.00	28.00	85.00	560.00
☐Autographed signatures ALLISON-SPINNER, back surcharged value and A-2-6-5	12.00	28.00	110.00	575.00
☐Autographed signatures ALLISON-NEW, back surcharged value and A-2-6-5	400.00	675.00	1650.00	5800.00

FIFTY-CENT NOTES

FOURTH ISSUE SPECIMENS AND PROOFS RARE

Face Design:
Bust
of Lincoln.

Back Design:
Green.

	A.B.P.	GOOD	V.FINE	UNC.
☐ Plain paper	16.00	23.00	60.00	575.00
☐ Paper with pink fibers	16.00	23.00	72.00	550.00

FIFTY-CENT NOTES

FOURTH ISSUE SPECIMENS AND PROOFS RARE

Face Design:
Bust
of Stanton.

Back Design:
Green
with "50."

	A.B.P.	GOOD	V.FINE	UNC.
☐ Red seal and signatures ALLISON-SPINNER, paper with pink fibers, blue ends	9.00	15.00	43.00	280.00

FIFTY-CENT NOTES

FOURTH ISSUE SPECIMENS AND PROOFS RARE

Face Design:
Bust of
Samuel
Dexter.

Back Design:
Green with
"50."

	A.B.P.	GOOD	V.FINE	UNC.
☐ Green seal, pink fibers, blue ends	8.00	12.00	24.00	200.00

FIFTY-CENT NOTES

FIFTH ISSUE SPECIMENS AND PROOFS RARE

Face Design:
Bust
of Crawford.

Back Design:
Green with
"50."

	A.B.P.	GOOD	V.FINE	UNC.
☐ Signatures ALLISON-NEW, paper with pink fibers, blue ends	6.00	10.00	20.00	90.00

FIFTY-CENT NOTES
FIFTH ISSUE SPECIMENS AND PROOFS RARE

Face Design:
Bust
of Seward.

Back Design:
Red &
Brown with
"$50–4%"

	A.B.P.	GOOD	V.FINE	UNC.
	75.00	100.00	825.00	1650.00

ERROR OR FREAK NOTES

Notes have been misprinted from time to time since the earliest days of currency. The frequency of misprintings and other abnormalities has increased in recent years due to heavier production and high-speed machinery. This has provided a major sub-hobby for note collectors. Freaks and errors have become very popular, their appeal and prices showing upward movement each year.

On the following pages we have pictured and described most of the more familiar and collectible Error Notes. Pricing is approximate only because many notes bearing the same general type of error differ in severity of error from one specimen to another. As a general rule, the less glaring or obvious errors carry a smaller premium value. Very valuable Error Notes include double denominations, or bills having the face of one denomination and reverse side of another.

Error and Freak Notes do turn up in everyday change. Specimens are located either in that fashion or from bank packs. As far as circulated specimens are concerned, some Error Notes have passed through so many hands before being noticed that the condition is not up to collector standards. This, of course, results in a very low premium valuation.

Values given below are for the specimens pictured and described. Different premiums may be attached to other specimens with similar errors, or notes showing the same errors but of different denominations.

MISMATCHED SERIAL NUMBERS

On ordinary notes, the serial number in the lower left of the obverse matches that in the upper right. When it fails to, even by the difference of a single digit, this is known as a "mismatched serial number." It occurs as the result of a cylinder or cylinders in the high-speed numbering machine becoming jammed. If more than one digit is mismatched, the value will be greater.

	V. FINE	UNC.
☐ $1 Federal Reserve Note, Series 1969, signatures Elston-Kennedy	143.00	330.00

	V. FINE	UNC.
☐ $1 Silver Certificate, Series 1957B, signatures Granahan-Dillon	132.00	270.00

	V. FINE	UNC.
☐ $1 Federal Reserve Note, Series 1977A, signatures Morton-Miller	121.00	270.00

INVERTED THIRD PRINT

The inverted third print is also known as "inverted overprint." The Treasury Seal, District Seal, Serial Numbers, and District Number are inverted on the obverse side of the note, or printed upside-down, caused by the sheet of notes (having already received the primary design on front and back) being fed upside-down into the press for this so-called "third print." (The back design is the "first print," the front is the "second print," and these various additions comprise the "third print." It is not possible to print these third print items at the same time as the obverse design, since they are not standard on every bill. At one time the signatures were included in the third print, but these are now engraved directly into the plate and are part of the second print.)

Though very spectacular, inverted third print errors are not particularly scarce and are especially plentiful in 1974 and 1976 series notes.

	V. FINE	UNC.
☐ $5 Federal Reserve Note, Series 1974, signatures Neff-Simon	160.00	291.00

	V. FINE	UNC.
☐ $2 Federal Reserve Note, Series 1976, signatures Neff-Simon	473.00	780.00

V. FINE   **UNC.**

☐$1 Federal Reserve Note, Series 1974, signatures Neff-Simon

          187.00   412.00

V. FINE   **UNC.**

☐$50 Federal Reserve Note, Series 1977, signatures Morton-Blumenthal

          467.00   715.00

V. FINE   **UNC.**

☐$20 Federal Reserve Note, Series 1974, signatures Neff-Simon

          236.00   506.00

V. FINE   **UNC.**

☐$10 Federal Reserve Note, Series 1974, signatures Neff-Simon

          220.00   440.00

COMPLETE OFFSET TRANSFER

Offset transfers are not, as is often believed, caused by still-wet printed sheets coming into contact under pressure. Though very slight offsetting can occur in that manner, it would not create notes as spectacular as those pictured here, in which the offset impression is almost as strong as the primary printing. These happen as a result of the printing press being started an instant or so before the paper is fed in. Instead of contacting the paper, the inked plate makes its impression upon the machine bed. When the paper is then fed through, it picks up this "ghost" impression from the bed, in addition to the primary impression it is supposed to receive. Each successive sheet going through the press will acquire the impression until all ink is totally removed from the machine bed. But, naturally, the first sheet will show the transfer strongest, and the others will be weaker and weaker. Obviously, the market value of such notes depends largely on the strength of the offset impression. The heavier and more noticeable it is, the more valuable the note will be—all other things being equal.

	V. FINE	UNC.
☐ $5 Federal Reserve Note, Series 1977, signatures Morton-Blumenthal, offset of reverse side of face		
Dark	148.00	385.00
Light	132.00	209.00

	V. FINE	UNC.
☐ $1 Federal Reserve note, Series 1974, signatures Neff-Simon, offset of reverse side of face.		
Dark	110.00	396.00
Light	110.00	203.00

PARTIAL OFFSET TRANSFER

The most logical explanation for this error is that a sheet of paper fed into the press incorrectly became mangled or torn, and part of the inked plate contacted the printing press bed. Therefore, wet ink was left on those portions of the press bed not covered by paper. When the next sheet was fed through, it received the correct impression, plus it acquired a partial offset transfer by contacting this wet area of the press bed. Just as with offset transfers, the first sheet going through the press following an accident of this kind will receive the strongest transfer, and it will become gradually less noticeable on succeeding sheets.

	V. FINE	UNC.
☐ $1 Federal Reserve Note, Series 1969D, signatures Banuelos-Schultz, offset of a portion of reverse side on face		
Dark	49.00	154.00
Light	44.00	143.00

PRINTED FOLD

Notes showing printed folds occur as the result of folds in the paper before printing, which probably happen most often when the sheet is being fed into the press. If the sheet is folded in such a manner that a portion of the reverse side is facing upward, as shown here, it will receive a part of the impression intended for its obverse. Naturally the positioning of these misplaced portions of printing is very random, depending on the nature and size of the fold.

	V. FINE	UNC.
☐ $20 Federal Reserve Note, Series 1977, signatures Morton-Blumenthal, Federal Reserve District seal and District number printed on reverse	159.00	341.00

THIRD PRINT ON REVERSE

The cause of this error is obvious, the sheet having been fed through the press on the wrong side (back instead of front) for the third impression or "third print." In the so-called third print, the note receives the Treasury and Federal Reserve District seals, district numbers, and serial numbers.

	V. FINE	UNC.
☐ $1 Federal Reserve Note, third print on reverse	165.00	378.00

BOARD BREAKS

The terminology of this error is misleading. It suggests that the fernlike unprinted areas were caused by a broken printing plate. Actually they must have resulted from something—probably linty matter—sticking to the printing ink. The assumption reached by the public, when it encounters such a note, is that the blank streaks were caused by the paper being folded in printing. This, however, is not possible, as that would yield an error of a much different kind (*see* Printed Fold).

It should be pointed out that board breaks are easily created by counterfeiters by erasing portions of the printed surface, and that the collector ought to examine such specimens closely.

	V. FINE	UNC.
☐ $20 Federal Reserve Note, board breaks on reverse	99.00	264.00

MISSING SECOND PRINT

The "second print" is the front face, or obverse of the note—the "first print" being the reverse or back. A note with a missing second print has not received the primary impression on its obverse, though the back is normal and the front carries the standard third print matter (Treasury Seal, serial numbers, etc.). These errors, while they probably occur frequently, are so easily spotted by B.E.P. checkers that such notes are very scarce on the market.

	V. FINE	UNC.
☐ $10 Federal Reserve Note, missing second print	275.00	715.00

PRINTED FOLD

This note was folded nearly in half before receiving the third print, which fell across the waste margin on the reverse side. Had the note not been folded, this waste margin would have been removed in the cutting process. This note, when unfolded, is grotesque in shape.

	V. FINE	UNC.
☐ $1 Federal Reserve Note, printed fold with Federal Reserve District seal, district numbers, and serial numbers on reverse. (Naturally, this note lacks the "third print" matter, such as the Treasury Seal, that was supposed to appear on the righthand side of the obverse.)	330.00	687.00

V. FINE   UNC.

☐ $5 Federal Reserve Note. Printed fold with entire Federal Reserve District seal, portion of another Federal Reserve District seal, and portion of two different serial numbers on the reverse. It may be hard to imagine how a freak of this nature occurs. This note was folded diagonally along a line bisecting the Lincoln Memorial building slightly to the right of center. The lefthand portion of the reverse side was thereby drawn down across the lefthand side of the obverse, extending well below the bottom of the note. It reached far enough down to catch the district seal intended for the note beneath it, as well as a bit of the serial number. This is why the two serial numbers are different; they were supposed to go on two different notes. Obviously, when something this dramatic happens in printing, not only one error note is created but several—at least—at the same time. Not all necessarily reach circulation, however.

550.00   1200.00

THIRD PRINT BLACK INK MISSING OR LIGHT

Though the machinery used is ultramodern, U.S. currency notes are printed by the same basic technique used when printing was first invented more than 500 years ago. Ink is spread on the metal plates and these are pressed on the sheets as they go through the press. Because the inking is manually fed (as is the paper), an even flow is usually achieved. When an under-inked note is found, it is generally merely "light," giving a faded appearance. But sometimes the plate will be very improperly inked, due to mechanical misfunction or some other cause, resulting in whole areas being unprinted or so lightly printed that they cannot be seen without close inspection. These are not especially valuable notes but counterfeit specimens are frequently made.

	V. FINE	UNC.

☐ $1 Federal Reserve Note, Series 1977, signatures of Morton-Blumenthal. Federal Reserve District seal and District numbers missing from lefthand side, remainder of "third print" material light but distinct. If the lefthand serial number was strong, there might be suspicion of this being a counterfeit.   99.00   286.00

THIRD PRINT GREEN INK MISSING OR LIGHT

In this case, the green, rather than the black, ink was applied too lightly to the printing plate.

	V. FINE	UNC.

☐ $5 Federal Reserve Note, Series 1977, signatures of Morton-Blumenthal   49.00   198.00

NOTE FOLDED DURING OVERPRINT

This note was folded as it was being overprinted and failed to receive the District seal and District numbers at the left side of its obverse. This kind of error, like all involving missing portions of printing, has been extensively counterfeited.

	V. FINE	UNC.
☐$2 Federal Reserve Note, Series 1976, signatures of Neff-Simon	103.00	231.00

FAULTY ALIGNMENT

Notes of this kind were formerly called "miscut," and sometimes still are. "Faulty alignment" is a more inclusive term which encompasses not only bad cutting but accidents in printing. If the sheet shifts around in the press, it will not receive the printed impressions exactly where they should be. Even if the cutting is normal, the resulting note will be misaligned; the cutting machine cannot correct botched printing. It is very easy to determine where the fault lies. If one side of the note has its design higher than the opposite side, this is a printing error. If the misalignment occurs equally on both sides, the problem was in cutting. Since the two sides are not printed in the same operation, it would be a one-in-a-million chance for them to become equally misaligned.

The value of such notes depends upon the degree of misalignment. Collectors are especially fond of specimens showing a portion—even if very slight, as with the one pictured of an adjoining note.

	V. FINE	UNC.
☐$5 Federal Reserve Note, bottom left of reverse shaved (or "bled"), corresponding portion of adjoining note just visible at top. This ranks as a "dramatic" specimen.		
Slight	66.00	176.00
Dramatic	71.00	291.00

INSUFFICIENT PRESSURE

Under-inking of the printing plate is not the only cause of weak or partially missing impressions. If the press is not operating correctly and the inked plate meets the sheet with insufficient pressure, the result is similar to under-inking. This probably happens as a result of a sheet going through just as the press is being turned off for the day, or at other intervals. Supposedly all action ceases at the instant of turnoff, but considering the rapidity of this operation, it is likely that a random sheet could pass through and be insufficiently impressed. The note pictured here received normal "third print," as is generally the case with notes whose first or second print is made with insufficient pressure.

	V. FINE	UNC.
☐$20 Federal Reserve Note, Series 1977, signatures of Morton-Blumenthal	148.00	385.00

PRINTED FOLD

This note, along with a large portion of the adjoining note, became folded after the second print. When it passed through the press to receive the third print or overprints (seals, serial numbers, etc.), these naturally failed to appear on the folded area.

	V. FINE	UNC.
☐$1 Federal Reserve Note, printed fold with overprints partially missing		
Small	88.00	231.00
Large	192.00	484.00

DOUBLE IMPRESSION

Double impressions have traditionally been traced to the sheet of notes passing through the press twice, which would be the logical explanation. However, in considering the method by which currency is printed, it would seem more likely that double impression notes have not made two trips through the press. They probably result from the automatic paper feed jamming. The sheet just printed fails to be ejected, and the printing plate falls upon it a second time instead of on a fresh sheet. This does not merely create a strong impression, but a twin, or a ghost, impression, since the sheet is not positioned exactly the same way for the second strike. Though the paper feed may not be operating properly, there will still be some slight movement—enough to prevent the second impression from falling directly atop the first.

	V. FINE	UNC.
☐$1 Federal Reserve Note, Series 1977A, signatures of Morton-Miller, double "second print" impression		
Partial	198.00	484.00
Complete	451.00	1045.00

DOUBLE IMPRESSION OF OVERPRINTS ("DOUBLE THIRD PRINT")

This note is normal as far as the primary obverse and reverse printings are concerned. It received twin impressions of the overprints or "third print." This was not caused by jamming of the paper feed as discussed above. Naturally, the serial numbers are different, as the automatic numbering machine turns with every rise and fall of the press.

	V. FINE	UNC.
☐ $20 Federal Reserve Note, Series 1950, signatures of		
Priest-Humphrey, double impression of overprints.		
Partial	275.00	632.00
Complete	506.00	863.00

THIRD PRINT (OR OVERPRINTS) SHIFTED

Whenever the overprints (serial number, seals, etc.) are out of position, vertically or horizontally, this is known as "third print shifted" or "overprints shifted." In the example pictured, shifting is extreme. This is a premium value specimen which would command the higher of the two sums quoted. Normally, the overprinting on a "shifted" note fails to touch the portrait, or touches it only slightly. The cause of this kind of error is a sheet feeding incorrectly into the press for the overprinting operation. As striking and desirable as these notes are to collectors, they often go unnoticed by the public.

	V. FINE	UNC.
☐ $100 Federal Reserve Note, Series 1969C,		
signatures of Banuelos-Schultz, third print shifted.		
Slight	231.00	522.00
Dramatic	220.00	451.00

INK SMEARS

Ink smearing is one of the more common abnormalities of currency notes. Generally it can be attributed to malfunction of the automatic inking device which inks the printing plate. When performing properly, ink is applied at a steady, controlled pace to the printing plate. A very minor disorder in the machine can dispense enough extra ink to yield very spectacular "smeared notes," such as the one illustrated. The value of ink smear notes depends upon the area and intensity of the smear. They are quite easily faked, so the buyer should be cautious.

	V. FINE	UNC.
☐$1 Federal Reserve Note, ink smear		
Small	27.00	99.00
Large	70.00	159.00

PRINTING FOLD

This note was crumpled along the right side prior to the third printing or application of overprints. Hence the "third print" matter on the lefthand side is normal, but portions of the overprint on the right appear on the note's reverse side.

	V. FINE	UNC.
☐$20 Federal Reserve Note, Series 1977,		
signatures Morton-Blumenthal.	137.00	308.00

BLANK CREASE

It occasionally happens that a note becomes creased prior to the reverse or obverse printing in such a way that a small fold is created. During the printing procedure this fold hides a portion of the note's surface, which fails to receive the impression. These notes are actually double errors—the cutting machine cuts them without knowledge of the fold, and when the fold is opened out the bill is then of larger than normal size. Since "crease errors" are difficult to spot in the Bureau of Engraving and Printing's checking, they find their way into circulation in rather sizable numbers. It is difficult to place standard values on them because the price depends on the exact nature of the specimen. The wider the crease, the more valuable the note will be. Premium values are attached to notes with multiple creases that cause the blank unprinted area to fall across the portrait.

	V. FINE	UNC.
☐ Blank crease note, any denomination. Value stated is collector premium over and above face value. (If note has additional value because of series, signatures, etc., this too must be added.)		
Single crease	33.00	93.00
Multiple crease	42.00	95.00

MIXED DENOMINATION

The two notes pictured are normal in themselves, and if they were not owned together as a set, no premium value would be attached to them. The error (which may be dubious to term as such) lies with their serial numbers. The $5 Note has a serial number one digit higher than the $1, suggesting that it was fed into the printing machine intended to print overprints (or "third prints") on $1 bills. Even when this does happen (probably infrequently), it is very difficult to obtain "matching" notes of the kind illustrated, in which the serial numbers are only a single digit apart. Even if you had a $5 Note and $1 Note (or other combination of denominations) from sheets that were fed one after the other, the odds on getting one-digit-apart serial numbers are extremely small.

The value is given for an Uncirculated set only, as there would be no possibility of finding such matched notes except in a bank pack. Once released into circulation, they may never again be mated.

	UNC.
☐Mixed denomination pair from bank pack, $5 Federal Reserve Note within pack of $1 Federal Reserve Notes	4100.00

BLANK REVERSE

U.S. currency has its reverse printed before the obverse—in other words, back before front. The only logical explanation for blank reverse notes is that blank paper found its way into the batch of sheets on which reverses had already been printed. They were then fed—without detection—into the press for application of the obverse. They continued to escape notice during printing of the overprints, and miraculously got into circulation.

	V. FINE	UNC.
☐$100 Federal Reserve Note, blank reverse	440.00	935.00

	V. FINE	UNC.
☐ $20 Federal Reserve Note, Series 1977, signatures of Morton-Blumenthal Blank reverse	176.00	440.00

	V. FINE	UNC.
☐ $10 Federal Reserve Note, Series 1974, signatures of Neff-Simon Blank reverse	176.00	385.00

	V. FINE	UNC.
☐ $1 Federal Reserve Note, Series 1977, signatures of Morton-Blumenthal Blank reverse	165.00	385.00

DOUBLE DENOMINATION COUNTERFEIT

This is a counterfeit or faked error. We include it to show the kind of work done by counterfeiters, and how such items can be made to resemble genuine errors. This happens to be a counterfeit of an error note that cannot exist in its genuine state. Thus, there can be no hesitancy in proclaiming it a fake. Anyone who is even slightly familiar with the way currency is printed should instantly recognize this item as a fraud.

Nevertheless, fakers succeed in selling (often at high prices) specimens of this kind, probably because some collectors want the impossible for their albums. Genuine double or twin denomination notes have the obverse of one denomination and the reverse of a different denomination. They do not consist of two obverses or two reverses, such as the one pictured. The note illustrated carries four serial numbers. For it to be genuine, it would have had to pass through the "third print" (overprinting) process twice. Obviously it was made by gluing a $1 and $5 Note together. Much more deceptive paste-ups are created with the notes correctly paired so that the obverse of one and reverse of the other shows. Beware!

INVERTED OBVERSE

U.S. currency is printed reverse first. Therefore, when the back and front do not face in the same vertical direction (as they should), the note is known as an "inverted obverse." The term "inverted reverse" is never used. This, of course, results from the sheet being fed through upside-down for the obverse or second print. Though these specimens are scarce in Uncirculated condition, they often pass through many hands in circulation before being spotted. The uninformed public is not even aware that a note with faces in opposite directions is an error and has premium value.

	V. FINE	UNC.
☐ $2 Federal Reserve Note, Series 1976, signatures of Neff-Simon, inverted obverse	174.00	770.00

MISSING THIRD PRINT

This error is also known as "missing overprint." It consists of a note released into circulation without having gone through the "third print" operation.

	V. FINE	UNC.
☐ $1 Federal Reserve Note, Series 1977, signatures Morton-Blumenthal, missing third print	198.00	440.00

FOREIGN MATTER ON OBVERSE

Sometimes foreign matter, usually paper scraps of one kind or another, gets between the printing plate and the sheet. This naturally results in the area covered being blank on the note. Because of the extreme pressure exerted in printing, the foreign matter is occasionally "glued" to the note and travels with it into circulation. If the appendage is paper, it will normally be found to be of the same stock from which the note is made—apparently a shred from one of the sheet margins that worked its way into a batch of sheets awaiting printing. The value of such notes varies greatly, depending on the size of the foreign matter and its placement. It's rare to find notes in which foreign matter became attached before the first or second print. Nearly always, they found their way to the note after the second print and before the third.

	V. FINE	UNC.
☐$1 Federal Reserve Note, Series 1974, signatures Neff-Simon, foreign matter on obverse	121.00	264.00

	V. FINE	UNC.
☐$1 Silver Certificate, Series 1935E, signatures of Priest-Humphrey. Foreign matter on obverse. More valuable than the preceding because of the note's age and the foreign matter being larger.	330.00	715.00

MISSING PORTION OF REVERSE DESIGN
(DUE TO ADHERENCE OF SCRAP PAPER)

In this instance, the foreign matter got in the way of the first print, or reverse printing. It prevented the covered area from being printed, but it later became dislodged and is no longer present. What appears on the illustration to be a strip of paper on the note is really the blank unprinted area once covered by the strip. Obviously a note that merely had a random strip of paper attached, over a normally printed design, would have no collector interest.

	V. FINE	UNC.
☐ $1 Federal Reserve Note, missing portion of reverse design due to adherence of scrap paper	121.00	262.00

OVERPRINT PARTIALLY MISSING

The overprint or third print on this note is normal on the righthand side and missing entirely on the left. This was caused by the note being folded (more or less in half, vertically) immediately before overprinting. Had the lefthand side been folded over the face, this would have interfered with the overprints on the righthand side. Instead, this specimen was folded over the reverse side, or downward, with the result that the missing portion of overprint did not strike the note at all—it simply hit the printing press bed. The reverse side of this note is normal.

	V. FINE	UNC.
☐ $1 Federal Reserve Note, Series 1963A, overprint partially missing	99.00	282.00

THIRD PRINT OFFSET ON REVERSE

This note is normal on the obverse but carries an "offset" of the third print or overprints on its reverse. It would appear that the overprints are showing through to the reverse, as if the note were printed on very thin paper. Actually, this "mirror image" is caused by a malfunction in the printing or paper-feeding machinery. The inked plate for printing the overprints contacted the machine bed without a sheet of paper being in place. Therefore, as the next sheet came through it received the normal overprint on its face and picked up the offset impression on its reverse from the machine bed. Each successive sheet going through the press also received an offset, but it naturally became fainter and fainter as the ink was absorbed. The value of a note of this kind depends on the intensity of the impression.

	V. FINE	UNC.
☐ $5 Federal Reserve Note, offset impression of overprints on reverse	137.00	297.00

CONFEDERATE MONEY

The Civil War Centennial of 1961–65 has generally been credited with sparking an interest in the collecting and study of Confederate or C.S.A. Notes. This, however, is not totally borne out by facts, as C.S.A. currency had advanced steadily in value since the 1940s. It rides a crest of popularity today surpassing the early 1960s. This is due in part to the exhaustive research carried out since that time and numerous books and articles published. Even today, some C.S.A. Notes would still appear to be undervalued based on their availability vs. regular U.S. issues.

History. It became apparent upon the outbreak of the Civil War that both sides would experience extreme coinage shortages, and each took to the printing of notes that could be exchanged in lieu of bullion or "real money" (which always meant coined money until the 1860s). The South suffered more serious difficulties than the North, as it did not have as many skilled printers or engravers at its command. Also, with the war being fought on its territory rather than the North's, there was an ever-present danger of sabotage to plants printing money or engaging in related activities. The Confederacy tried by all available means to satisfy the currency demand and succeeded in distributing quite a large quantity of notes. Its shortage was taken up by notes issued by private banks, individual states, counties, railroads, and private merchants. Merchant tokens, to take the place of rapidly disappearing small change, poured forth in abundance during this period. All told, the Confederate Congress authorized the printing of about one and a half billion dollars' worth of paper currency. It is impossible to determine the total actually produced, but it would appear that this figure was far surpassed. At the war's conclusion, these notes were worthless, as the C.S.A. no longer existed and the federal government refused to redeem them. Many were discarded as scrap, but a surprising number were held faithfully by their owners who believed "the South will rise again." The South did indeed rise, industrially and economically, and those old C.S.A. Notes rose, too. They still aren't spendable, but many are worth sums in excess of face value as collectors' pieces. Until about 1900, however, practically no value was placed on Confederate currency—even by collectors.

Designs. Some surprising designs will be observed, including mythological gods and goddesses that seem to relate very little to the Southern artistic or cultural climate of the 1860s. Many scholarly efforts have been made to explain away the use of such motifs, but the simple fact is that they appeared not so much by choice as by necessity. Southern printers, not having the facilities of their Northern counterparts, were compelled to make do with whatever engravings or "stock cuts" were already on hand, as inappropriate as they might have proved. However, a number of original designs were created reflecting unmistakably regional themes and at times picturing heroes or leaders of the Confederacy. Slaves at labor, used as a symbol of the South's economic strength and its supposed advantage over the North, where labor was hired, was a frequent motif. Sailors were also depicted, as well as railroad trains and anything else that appeared symbolic of Southern industry. Probably the most notable single design, not intended to carry the satirical overtones it now possesses, is "General Francis Marion's Sweet Potato Breakfast" on the $10 1861 issue note.

In general, the C.S.A. Notes are not so badly designed a group as might be anticipated in light of conditions. The designing was, in fact, several leagues improved over the printing, which often left much to be desired. George Washington is depicted—not for being the first U.S. President but as a native son of Virginia. Jefferson Davis, President of the C.S.A., is among the more common portraits. He became even more disliked in the North than he otherwise might have been because of his picture turning up on currency. But after the war he took a moderate stand

and erased the old ill feelings; he even had words of praise for Lincoln. Other individuals whose portraits (not necessarily very faithful) will be encountered are:

- John C. Calhoun, U.S. Senator who led the battle for slavery and Southern Rights (later called "states' rights")
- Alexander H. Stephen, Davis' Vice-President of the C.S.A.
- Judah P. Benjamin, holder of various official titles in the Southern government
- C.G. Memminger, Secretary of the Treasury and Secretary of War
- Lucy Pickens, wife of South Carolina's governor and the only woman (aside from mythological types) shown on C.S.A. currency
- John E. Ward
- R.M.T. Hunter

Printers. The study of printers of C.S.A. Notes is complex, made no less so by the fact that some contractors produced only plates, others did only printing (from plates procured elsewhere), and some did both. The principal Southern printer was the lithography firm of Hoyer & Ludwig of Richmond, Virginia. Also located in Richmond were Keatinge & Ball, which did commendable, if not exactly inspired, work, and B. Duncan, who also worked in Columbia, South Carolina. Another firm involved in quite a bit of note printing was J.T. Paterson of Columbia. The so-called "Southern Bank Note Company" was a fictitious name used to disguise the origin of notes prepared in the North. Some early notes were marked "National Bank Note Co., New York," but it was subsequently decided to remove correct identification from the notes of this printer, undoubtedly on the latter's request (fearing prosecution for aiding the enemy).

Cancellations. Two varieties of cancels are commonly found on C.S.A. Notes. First is the Cut Cancel (CC), in which a knife or similar instrument has been used to make piercings in a design or pattern. Unless roughly executed, such cuts do not materially reduce a specimen's value. In the case of some notes, examples without cancellation are almost impossible to find. The COC, or Cut-Out Cancel, is more objectionable because, instead of merely leaving slits, a portion of the paper was removed. The reduction of value for a Cut-Out Cancel averages around 25 percent. These are considered "space fillers" if the issue is fairly common, but a rare note with a COC may be very desirable. Pen Cancellations (PC) are far less frequently encountered. These show the word "Canceled" written out by hand across the note's face, in ink. Unless the ink is heavy or blotchy, a Pen Cancel will not have too much bearing on value. As the note is not physically injured, it would seem to be the least offensive of the three varieties. Whenever a note is being sold, presence of a cancel, of whatever type, should be plainly spelled out. Some collectors are not interested in canceled specimens. In time, as the scarce issues become even scarcer, they will probably have to be accepted as a fact of life.

Signatures. The first six notes issued, the four from Montgomery and T5 & 6 from Richmond, were hand-signed by the Register and Treasurer themselves. Thereafter, because the Treasury Secretary felt hand signatures helped prevent counterfeiting, and because of the quantities of notes spewing forth, clerks were hired to sign "for Register" and "for Treasurer." There were about 200 different people who signed for each Treasury official, making for thousands of signature combinations. Mostly the clerks were women, many the wives or daughters of soldiers who had been killed in action. Since the notes were signed in Richmond through April of 1864 (when all operations were removed to Columbia, South Carolina), most of the signers were from there. Some moved to Columbia, and others were hired there.

It is most interesting to many people to find that they had relatives who signed Confederate money, and many people search for such notes. A complete listing of all the names from the Confederate Records appears in Colonel Criswell's extensive book, *Confederate and Southern States Currency*.

Condition Grades. While condition standards are basically the same for Confederate currency as other notes of their age, some allowance must be made for paper quality and deficiencies in printing and cutting. These matters have nothing to do with the preservation or wear and can be observed just as frequently in Uncirculated specimens as in those in average condition. Without a source of good paper, printers were obliged to use whatever was most easily and quickly obtainable. Often the paper was thin, or stiff, or contained networks of minute wrinkles which interfered with printing. Cutting was generally not done by machine, as in the North, but by hand with a pair of scissors—workers actually took the sheets and cut apart notes individually. When paper-cutting devices were employed, they were apparently not of the best quality. In any case, regular edges on C.S.A. Notes are uncommon, and their absence does not constitute grounds for classifying an otherwise perfect specimen in a condition grade below Uncirculated. When the occasional gem is located—a well-printed, well-preserved note on good paper, decently cut—its value is sure to be higher than those listed. The collector is not advised to confine himself to such specimens, as his activities would become seriously limited.

Uncirculated—UNC. An Uncirculated note shows no evidence of handling and is as close to "new condition" as possible. An Uncirculated specimen may, however, have pinholes or a finger smudge, which should be mentioned in a sales offering. If these are readily noticeable, the note deserves to be classified as "Almost Uncirculated." Crispness is hardly a criterion of uncirculation as this quality is expected in notes graded as low as Very Fine.

Almost Uncirculated—A.U. Similar to the above grade, but not quite as good as an Uncirculated specimen. The note bears no indication of having actually circulated but has minor flaws resulting from accident or mishandling, such as individuals' counting crinkles.

Extremely Fine—X.F. An X.F. note is on the borderline between Uncirculated and Circulated. It has not been heavily handled but may reveal several imperfections: a pinhole, finger smudge, counting crinkles, or a light wallet fold. The fold is not so heavy as to be termed a crease.

Very Fine—V.F. Has been in circulation but is not worn or seriously creased. It must still be clean and crisp, without stains or tears. Fine to Very Fine condition is considered the equivalent of "Average Circulated" but not "Average" condition (which is another term for poor).

Fine—F. A note that has been in circulation and shows it, but has no physical injuries or just slight ones.

Very Good—V.G. A well-circulated note bearing evidence of numerous foldings. It may possibly have creased corners and wrinkles as well as light staining, smudging, or pinholes, but major defects (such as a missing corner) would place it into an even lower category.

Good—G. Good notes have been heavily circulated, worn, possibly stained or scribbled on edges, could be frayed or "dog-eared." There may be holes larger than pin punctures, but not on the central portion of design. This is the lowest grade of condition acceptable to a collector, and only when nothing better is available. Unless very rare, such specimens are considered space-fillers only.

Average Buying Prices—A.B.P. The Average Buying Prices given here are the approximate sums paid by retail dealers for specimens in Good condition. As selling prices vary, so do buying prices, and in fact they usually vary more. A dealer who is overstocked on a certain note is sure to offer less than one who has no specimens on hand. The dealer's location, size of operation, and other circumstances will also influence the buying price. We present these figures merely as approximate guides to what sellers should expect.

Type Numbers. Each Confederate Note pictured has a "Type" number as well as a "regular" Criswell catalog number. The Criswell numbers are listed in the beginning of each of the price listings, and the Type numbers appear immediately following in parentheses. These numbers are used for identification and are cross-referenced in Grover Criswell's publications.

FOR MORE INFORMATION

Considered to have been the foremost authority on Confederate currency, the late Col. Grover Criswell has a variety of books available. His last release, *Confederate and Southern States Currency* ($75), covers all the currency issued by the Confederate States Central Government, the Southern States, the Indian Territories, the Florida Republic and Territory, and the Republic and Independent Government of Texas. This edition also gives interesting discovery information that you are sure to enjoy. There are also current market values listed, as well as rarities. This is the best reference available for the serious collector, libraries, and the casual reader.

CONFEDERATE STATES OF AMERICA—
1861 ISSUE, MONTGOMERY, ALABAMA
$1,000,000 authorized by "Act of March 9th."
Written dates "1861."
"NATIONAL BANK NOTE CO., NY"

TYPE
1

Face Design: Green and black, bears "Interest Ten Cents Per Day," 607
issued. John C. Calhoun left, Andrew Jackson right.

CRISWELL	NOTE	A.B.P.	GOOD	UNC.
☐1	$1000	6500.00	8150.00	51,000.00

"NATIONAL BANK NOTE CO., NY"

TYPE
2

Face Design: Green and black, bears "Interest Five Cents Per Day," 607
issued. Cattle crossing a brook.

CRISWELL	NOTE	A.B.P.	GOOD	UNC.
☐2	$500	6500.00	8400.00	52,000.00

CONFEDERATE STATES OF AMERICA—
1861 ISSUE
"NATIONAL BANK NOTE CO., NY"

TYPE 3

Face Design: Green and black, bears "Interest One Cent Per Day." Railway train, Minerva left.

CRISWELL	NOTE	A.B.P.	GOOD	UNC.
☐3	$100	2800.00	6300.00	30,000.00

"NATIONAL BANK NOTE CO., NY"

TYPE 4

Face Design: Green and black, bears "Interest Half A Cent Per Day." Negroes hoeing cotton.

CRISWELL	NOTE	A.B.P.	GOOD	UNC.
☐4	$50	3150.00	5000.00	27,000.00

CONFEDERATE STATES OF AMERICA—1861 ISSUE
"AMERICAN BANK NOTE CO., NY"
(Though ostensibly by the "SOUTHERN BANK NOTE CO.")

TYPE
5

Face Design: Green and black, red fibre paper, bears "Interest One Cent Per Day." Railway train, Justice left and Minerva right.

CRISWELL	NOTE	A.B.P.	GOOD	UNC.
☐5	$100	550.00	850.00	2775.00

TYPE
6

Face Design: Green and black, red fibre paper, bears "Interest Half A Cent Per Day." Pallas and Ceres seated on bale of cotton, Washington at right.

CRISWELL	NOTE	A.B.P.	GOOD	UNC.
☐6	$50	360.00	600.00	2500.00

CONFEDERATE STATES OF AMERICA—1861 ISSUE
$20,000,000 authorized by "Act of May 16th, 1861"
(All lithographic date "July 25th, 1861")
"HOYER & LUDWIG, RICHMOND, VA"

TYPE
7

Face Design: Ceres and Proserpina flying, Washington left.

CRISWELL	NOTE	A.B.P.	GOOD	UNC.
☐7-13	$100	425.00	600.00	2500.00

TYPE
8

Face Design: Washington, Tellus left.

CRISWELL	NOTE	A.B.P.	GOOD	UNC.
☐14-22	$50	90.00	110.00	3850.00

CONFEDERATE STATES OF AMERICA—1861 ISSUE

TYPE XXI

Face Design: Exists in a variety of colors.

CRISWELL	NOTE	A.B.P.	GOOD	UNC.
☐XXI	$20	75.00	140.00	365.00

The above type notes were bogus. For years it was thought they were a regular Confederate issue, and evidence exists that they were circulated as such. No collection of Confederate Notes is complete without one. There is no evidence as to who the printer was, but the authors have reason to believe he was located somewhere in Ohio. It is not a product of S.C. Upham, of Philadelphia, the well-known counterfeiter of Confederate Notes.

TYPE 9

Face Design: Large sailing vessel, "20" at left.

CRISWELL	NOTE	A.B.P.	GOOD	UNC.
☐23-33	$20	45.00	110.00	425.00

CONFEDERATE STATES OF AMERICA—1861 ISSUE

TYPE
10

Face Design: Liberty seated by eagle, with shield and flag.

There are at least forty-two minor varieties of this note, including a supposed ten or eleven stars on shield. Usually the stars are so indistinct that a note may show from six to fifteen stars. The other differences are minute changes in the size of the "10" in the upper corners. We list only the major type.

CRISWELL	NOTE	A.B.P.	GOOD	UNC.
☐ 34-41	$10	85.00	125.00	3200.00

TYPE
11

Face Design: Liberty seated by eagle, sailor left.

CRISWELL	NOTE	A.B.P.	GOOD	UNC.
☐ 42-45	$5	250.00	700.00	23,500.00

CONFEDERATE STATES OF AMERICA—1861 ISSUE
(Written date "July 25th, 1861")
"J. MANOUVRIER, NEW ORLEANS"

TYPE
12

Face Design: CONFEDERATE STATES OF AMERICA in blue on blue reverse.

CRISWELL	NOTE	A.B.P.	GOOD	UNC.
☐46-49	$5	525.00	1040.00	8400.00

$100,000,000 authorized by "Act of Aug. 19th, 1861."
$50,000,000 authorized by "Act of Dec. 24th, 1861."
"HOYER & LUDWIG, RICHMOND, VA"

TYPE
13

(Lithographic date "September 2nd, 2d, & s, 1861")
Face Design: Negroes loading cotton, sailor left.

CRISWELL	NOTE	A.B.P.	GOOD	UNC.
☐50-58	$100	60.00	100.00	3250.00

CONFEDERATE STATES OF AMERICA—1861 ISSUE

TYPE
14

Face Design: Moneta seated by treasure chests, sailor left.

CRISWELL	NOTE		A.B.P.	GOOD	UNC.
☐59-78	$50		45.00	75.00	375.00

"SOUTHERN BANK NOTE CO., NEW ORLEANS"

TYPE
15

Face Design: Black and red on red fibre paper. Railway train, Justice right, Hope with anchor left.

CRISWELL	NOTE		A.B.P.	GOOD	UNC.
☐79	$50		950.00	1500.00	12000.00

CONFEDERATE STATES OF AMERICA—1861 ISSUE
"KEATINGE & BALL, RICHMOND, VA"

TYPE
16

Face Design: Black and green, red fibre paper. Portrait of Jefferson Davis.

CRISWELL	NOTE	A.B.P.	GOOD	UNC.
☐80-98	$50	120.00	175.00	1400.00

"HOYER & LUDWIG, RICHMOND, VA"

TYPE
17

Face Design: Black with green ornamentation, plain paper. Ceres seated between Commerce and Navigation, Liberty left.

CRISWELL	NOTE	A.B.P.	GOOD	UNC.
☐99-100	$20	255.00	325.00	2600.00

CONFEDERATE STATES OF AMERICA—1861 ISSUE
"HOYER & LUDWIG, RICHMOND, VA"

TYPE
18

Face Design: Large sailing vessel, sailor at capstan left.

CRISWELL	NOTE	A.B.P.	GOOD	UNC.
☐101-136	$20	40.00	75.00	200.00

"SOUTHERN BANK NOTE CO., NEW ORLEANS"

TYPE
19

Face Design: Black and red on red fibre paper. Navigator seated by charts,
Minerva left, blacksmith right.

CRISWELL	NOTE	A.B.P.	GOOD	UNC.
☐137	$20	700.00	1100.00	6000.00

CONFEDERATE STATES OF AMERICA—1861 ISSUE
"B. DUNCAN, COLUMBIA, SC"

TYPE
20

Face Design: Industry seated between cupid and beehive, bust of A. H.
Stephens left.

CRISWELL	NOTE		A.B.P.	GOOD	UNC.
☐139-140	$20		50.00	75.00	300.00

"B. DUNCAN, RICHMOND, VA"

CRISWELL	NOTE		A.B.P.	GOOD	UNC.
☐141-143	$20		45.00	70.00	315.00

"KEATINGE & BALL, COLUMBIA, SC"

TYPE
21

Face Design: Portrait of Alexander H. Stephens.

YELLOW-GREEN ORNAMENTATION

CRISWELL	NOTE		A.B.P.	GOOD	UNC.
☐144	$20		150.00	220.00	2000.00

DARK-GREEN ORNAMENTATION

CRISWELL	NOTE		A.B.P.	GOOD	UNC.
☐145-149	$20		110.00	225.00	1900.00

CONFEDERATE STATES OF AMERICA—1861 ISSUE
"SOUTHERN BANK NOTE CO., NEW ORLEANS"

**TYPE
22**

Face Design: Black and red, red fibre paper. Group of Indians, Thetis left, maiden with "X" at right.

CRISWELL	NOTE		A.B.P.	GOOD	UNC.
☐150-152	$10		250.00	425.00	2600.00

"LEGGETT, KEATINGE & BALL, RICHMOND, VA"

**TYPE
23**

Face Design: Black and orange/red. Wagon load of cotton, harvesting sugar cane right. John E. Ward left.

CRISWELL	NOTE		A.B.P.	GOOD	UNC.
☐153-155	$10		350.00	550.00	3750.00

CONFEDERATE STATES OF AMERICA—1861 ISSUE
"LEGGETT, KEATINGE & BALL, RICHMOND, VA"

TYPE
24

Face Design: Black and orange/red. R.M.T. Hunter left, vignette of child
right.

CRISWELL	NOTE	A.B.P.	GOOD	UNC.
☐156-160	$10	100.00	195.00	1200.00

"KEATINGE & BALL, RICHMOND, VA"

CRISWELL	NOTE	A.B.P.	GOOD	UNC.
☐161-167	$10	75.00	140.00	1000.00

"KEATINGE & BALL, RICHMOND, VA"

TYPE
25

Face Design: Hope with anchor, R.M.T. Hunter left, C. G. Memminger right.

CRISWELL	NOTE	A.B.P.	GOOD	UNC.
☐168-171	$10	65.00	110.00	700.00

CONFEDERATE STATES OF AMERICA—1861 ISSUE
"KEATINGE & BALL, RICHMOND, VA"

TYPE
26

Face Design: Hope with anchor, R.M.T. Hunter left, C.G. Memminger right.

Face Design: *Solid red "X" and "X" overprint.

CRISWELL	NOTE	A.B.P.	GOOD	UNC.
☐173-184	$10	75.00	125.00	925.00

*There are three types of red "X" and "X" overprints. That section of the note on which the overprints appear is illustrated in double size.

Face Design: *Coarse lace "X" and "X" red overprint.

CRISWELL	NOTE	A.B.P.	GOOD	UNC.
☐189-210	$10	70.00	110.00	700.00

CONFEDERATE STATES OF AMERICA—1861 ISSUE

Face Design: Fine lace "X" and "X" red overprint.*

CRISWELL	NOTE	A.B.P.	GOOD	UNC.
☐211–214	$10	65.00	110.00	705.00

TYPE 27

Face Design: Liberty seated by shield and eagle.

CRISWELL	NOTE	A.B.P.	GOOD	UNC.
☐221-229,	$10	1650.00	6000.00	45,000.00

CONFEDERATE STATES OF AMERICA—1861 ISSUE
"HOYER & LUDWIG, RICHMOND, VA"

TYPE 28

Face Design: Ceres and Commerce with an urn.

CRISWELL	NOTE	A.B.P.	GOOD	UNC.
☐230-234	$10	45.00	75.00	700.00

"J. T. PATERSON, COLUMBIA, SC"

CRISWELL	NOTE	A.B.P.	GOOD	UNC.
☐235-236	$10	50.00	85.00	700.00

"B. DUNCAN, RICHMOND, VA"

TYPE
29

Face Design: Negro picking cotton.

CRISWELL	NOTE	A.B.P.	GOOD	UNC.
☐237	$10	110.00	250.00	1700.00

CONFEDERATE STATES OF AMERICA—1861 ISSUE
"B. DUNCAN, COLUMBIA, SC"

TYPE
30

Face Design: Gen. Francis Marion's "Sweet Potato Dinner." R. M. T. Hunter left, Minerva right.

CRISWELL	NOTE	A.B.P.	GOOD	UNC.
☐238	$10	50.00	100.00	380.00

NO ENGRAVER'S NAME

CRISWELL	NOTE	A.B.P.	GOOD	UNC.
☐239-241	$10	45.00	65.00	370.00

"SOUTHERN BANK NOTE CO., NEW ORLEANS"

TYPE
31

Face Design: Black and red on red fibre paper. Minerva left; Agriculture, Commerce, Industry, Justice, and Liberty seated at center; statue of Washington right.

CRISWELL	NOTE	A.B.P.	GOOD	UNC.
☐243-245	$5	135.00	245.00	1850.00

CONFEDERATE STATES OF AMERICA—1861 ISSUE
"LEGGETT, KEATINGE & BALL, RICHMOND, VA"

TYPE
32

Face Design: Black and orange/red. Machinist with hammer, boy in oval left.

CRISWELL	NOTE	A.B.P.	GOOD	UNC.
☐246-249	$5	350.00	425.00	3500.00

"LEGGETT, KEATINGE & BALL, RICHMOND, VA"

TYPE
33

Face Design: Black and white note with blue-green ornamentation. C.G. Memminger, Minerva right.

CRISWELL	NOTE	A.B.P.	GOOD	UNC.
☐250-256	$5	75.00	150.00	1400.00

CONFEDERATE STATES OF AMERICA—1861 ISSUE
"KEATINGE & BALL, RICHMOND, VA"

TYPE
34

Face Design: C.G. Memminger, Minerva right.

CRISWELL	NOTE	A.B.P.	GOOD	UNC.
☐262-270	$5	50.00	110.00	950.00

"HOYER & LUDWIG, RICHMOND, VA"

**TYPE
35**

Face Design: Loading cotton left, Indian princess right.

CRISWELL	NOTE	A.B.P.	GOOD	UNC.
☐271	$5	2200.00	6700.00	80,000.00

CONFEDERATE STATES OF AMERICA—1861 ISSUE
"HOYER & LUDWIG, RICHMOND, VA"

**TYPE
36**

Face Design: Ceres seated on bale of cotton, sailor left.

CRISWELL	NOTE	A.B.P.	GOOD	UNC.
☐272	$5	45.00	75.00	415.00

"J. T. PATERSON & CO., COLUMBIA, SC"

CRISWELL	NOTE	A.B.P.	GOOD	UNC.
☐274	$5	30.00	55.00	275.00
☐276-282	$5	30.00	55.00	275.00

CONFEDERATE STATES OF AMERICA—1861 ISSUE
"B. DUNCAN, RICHMOND, VA"

TYPE
37

Face Design: Sailor seated beside bales of cotton, C.G. Memminger left,
Justice and Ceres right.

CRISWELL	NOTE	A.B.P.	GOOD	UNC.
☐284	$5	60.00	110.00	700.00

"B. DUNCAN, COLUMBIA, SC"

CRISWELL	NOTE	A.B.P.	GOOD	UNC.
☐285	$5	60.00	150.00	700.00

"B. DUNCAN, COLUMBIA, SC"

TYPE
38

Face Design: Personification of South striking down Union, J.P. Benjamin
left. Dated "September 2, 1861" through an error. No Confederate Note less
than $5 was authorized in 1861.

CRISWELL	NOTE	A.B.P.	GOOD	UNC.
☐286	$2	260.00	375.00	800.00

CONFEDERATE STATES OF AMERICA—1862 ISSUE
$165,000,000 Authorized by "Act of April 17th."
"HOYER & LUDWIG, RICHMOND, VA."

TYPE 39

Face Design: Railway train, straight steam from locomotive, milkmaid left. Bears "Interest at Two Cents Per Day."

CRISWELL	NOTE	A.B.P.	GOOD	UNC.
☐287-289	$100	55.00	85.00	200.00

Dated May 5 to May 9, 1862
J.T. PATERSON, COLUMBIA, S.C. (At Lower Left)

☐290-293	$100	45.00	75.00	160.00

VARIOUS WRITTEN DATES, MAY THROUGH OCTOBER, 1862

J.T. PATERSON, COLUMBIA, S.C. (At Lower Right)

☐294-296	$100	45.00	75.00	160.00

VARIOUS WRITTEN DATES, MAY THROUGH OCTOBER, 1862

TYPE 40

"J.T. PATERSON, COLUMBIA, S.C."
Face Design: Railway train, diffused steam from locomotive, milkmaid left. Bears "Interest at Two Cents Per Day."

CRISWELL	NOTE	A.B.P.	GOOD	UNC.
☐298-309	$100	48.00	75.00	200.00

VARIOUS WRITTEN DATES, MAY THROUGH OCTOBER, 1862

CONFEDERATE STATES OF AMERICA—1862 ISSUE
"KEATINGE & BALL, COLUMBIA, S.C."
On the following notes there are two types of ornamental
scrolls in the upper right corners.

**TYPE
41**

Face Design: "Hundred" overprint in orange/red. Bears "Interest at Two
Cents Per Day." Negroes hoeing cotton, J.C. Calhoun left, Columbia right.

CRISWELL	NOTE	A.B.P.	GOOD	UNC.
☐310-314	$100	105.00	90.00	275.00

Dated "August 26th, 1862" (Date all written, scroll No. 1.)

☐315-324	$100	55.00	100.00	200.00

Written dates, AUG. to DEC. "1862." ("186" of date is engraved.)

☐325-331	$100	55.00	95.00	200.00

Dated January 1 to January 8, 1863.

CONFEDERATE STATES OF AMERICA—1862 ISSUE
$5,000,000 authorized by "Act of April 18th, 1862"
$5,000,000 authorized by "Act of September 23rd, 1862"
"B. DUNCAN, COLUMBIA, S.C."

TYPE
42

Face Design: Personification of South striking down Union, J.P. Benjamin left.

CRISWELL	NOTE	A.B.P.	GOOD	UNC.
☐334-337	$2	40.00	50.00	375.00

TYPE
43

Face Design: "2" and "Two" in green overprint. Personification of South striking down Union, J.P. Benjamin left.

CRISWELL	NOTE	A.B.P.	GOOD	UNC.
☐338	$2	50.00	90.00	1650.00

CONFEDERATE STATES OF AMERICA—1862 ISSUE

TYPE
44

Face Design: Steamship at sea. Lucy Holcombe Pickens right. Liberty left.

CRISWELL	NOTE	A.B.P.	GOOD	UNC.
□339-341	$1	50.00	70.00	275.00

TYPE
45

Face Design: "1" and "One" green overprint. Steamship at sea. Lucy Holcombe Pickens right. Liberty left.

CRISWELL	NOTE	A.B.P.	GOOD	UNC.
□342-342A	$1	60.00	110.00	1750.00

CONFEDERATE STATES OF AMERICA—1862 ISSUE
"HOYER & LUDWIG, RICHMOND, VA."
This is a Sept. 2, 1861 note, dated through error
"September 2, 1862." No engravers' name, appears,
but it is a product of Hoyer & Ludwig, Richmond, VA.

TYPE
46

Face Design: Ceres reclining on cotton bales. R.M.T. Hunter at right.

CRISWELL	NOTE	A.B.P.	GOOD	UNC.
☐343-344	$10	45.00	85.00	600.00

(Essay Note, Printed Signatures.)
"KEATINGE & BALL, COLUMBUS, S.C."

TYPE
47

Face Design: Liberty seated on bale of cotton. R.M.T. Hunter right.

CRISWELL	NOTE	A.B.P.	GOOD	UNC.
☐345	$20		EXTREMELY RARE	

CONFEDERATE STATES OF AMERICA—1862 ISSUE
(Essay Note, Printed Signatures.)
"KEATINGE & BALL, COLUMBUS, S.C."

TYPE
48

Face Design: Ceres holding sheaf of wheat. R.M.T. Hunter right.

CRISWELL	NOTE	A.B.P.	GOOD	UNC.
☐346	$10		EXTREMELY RARE	

CONFEDERATE STATES OF AMERICA—1862 ISSUE
$90,000,000 authorized by "Act of Oct. 13th, 1862"
"KEATINGE & BALL, COLUMBIA S.C."

TYPE
49

Face Design: Fancy green reverse. Lucy Holcombe Pickens. George W. Randolph right.

CRISWELL	NOTE	A.B.P.	GOOD	UNC.
☐347-349	$100	135.00	300.00	1350.00

CONFEDERATE STATES OF AMERICA—1862 ISSUE
"KEATINGE & BALL, RICHMOND, VA." (THIRD SERIES)

TYPE 50

Face Design: Black and green. Ornate green reverse. Jefferson Davis.

CRISWELL	NOTE	A.B.P.	GOOD	UNC.
☐350-356	$50	135.00	225.00	1950.00

"KEATINGE & BALL, COLUMBIA, S.C." (THIRD SERIES)

CRISWELL	NOTE	A.B.P.	GOOD	UNC.
☐357-362	$50	80.00	180.00	720.00

CONFEDERATE STATES OF AMERICA—1862 ISSUE
"KEATINGE & BALL, COLUMBIA, S.C."

TYPE 51

Face Design: Fancy blue reverse. State Capitol at Nashville, Tennessee. A.H. Stephens.

CRISWELL	NOTE	A.B.P.	GOOD	UNC.
☐363-368	$20	85.00	150.00	850.00

CONFEDERATE STATES OF AMERICA—1862 ISSUE

TYPE
52

Face Design: Fancy blue reverse. State Capitol at Columbia S.C., R.M.T.
Hunter. Printed on pink paper.

"B. DUNCAN."

CRISWELL NOTE	A.B.P.	GOOD	UNC.
☐ 369-375IB $10	35.00	60.00	195.00

"EVANS & COGSWELL"

CRISWELL NOTE	A.B.P.	GOOD	UNC.
☐ 376-378 $10	35.00	60.00	195.00

TYPE
53

Face Design: Fancy blue reverse. State Capitol at Richmond, VA., C.G.
Memminger. Printed on pink paper.

There are many varieties of printers names on notes of
this issue, though all have the same engraver's names. In
general, the only valuable ones are those with two "Printers"
names.

CRISWELL NOTE	A.B.P.	GOOD	UNC.
☐ 379-390 $5	35.00	60.00	175.00

Face Design: Judah P. Benjamin. Printed on pink paper.

CRISWELL	NOTE		A.B.P.	GOOD	UNC.
☐391-396	$2		45.00	130.00	325.00

TYPE 54

Face Design: Clement C. Clay. Printed on pink paper.

CRISWELL	NOTE		A.B.P.	GOOD	UNC.
☐397-401	$1		50.00	130.00	390.00

TYPE 55

CONFEDERATE STATES OF AMERICA—1863

$50,000,000 authorized monthly, from April 1863 to January 1864, "By Act of March 23rd, 1863."

All notes of this year dated April 6th, 1863, but a red overprinted date appears on all the $5, $10, $20, $50, and $100 denominations showing the year and month of issue.

"KEATINGE & BALL, COLUMBIA, S.C."

Face Design: Green reverse. Lucy H. Pickens. Two soldiers left. George W. Randolph right.

TYPE 56

CRISWELL	NOTE		A.B.P.	GOOD	UNC.
☐402-404	$100		85.00	120.00	425.00

"KEATINGE & BALL, RICHMOND, VA."

TYPE 57

Face Design: Green and black, ornate green reverse, Jefferson Davis.

CRISWELL	NOTE		A.B.P.	GOOD	UNC.
☐406-417	$50		60.00	110.00	365.00

CONFEDERATE STATES OF AMERICA—1863

TYPE 58

Face Design: Fancy blue reverse. State Capitol at Nashville, TN., A.H. Stephens.

CRISWELL	NOTE		A.B.P.	GOOD	UNC.
☐418-428	$20		60.00	70.00	325.00

TYPE 59

Face Design: Blue back. State Capitol at Columbia, S.C., R.M.T. Hunter.

CRISWELL	NOTE	A.B.P.	GOOD	UNC.
☐429-447	$10	30.00	60.00	210.00

Engravers' names on lower margin.

TYPE 60

Face Design: Fancy blue reverse. State Capitol at Richmond, VA. C.G. Memminger.

CRISWELL	NOTE	A.B.P.	GOOD	UNC.
☐448-469	$5	30.00	60.00	210.00

Pink Paper.

TYPE 61

Face Design: Judah P. Benjamin.

CRISWELL	NOTE	A.B.P.	GOOD	UNC.
☐470-473	$2	80.00	90.00	325.00

TYPE 62

Face Design: Clement C. Clay. Pink Paper.

CRISWELL	NOTE	A.B.P.	GOOD	UNC.
☐ 474-484	$1	30.00	60.00	325.00

"ARCHER & DALY. RICHMOND, VA."

TYPE 63

Face Design: Bust of Jefferson Davis. Pink Paper.

CRISWELL	NOTE	A.B.P.	GOOD	UNC.
☐ 485-488	50 Cents	25.00	50.00	85.00

CONFEDERATE STATES OF AMERICA—1864

$200,000,000 was authorized by "Act of February 17th, 1864."
All notes of this year are dated "Feb. 17th, 1864."

The actual amount issued was probably ten times the figure given above and the amount printed even greater. Thus there are many minor varieties of each type including color variations, flourishes, and more signature combinations than any other year. The authors list only the **important** types. The most common Confederate Notes appear in this year.

"KEATINGE & BALL, COLUMBIA, S.C."

TYPE
64

Face Design: Reddish horizontal line background. Equestrian statue of Washington and Confederate flag at left. Gen. T.J. "Stonewall" Jackson right.

CRISWELL	NOTE	A.B.P.	GOOD	UNC.
☐489-489A	$500	200.00	350.00	850.00

"A CONFEDERATE COUNTERFEIT."
Same as $100 Note illustrated on the next page, but
1/4 inch narrower, and 1/4 inch shorter.
This note only exists in Serial Letter "D."

CRISWELL	NOTE	A.B.P.	GOOD	UNC.
☐ 492	$100	75.00	95.00	245.00

Although a counterfeit, this note was listed in Bradbeer as a genuine, and evidence exists proving that it was accepted as such in the Confederacy. It is an excellent copy, in some ways better engraved than the genuine, but is easily distinguishable by its small size. The authors list it herein with the regular issues because few collectors desire to be without one. It is by far the most popular Confederate counterfeit.

**TYPE
65**

Face Design: Reddish network background. Intricate blue reverse with "Hundred" in large letters. Lucy Pickens. Two soldiers left. George W. Randolph right.

CRISWELL	NOTE		A.B.P.	GOOD	UNC.
□490-494	$100		55.00	120.00	295.00

**TYPE
66**

Face Design: Reddish network background. Intricate blue reverse with "Fifty" in large letters. Jefferson Davis.

CRISWELL	NOTE		A.B.P.	GOOD	UNC.
□495-503	$50		50.00	85.00	240.00

**TYPE
67**

Face Design: Reddish network background. Intricate blue reverse with "Twenty" in large letters. State Capitol at Nashville, TN. A.H. Stephens right.

CRISWELL	NOTE		A.B.P.	GOOD	UNC.
□504-539	$20		30.00	70.00	105.00

"KEATINGE & BALL, COLUMBIA, S.C."
("PTD. BY EVANS & COGSWELL" On left end)

**TYPE
68**

Face Design: Reddish network background. Intricate blue reverse with "Ten" in large letters. Horses pulling cannon. R.M.T. Hunter at right.

CRISWELL	NOTE	A.B.P.	GOOD	UNC.
☐540-553	$10	22.00	27.00	75.00

"KEATINGE & BALL, COLUMBIA, S.C."

**TYPE
69**

Face Design: Reddish network background. Intricate blue reverse with "Five" in large letters. State Capitol at Richmond, VA. C.G. Memminger at right.

CRISWELL	NOTE	A.B.P.	GOOD	UNC.
☐558-565	$5	22.00	27.00	75.00

**TYPE
70**

Face Design: Reddish network background. Judah P. Benjamin.

CRISWELL	NOTE	A.B.P.	GOOD	UNC.
□566-571	$2	45.00	80.00	180.00

**TYPE
71**

Face Design: Reddish network background. Clement C. Clay.

CRISWELL	NOTE	A.B.P.	GOOD	UNC.
□572-577	$1	50.00	90.00	250.00

"ENGRAVED BY ARCHER & HALPIN, RICHMOND, VA."

**TYPE
72**

Face Design: Bust of Jefferson Davis. Pink Paper.

CRISWELL	NOTE	A.B.P.	GOOD	UNC.
□578-579	50 Cents	20.00	45.00	80.00

The Blackbooks!

HOUSE OF COLLECTIBLES SERIES

Title	ISBN	Price	Author

The Official® Price Guides to

Title	ISBN	Price	Author
America's State Quarters	0609807706	$6.99	Ganz
American Arts & Crafts, 3rd ed.	060980989X	$21.95	Rago
American Patriotic Memorabilia	0609810146	$16.95	Pollack
Classic Video Games	0375720383	$16.95	Ellis
Clocks	0609809733	$19.95	Korz
Collecting Books, 4th ed.	0609807692	$18.00	Tedford/Goudey
Collector Knives, 14th ed.	1400048346	$17.95	Price
Collector Plates, 7th ed.	0676601545	$19.95	Rinker Ent.
Costume Jewelry, 3rd ed.	0609806688	$17.95	Miller
Dinnerware of the 20th Century	0676600859	$29.95	Rinker
Glassware, 3rd ed.	067660188X	$17.00	Pickvet
Hake's Character Toys, 4th ed.	0609808222	$35.00	Hake
Hislop's International Fine Art	0609808745	$20.00	Hislop
Indian Arrowheads, 8th ed.	0609810537	$26.00	Overstreet
Kiss Collectibles	1400050294	$18.00	Floren
Military Collectibles, 6th ed.	0676600522	$20.00	Austin
Mint Errors, 6th ed.	0609808559	$15.00	Herbert
Movie Autographs and Memorabilia	1400047315	$20.00	Cohen
Native American Art	0609809660	$24.00	Reno
Overstreet Comic Book Grading Guide	0609810529	$24.00	Overstreet/Blumberg
Overstreet Comic Books, 34th ed.	1400046696	$25.00	Overstreet
Overstreet Indian Arrowheads, 7th ed.	0609808699	$24.00	Overstreet
Pottery & Porcelain, 8th ed.	0876378939	$18.95	Duke
Quilts, 2nd ed.	1400047978	$16.00	Barach
Records, 16th ed.	0609809083	$25.95	Osborne
Vintage Fashion and Fabrics	0609808133	$17.00	Smith

The Official® Guides to

Title	ISBN	Price	Author
Coin Grading and Counterfeit Detection, 2nd ed.	0375720502	$19.95	PCGS
Flea Market Prices, 2nd ed.	1400048893	$14.95	Rinker
How to Make Money in Coins Right Now, 2nd ed.	0609807463	$14.95	Travers
Directory to U.S. Flea Markets, 8th ed.	0609809229	$14.00	Werner
One-Minute Coin Expert, 4th ed.	0609807471	$7.99	Travers
Stamp Collector's Bible	0609808842	$22.00	Datz

The Official® Beckett Sports Cards Price Guides to

Title	ISBN	Price	Author
Baseball Cards 2006, 25th ed.	0375721002	$7.99	Beckett
Basketball Cards 2006, 14th ed.	0375721045	$7.99	Beckett
Football Cards 2006, 29th ed.	0375721029	$7.99	Beckett

The Official® Blackbook Price Guides to

Title	ISBN	Price	Author
U.S. Coins 2006, 44th ed.	1400048443	$7.99	Hudgeons
U.S. Paper Money 2006, 38th ed.	1400048451	$6.99	Hudgeons
U.S. Postage Stamps 2006, 28th ed.	140004846X	$8.99	Hudgeons
World Coins 2006, 9th ed.	1400048478	$7.99	Hudgeons

Instant Expert

Title	ISBN	Price	Author
Collecting Oriental Rugs	0375720448	$12.95	Ware
Collecting Teapots	0375720456	$12.95	Rousmaniere
Collecting Art Deco	0375720421	$12.95	Fusco
Collecting Books	0375720545	$12.95	Budman